T0277077

HITLER'S VALKYRIE

THE UNCENSORED BIOGRAPHY OF UNITY MITFORD

DAVID R.L. LITCHFIELD

To Robert Kearns and Caroline Schmitz

First published 2013
This paperback edition 2015

The History Press
The Mill, Brimscombe Port
Stroud, Gloucestershire, GL5 2QG
www.thehistorypress.co.uk

British Library Cataloguing in Publication Data.
A catalogue record for this book is available from the British Library.

ISBN 978 0 7509 6088 5
Typesetting and origination by Thomas Bohm, User Design,
Illustration and Typesetting
Printed and bound in Great Britain by TJ International Ltd

CONTENTS

INTRODUCTION

Hitler's Valkyrie is the first independent, unexpurgated biography of the Honourable Unity Valkyrie Freeman-Mitford. It is also the first biography of Unity Mitford to give a full explanation of her astonishing social, political, sexual and transcendental relationship with Adolf Hitler.

The remarkable and much-loved Mitford family has remained largely unrepentant concerning their enthusiastic support of Hitler, the Nazis, Oswald Mosley and British fascism. But having initially encouraged Unity's affair with Hitler, after the war they distanced themselves by insisting that she had in fact been a rather unintelligent, clumsy lump of a girl, whose unrequited relationship with one of the most terrifying dictators of all time was a mere romantic obsession.

Following further research and the reinterpretation of existing, often contradictory evidence, plus new information supplied by the author's own family and friends, *Hitler's Valkyrie* will reveal that while she was, like Hitler, an extreme fantasist, there was little of the previously claimed juvenile romantic about Unity. She (and her sister Diana) could in fact have more accurately been compared with the wonderfully promiscuous Jane Digby (Lady Ellenborough, a nineteenth-century English aristocrat, famed for her extravagant and exotic sexual adventures) than with any sentimentally romantic Jane Austen inspired character.

This is also the first book to explain how and why a maniacally ambitious Austrian, who was already subject to the demands of a physically attractive mistress *and* had only recently achieved dictatorial power over Germany *and* was equally determined to gain world domination *and* achieve the creation of a Jew-free, Nordic master race, could find the time, let alone the motivation, to devote to a young, upper-class English girl.

Hitler's Valkyrie answers the questions of how and why an unmarried, 21-year-old girl with a conspicuously liberal attitude towards her own sexuality could spend so much time, often alone and unchaperoned, in the company of a man twenty-five years her senior without causing a major scandal; and why her parents displayed such obvious pride in her having been conceived in a town called Swastika, had seen fit to christen her Valkyrie (a female figure of Norse mythology and 'chooser of the slain' who accompany their slaughtered warrior heroes to the afterlife hall of Valhalla where they attend to their various needs) and generously financed her life in Munich, while subsequently claiming that they had wanted nothing more than for her to return home.

There is also the question of the motivation for her extremely active sex life, much of it with SS officers, Sturmführers or 'Storms' as Unity referred to them, and what it may have contributed to her spiritual and physical relationship with 'my Führer'.

For the privileged few, the period following the First World War, when, despite financial pressures, Britain was at her imperial zenith, was a golden era. It was an endless summer of white floppy sun hats, cucumber sandwiches, goat carts and racquet presses, but also an era in which the ruling classes' fear of communism encouraged a surprising amount of enthusiasm for fascism and Adolf Hitler. It was enough for many to be quite accepting of the Mitfords' role as the first family of fascism, though somewhat reassuringly, not enough for Oswald Mosley and the British Union of Fascists to win one single seat in Parliament.

Meanwhile, Unity and her sisters were developing a reputation as a one-off icon of eccentricity, much loved by the new, socially ambitious English middle class. *Hitler's Valkyrie* also reminds us of the Mitford girls' obsessive fascination with themselves, their parents, aunts, uncles, cousins and only brother, combined with a quite remarkable conviction that all other 'PLU' (People Like Us) shared this fascination. Of course, many did, and still do.

But our fascination with the Mitford girls did not develop by chance. Nor did it do so merely because they were, as described by various acolytes, 'glamorous', 'romantic', 'scaldingly witty', 'born storytellers', 'mad', 'eccentric', 'remarkable' and 'brilliant', were related to Winston Churchill and married into both Ireland's fabulously wealthy 'beerage' and the upper echelons of English aristocracy, many of whom shared their enthusiasm for fascism. It was in fact, as this book will explain, skilful promotion that so successfully established the girls as celebrities and the name Mitford as a brand leader in the world of middle-class social, political and literary culture. Many still consider the Mitfords to be a deeply wonderful, aristocratic family, typical of everything that is – or was – best about England's green and pleasant land.

They were such a perfect reflection of the times that it was often difficult to believe that the Mitford family had not been invented by Evelyn Waugh, though in part, of course, they had. For it was Waugh who, while embracing many of the Mitford girls' expressions and anecdotes in his own writing, assisted and encouraged Unity's elder sister Nancy to write a series of best-selling, popular novels based on a satirical view of the Mitford family, their competitive snobbery and extreme political convictions. It was Nancy's 'brilliance' in injecting sufficient, often quite vicious humour into the recounting of their often appalling views and actions that made them not just socially acceptable but positively magnetic to their increasingly adoring public.

The Mitford girls were also fortunate in having a splendidly handsome, grumpy old father in Lord Redesdale, who could be and would be endlessly caricatured. But of even greater value to the development of their fame and fortune was their ambitious mother, Sydney, who in her initial determination to marry off her six daughters, developed an astonishing ability to obtain coverage of their 'goings on' in the social columns of national newspapers; despite the fact that, in truth, the upper echelons of the aristocracy, including the Duke of Devonshire, considered such self-promotion to be extremely vulgar and not at all the thing. This form of promotion also involved her in the quite shameless exploitation of Unity's relationship with Hitler, including her leaking the story of their possible marriage. All of which resulted in her daughters' ever-increasing celebrity status and Nancy's burgeoning book sales.

Then there is the question of how and why Adolf Hitler, who to this day the Mitfords and their friends and acquaintances still describe as 'charming' and 'delightful', saw fit to persuade 'my Valkyrie' and the four other women in his life to commit – or attempt to commit – suicide and the part this necromantic element in his make-up would play in his responsibility for causing the death of 70 million people.

It should be noted that Hitler's necromancy took the form of an obsession with death and his God-like control over who lived and died, rather than the more classical form of necromancy, which involves attempting to raise or communicate with the dead by means of occult practices.

It is perhaps understandable why, following Unity's death in 1948, when even the Mitfords had begun to appreciate that Hitler had become somewhat less socially acceptable, Unity's mother and, more recently, her sister, 'Debo' Devonshire, worked towards 'putting the record straight' concerning Unity. In so doing, Debo described her sister's worship of the Führer as a mere 'friendship'. But *Hitler's Valkyrie* will also examine why when Unity died, her mother, rather than quietly grieve, chose to take issue with the *Daily Mail* concerning her daughter's obituary, entitled 'The Secret Life of Unity Mitford', by their man in Germany, George Ward Price; the same pro-Nazi George Ward Price who, prior to the outbreak of war had admiringly described Unity as 'a spirited young English girl' while encouraging her relationship with Hitler.

But after the war, when such attitudes were a great deal less acceptable, George had used Unity's obituary to absolve her, by giving the impression that her relationship was little more than a pose and her suicide a tragic form of exhibitionism. While one had to admire Sydney's apparent loyalty, predictably her protest only helped to remind the public of her commitment to fascism. However, her defensive reaction may have resulted from the pressure she had been under in hiding Unity's true secrets; secrets that would go with her to the grave and beyond but which can now, finally, be made known.

I

DAWN OF THE DAUGHTERS OF ALBION

1264–1904

And did those feet in ancient time
Walk upon England's mountains green?
William Blake

Late one night in pre-war Munich, a young woman dressed in a black jacket, long black skirt, boots and gauntlets, accompanied by six SS officers in full uniform, climbed the dark stairs to her apartment. Once inside she removed her gloves and lit two large ecclesiastical candles either side of her bed, the head of which was draped with enormous swastika banners. The candlelight also revealed silver framed portraits of Adolf Hitler on the side tables.

As she stepped out of her skirt, she was seen to be wearing no underwear apart from black stockings. She then took a Nazi armband and pulled it down over her eyes before lying down, spread-eagled. One of the men bound her hands and feet to the four corners of the bed while another, in what was obviously a familiar ritual, wound up the gramophone and dropped the needle on a record of *Horst-Wessel-Lied*, the iconic Nazi anthem. The other officers removed their boots, belts and uniforms. Then, as the pounding marching song broke the silence, they took it in turns to swiftly and aggressively mount her.

Could this young girl have been the same Unity Valkyrie Freeman-Mitford, daughter of Lord and Lady Redesdale, that her family and friends insisted was a virginal, innocent romantic? Her Austro-Hungarian society friends, the Baroness 'Gaby' Bentinck and 'Milly' Howard-Brown, were certainly quite convinced it was. But then much about Unity and the Mitford family was – and is – not quite what it seemed.

According to Jonathan Guinness, author of *The House of Mitford*, Bertie Mitford, Unity's paternal grandfather, used to claim that Sir Bernard Burke of *Burke's Peerage* fame had once informed him that the Mitfords were descended from 'perhaps' the two oldest Saxon families in England, a statement designed to suggest that they pre-dated the Norman Conquest: 'Whether or not the Mitfords were Saxon, they were certainly medieval. Belonging to the landed gentry of Northumberland, they remained for centuries locally prominent, without ever becoming nationally distinguished.' But in reality Lord and Lady Redesdale and their children's connection to those of their forefathers who had qualified as landed gentry was tenuous to say the least and the conditions of their inheritance highly fortuitous. It should also be said that without a degree of propitious genealogy, and the Mitford girls' flair for self-publicity, combined with a small quantity of indulgent, but highly successful literary endeavour and Adolf Hitler's astonishing relationship with Unity, they would probably have remained profoundly 'un' distinguished.

There is evidence to suggest that during the reign of Charles II one Robert Mitford, born in 1612, managed to recover the family castle, or what was left of it, and the small town of Mitford near Morpeth, confiscated by Henry III as punishment for some treacherous act of skulduggery some 400 years earlier.

For the next hundred years or so, while the Civil War came and went, the new Mitford line was sufficiently successful in trade for a great-grandson, yet another John Mitford, to gain adequate education to qualify as a barrister; being called to the bar in 1777. Three years later, rather precociously, he published a book known as 'Mitford on Pleadings', which was said to have been much read, 'even making him a fair amount of money; it continued to be read for a century afterwards'.[1]

However, it seems more likely that the considerable quantity of money he made which enabled him to return to Northumberland and invest in a much more comfortable and less draughty country seat in Redesdale would likely have resulted from some far less socially acceptable and 'busier' activity than writing a law book.

By the law of averages, barristers are quite likely to spend at least half their working life being paid to lie on other peoples' behalf, a skill which of course also qualifies them for a career in politics. So it was that John Mitford entered Parliament where he soon established his natural affinity with politics by rapidly and successively achieving the roles of Solicitor General, Attorney General and Speaker of the House of Commons. It was hardly surprising that after this seemingly mercurial rise to political eminence he should soon be 'raised to the peerage as Lord Redesdale and appointed Lord Chancellor of Ireland'.[2]

The first Lord Redesdale's most enduring achievement during his term of office was the coining of the phrase, 'I find that there is in Ireland one law for the rich and another for the poor.' But while he may have voiced concern for the human rights of individual Catholics, like many other Protestants he opposed the political power of the Roman Catholic Church, manifested by his preventing Catholics from being granted positions of political power.

Predictably, the situation ended in tears when, in 1806, he made a serious error of judgement by refusing to grant the Catholic Lord Cloncurry (the Irish republican, politician and landowner) the post of magistrate. Cloncurry's successful legal challenge of his decision resulted in the first Lord Redesdale being obliged to resign.

However, his fall from grace was compensated, at least in a material and financial sense, in 1808, by the totally unexpected inheritance of the Batsford House and estate, which included many thousands of acres of Cotswold countryside. This seemingly miraculous windfall resulted from the death of Thomas Freeman, his uncle only by marriage, with whom he shared no blood relatives and whose only other surviving relative, a childless granddaughter, had also died shortly afterwards.

In memory (and presumably in appreciation) of Thomas Freeman, the family name was legally changed to Freeman-Mitford. One supposes it was the least Redesdale could have done to give the inheritance a modicum of credibility. Without this legacy, for which the Mitfords didn't have to raise a finger, their lives would have been considerably less privileged.

Having inherited Batsford in 1830, the second Lord Redesdale, John Thomas, had settled comfortably into his position as an upstanding member of the squirearchy, an amateur theologian and master of the Heythrop Hunt, while remaining 'active in managing the House of Lords in the interests of the Conservative Party'.[3] As a result, the Mitford history included yet another stroke of ironic social advancement when Benjamin Disraeli, Great Britain's only Jewish prime minister (albeit converted to Anglicism), rewarded him with an additional step up the peerage ladder as the Earl of Redesdale.

In his position as the Second Lord Redesdale, 'The Great Dictator', as John Thomas was known, refused to make any attempt to create a son and heir to inherit the position of the Third Lord Redesdale. Instead, he chose to live with his sister in what Jonathan Guinness insisted was 'perfect and celibate amity'. Though how he could have known why such an arrangement should qualify as either 'perfect' or 'celibate' remains a mystery.

As a result of the shortage of suitable breeding stock that would (hopefully) result from such a relationship, the earl chose to leave his substantial estates to his first cousin twice removed in the form of

Algernon Bertram Freeman-Mitford, or 'Bertie' (pronounced Barty in the old English habit of pronouncing 'e' as 'a'), whose brother, Henry his Lordship, had disinherited as a result of having married a German girl and moved back to the country of her birth. Unfortunately, as Bertie lacked the required inheritance qualifications, the old man took both his titles to the grave with him in 1886, obliging Bertie to start again at the bottom of the peerage ladder. But in 1902, as a result of services to queen and country and his formidable social ambition, he would also be ennobled, taking the title of Baron Redesdale.

*   *   *

Bertie's grandfather, Henry Mitford of Exbury, was a captain in the Royal Navy until Christmas Eve 1803 when his first command, the *York*, 'went down with all hands in a fog in the North Sea'[4]. It was an ignominious end to an unremarkable naval career.

He left two daughters by his first marriage and an unfortunately pregnant second wife called Mary, who gave birth to a fatherless son, Henry-Reveley Mitford. Mary soon married again and together with his older half-sisters, Henry-Reveley was abandoned by his mother and stepfather and brought up by his grandfather, the noted historian William Mitford; apparently a deeply unpleasant but financially privileged man.

As a result of this arrangement, instead of a happy childhood Bertie's father was blessed with a good education and private means, without which it would have been quite impossible to have even thought of going to Oxford, let alone taken up a post as attaché to the British Legation in Florence. Then, as now, the city contained 'a colony of cultivated English people, drawn to the place by a love of the arts or of the climate; some of them, perhaps being attracted by the somewhat looser conventions which in all generations prevail among people who live abroad'.[5] According to Jonathan and Catherine Guinness, it was among this 'agreeable society' that Henry

Reveley met Lady Georgina Ashburnham, whose father, the Earl of Ashburnham, owned a Florentine villa.

Henry left the Foreign Service shortly after their marriage in 1828, following the death of his grandfather and the subsequent inheritance of a house at Exbury on the Solent. There he adopted the life of a country squire, with the customary seat on the magistrates' bench. Several children were born to the marriage, of whom three boys survived: twins named Percy and Henry, born in 1833, and Bertie, born on 24 February 1837, who in truth was fathered by Lady Georgina's lover, Francis Molyneux, the youngest son of the second Earl of Sefton. It was said, rather cruelly, that Henry, 'being a somewhat naïve innocent with little strength of character, never suspected a thing'.[6]

Rumours that Francis Molyneux was Bertie's real father persisted for centuries. They resurfaced as late as 1941, when Deborah Mitford was about to marry the then Lord Andrew Cavendish, son of the 10th Duke of Devonshire. 'The Duke was chatting to a friend in his club about it, and went to get a *Burke's Peerage* to look up the Mitfords. "If you want to see who they really are," said the friend, "look under Sefton."'

*   *   *

The maternal side of the Mitford family was also not without its skeletons, though in this case they were far less grand; almost a Dickensian cliché in fact. The action in question was perpetrated in 1844 by Thomas Milner-Gibson, a Suffolk landowner and Liberal politician, who returned home one evening with a blond, three-year-old boy whom he introduced to his wife Susanna as Thomas Gibson Bowles, his extremely fortunate but illegitimate son. He admitted the boy's mother was his mistress, Susannah (with an 'h') Bowles, a servant and daughter of William Bowles, a brushmaker. Susannah apparently worked as a servant in the London town house of Milner-Gibson, at 48 Eaton Square. It was the same house in which Thomas Bowles had been conceived.

While he settled the boy's mother into a small house in Gravesend, and presumably supplied her with an allowance, his wife, who had already lost a previous son, somewhat surprisingly welcomed the new foster son as her own.

Thomas Bowles grew up much loved by his father and stepmother, who made his childhood happy and secure. Thomas assumed his role as eldest son, apparently none the worse for his parental substitution, his stepmother giving birth to a further two surviving sons. But it was Thomas who his father would favour, taking him sailing and introducing him to country sports and politics. He appeared also to have been the brightest of the boys. While Thomas' relations with both his father and stepmother remained close and warm to the end of their lives, no mention was ever made of his relationship with his real mother.

One disadvantage, if it could be considered such a thing, which was said to have been 'imposed by his illegitimacy', was that the boy could not attend any English public school. However, it was difficult to comprehend how the schools would have known, apart from the fact that his father had not seen fit to honour the boy with his own name. But perhaps the bright young boy was also sufficiently intelligent to have used it as a means of avoiding what he knew to be the ghastliness of English public schools at that time. It was thus perhaps as a result of his stepmother's love of France, and their collusion, that he was enrolled at a school in Normandy. From there Thomas progressed to King's College, London, before being nominated by his father to a position as a junior clerk in the Legacy and Succession Duty office at Somerset House.

Unsurprisingly, Thomas Bowles soon found his work as a clerk to be as boring as Bertie Mitford was finding his endless copying of dispatches at the Foreign Office; where he had arrived via Eton and Oxford. But while Bertie busied himself both socially and physically, playing racquets at the same club as the Prince of Wales, Thomas discovered a cure for his boredom and a supplement to his income by submitting social stories to *The Morning Post*. He soon proved himself to be a natural journalist and also enjoyed considerable self-assurance which, combined with a degree of sensitivity, empowered him with a great deal of persuasive charm.

★   ★   ★

Bertie may have found the Foreign Office to be 'blindingly tedious' but he was more than appreciative of the social advantages it offered. 'A clerk in the FO at that time carried with him a passport to all that was best in political, diplomatic, literary and artistic society', and being both bright, gregarious and extremely ambitious he was said to have royally exploited these social opportunities: 'Bertie met, and impressed, Benjamin Disraeli … [He] also became rather a favourite of the Palmerstons. He met Thackeray at dinner with the Pre-Raphaelite artist Sir John Millais. He also came to know the Prince of Wales, at whose wedding in 1863 he was a gentleman usher.'[7]

Algernon Bertram Freeman-Mitford's first foreign posting was to St Petersburg, while his next was Peking in 1865, from where he wrote long and detailed letters home. These same letters would become the basis of his book, *The Attaché at Peking*.

Apart from developing his extreme right-wing political views, Bertie's main occupation was learning to speak Chinese. This was in the days when raising one's voice was usually considered a perfectly acceptable means of communicating with foreigners; army officers being advised to use their swagger sticks for additional emphasis.

★   ★   ★

Meanwhile, in order to devote more time to the fulfilment both of his entrepreneurial and journalistic ambitions, the Mitford girls' maternal grandfather, Thomas Gibson Bowles, resigned from the civil service. While he was said to be capable of selling any story he cared to write, he yearned for the freedom and excitement to be gained from publishing his own magazine. So, with virtually no resources to found and edit a new weekly magazine, he launched *Vanity Fair* whose title, taken from Thackeray's novel, was suggested by his friend Frederick Burnaby, an officer in the Royal Horse Guards, or 'Blues'. Burnaby also became a contributor to the magazine, providing it with a large proportion of its social gossip; much to the annoyance of his fellow officers.

The magazine also contained political comment both foreign and domestic, as well as social news, humour and arts criticism. By 1870 *Vanity Fair* was established and profitable. It could also be considered the first step in what would prove to be the Mitfords' personal capitalisation of their knowledge of the press.

*   *   *

In 1866, after less than a year in China, Bertie Mitford was posted to Yokohama in Japan; a country that was to have a profound effect upon him. It appeared that the major reason for his affinity with the country was the martial spirit it shared with medieval Europe, complete with Samurai knights in armour. Since 1185 Japan had remained a feudal country in the sense that medieval Europe had been feudal. Perhaps because of this it had also retained a constitutional monarchy and little interest in democracy. Shogun warlords and their clans ran the country, while the emperor's role comprised little more than that of a ceremonial figurehead with limited real power. It was hardly surprising that Japan would so readily adopt fascism and ally itself to Hitler and the Nazi Party, or that Bertie would be so enamoured with the country. He explicitly compared the Samurai with the class of which he considered himself to be a member, namely the English aristocracy, with its roots in medieval chivalry. Bertie was, of course, a screaming snob and a rank fascist at heart, qualities that most of the Mitfords would inherit in various degrees.

By the time Bertie returned home in 1870, he claimed to have become fluent in Japanese, though one of the family told how, having stopped in the park in Paris to speak to a small Japanese child in their own tongue, 'They couldn't understand a word he said!'

*   *   *

Despite much of the population living in abject poverty, Britain was now the richest country on earth and at the height of its imperial power. Germany, on the other hand, had yet to become a unified nation. However, that hadn't prevented their successful invasion of Queen Victoria's German-speaking Court, which was largely the result of her having married most of her children off to Protestant German princes.

After the Austro-Prussian War of 1866, the North German Confederation came into existence as a military alliance of the twenty-two princely states of northern Germany with the kingdom of Prussia as their leader. After the Franco-Prussian war in 1871 the Confederation was joined by the southern states of Bavaria, Württemberg and Baden, and parts of the Grand Duchy of Hesse, to form the second German Empire with the King of Prussia, William I, as its president and Otto von Bismarck as chancellor.

With the Prussians' propensity for violence, both ritualised and realised, and increasing industrial and colonial competition between Germany, Britain and America, a full-scale confrontation between the three was inevitable. Perhaps it should have been predictable that the human catalyst for a later war, though little more than an enthusiastic participant in the first conflict, would be a man from a country whose descent into chaos had already started.

Hitler was born in 1889 into an almost ungovernable Austro-Hungarian Empire of dual sovereignty, eleven principal national groups and eight languages (for the various Slavic peoples). Still largely under the control of the Catholic Church and the Habsburg monarchy, it was this old, imperial order to which Hitler's customs-officer father had devoted his life, and which he brutally forced his son to adopt.

Rarely a day went by that the young boy did not receive a vicious beating, whose legal limit of severity was 'to within an inch of his life'. In addition to this savage and joyless existence, when he was still only 11 years old Hitler suffered the tragic death of his younger brother. The death of his father in 1903 (which was followed by his beloved mother's demise in 1907) must at least have brought him some small degree of relief.

Desperate to rise above his father's hated subservience to the monarchy, Hitler had intended to devote his life to art and culture. However, his father had forced him to attend a *Realschule* (technical school) in Linz where he failed his exams, only receiving any appreciation for his diligence in drawing and gymnastics.

Despite his having been expelled from a second *Realschule* in Linz at the age of 17 and rejected by the Vienna Academy of Fine Arts, Hitler attended the local theatre, joined the musical club and a local library and tried desperately to move into a better class of society. But instead of being accepted as middle class, he found himself treated as a rough-hewn provincial and an outsider among the sons of academics.

It was hardly surprising that the suffering and rejection of Hitler's childhood and youth resulted in his withdrawal into his own complex fantasy world. There he dreamt of a new world order, whose style and content was massively influenced by the monumental style and content of Richard Wagner's operas and writing. Its importance to him was illustrated by his attendance at forty performances of *Tristan und Isolde* while still in his teens; immersing himself in Teutonic legend and Nordic mythology while rejecting the oppressive Catholic Church.

Increasingly, Hitler also adopted the prejudices, slogans, anxieties and demands of contemporary upper-class Viennese society. Among the elements were anti-Semitism and Social Darwinism, the latter advocating a rigorous process of selective extermination and breeding that was believed to be capable of preventing faulty lines of evolution and assuring one nation's superiority over all others; in other words, the master race theory. He also readily adopted a deep hatred of socialism.

In 1905 Hitler was still only 16 when he moved to Vienna, the bourgeois German city of Georg Ritter von Schönerer, the far right Pan-German politician, and Karl Lueger, the city's self-professed anti-Semitic mayor and a serious disciple of various occult organisations and theories. Schönerer was also obsessed with being overwhelmed by foreigners, considering the presence of the Jews, Roman Catholics, Slavs, Habsburgs and socialists to be a threat to the ever-increasing climate of nationalism. On their watch-chains, his followers wore the insignia of the committed anti-Semite in the shape of a hanged Jew, while Schönerer also coined the pseudo-medieval greeting '*heil*' and insisted on his followers referring to him as the 'Führer'.

*   *   *

In 1870, reluctant to join White's because of its restrictions on smoking, the Prince of Wales formed a new club, the Marlborough, which Bertie Mitford also joined. In the spring of 1871 his book, *Tales of Old Japan*, was published by Macmillan and enjoyed considerable success.

At the age of 37, having very nearly succumbed to illness in Japan, Bertie decided that it was time to leave the diplomatic service and settle down. He was rewarded for his foreign service with a post that was socially acceptable, congenial and remarkably stress free. He also found an 'entirely suitable wife' (referring no doubt both to her social and financial position) and bought Lindsey House in Cheyne Walk, Chelsea, where he was to live until he inherited Batsford in 1886.

The post of Secretary to the Board of Works appeared to be quite stultifying compared with his previous endeavours but Bertie displayed equal diligence and did work of lasting importance in the improvement of London parks and the restoration of the Tower of London. Meanwhile, his new wife, Lady Clementine Ogilvy, daughter of the 10th Earl of Airlie, added immeasurably to his social standing. At 21 she was sixteen years younger than Bertie.

One of the more interesting rumours that circulated in the family was that before transferring his affections to Clementine, Bertie had been having an affair with her mother, Blanche, the Countess Airlie, who was said to have strongly resented his relationship with her daughter. But her reputed bad humour failed to prevent their marriage on 31 December 1874 in the chapel of the family's Cortachy Castle, at the foot of Glen Prosen in eastern Scotland. It was a grand affair, celebrated with feasting and bagpipes in the kind of feudal setting most calculated to appeal to 'Dirty' Bertie, who may quite well have continued his affair with his mother-in-law even after the wedding and subsequent breeding programme with her daughter.

★   ★   ★

At the same time as Thomas Bowles was establishing his publishing company, he was also developing what appeared to be a social conscience, which was somewhat at odds with such a commitment to free enterprise. He wondered, 'Is it not strange that men should be found who can amass a fortune out of the blood and bone of their fellows, and who yet thoroughly believe that they have no duties to fulfil towards them?' Albeit, his charitable and moral view of mankind was largely confined to white Protestants; such undoubtedly unusual thinking, particularly amongst the privileged of the time, should not be confused with liberalism, or even worse, socialism.

He had also adopted an extreme dislike for the English class system and a deep distrust of groups in general, remarking, 'We seem to think that when we follow a multitude to do evil, the evil thereby becomes good.'

Thomas Bowles had a particularly forthright character, which resulted in his aggressive rudeness to anyone unwise enough to express disagreement with his opinions. Fortunately, he also never lost his power to charm, an accomplishment that his future in-law, Lady Clementine Mitford, never failed to find extremely irritating.

While Bertie had been busy acquiring a family and securing his future, Thomas was indulging a passion for the sea and sailing that he had inherited from his father, who had taught him how to handle sailing ships and navigate like a professional. Having obtained his master mariner's certificate in 1874, Thomas invested in a yacht called *Billy Baby*. Only then did he consider marriage. Jessica was seemingly like all young gals of that time, described as 'tall, fair-haired and slim. She was the youngest daughter of Major-General Charles Evans-Gordon, said to be descended from that other 'notable' Scots family, 'the Gordons of Lochinvar'. Unfortunately, her father and her five brothers were deeply unimpressed both by Thomas'[8] ebullience and his birthright. Even so, the couple's mutual attraction and determination was rewarded with their marriage, which finally took place in 1876.

They settled at Cleeve Lodge in Kensington where Jessica, despite her physical frailty and lack of enthusiasm for motherhood, gave birth to four children. Tragically, though somewhat predictably, she died during her fifth pregnancy when Sydney, the Mitford girls' mother, was still only 7 years old.

*　　*　　*

David Mitford was born on 13 March 1878. He was Bertie's third child and second son, and was grumpy from birth. Fortunately he was also 'strikingly handsome' and endowed with 'his father's luminous blue eyes'. Some also saw fit to mention that he 'took early to field sports, most especially shooting'.

Surprisingly, Bertie sent David not to Eton, but to Radley. 'Because he thought that David would behave badly and hinder [his elder brother] Clement in his Eton career.' It appears that David may have also lacked the necessary academic abilities to justify such investment, as he also failed to follow his brother to Summer Fields preparatory school; leaving him free to roam the countryside and concentrate on his ferrets, rod, lurcher and gun. Predictably, following such a profound lack of preparation, his stay at Radley proved notably unremarkable; achieving little, apart from establishing his social position.

David apparently planned to go into the army but failed to get into Sandhurst; another demonstration of his lack of even the most basic academic abilities. Determined that the boy should 'amount to *something*', Bertie found him a job tea planting in Ceylon; a position that was often awarded to 'remittance boys'. But for some unexplained reason, David returned home after a few years. It may have been due to his undiminished determination to serve in the army, for the outbreak of the Boer War in 1899 gave him the opportunity to join the Northumberland Fusiliers, a regiment with undoubted family connections but a great deal less social status than the 10th Hussars, into which his golden elder brother was commissioned, presumably after some considerable financial investment on the part of his father; as was 'the done thing' at the time.

Meanwhile, as a result of his father's refusal to invest in his younger son's commission, David was obliged to join up in the ranks. It was a courageous act of determination, but David paid a heavy price for his bravery and commitment when he was badly wounded. His injuries resulted in the loss of one of his lungs and his being 'invalided out' of the regiment. Such a debilitating injury should also have rendered him unfit for any further military service.

By now it had been accepted that he was not very good at reading or writing and it was said, rather generously, that none of Bertie's nine children inherited his intellectual interests. Unfortunately, this did not include his political views, which David certainly did inherit. He was also said to have possessed a distinct way with words, whatever that may have meant, for his use of words appeared to have been quite typical, if somewhat limited, for someone of his socio-political persuasion, and would by modern standards have appeared almost comical, peppered with evidence of his firm belief in his own social, political and racial superiority. Sydney Bowles, on the other hand, while rebelling against her father and developing extreme right-wing views, inherited Thomas' confidence as a prolific writer; with a useful knowledge of the press.

★   ★   ★

The pomp and splendour of Britain's aristocracy was threatened by a fatal decline in the 1880s. Much of the trouble was economic, based on the fact that the land, the territorial holdings, those broad acres that defined one's membership of the upper classes, were becoming less of an asset and more of a liability as time passed.

The debts and mortgages that encumbered most estates were easy enough to service in the mid-1800s, when farming was profitable, but as incomes fell the debt burden became more difficult to sustain. Taxation also became a major problem, especially in the form of death duties. Worse still were the great houses at the centre of the large estates, all of which were remorseless drains on the unstable incomes from the surrounding fields and needed endless repair and refurbishment. It was a constant fight against dry rot, leaking roofs and disintegrating stonework.

There was also the problem of labour. The days of peasant farmers who would work all hours that God made for little more than subsistence food and a hovel were long since gone, as agricultural labour increasingly moved to the urban environment created by the Industrial Revolution. Labour-saving machinery was being developed, but landowners such as David Mitford were reluctant to invest the necessary capital. The management of estates wasn't helped by the habit of insisting that the eldest son should inherit, regardless of his intelligence or suitability. They often possessed little knowledge of farming; considering it beneath them. Instead, they regarded the sole purpose for a gentleman's interest in woods, fields and streams to be that of blood and field sports. The ownership of land was generally accepted as a qualification for ennoblement rather than a commercial asset; financial endeavour still being considered somewhat vulgar.

With the inclement agricultural conditions and the ever-increasing power of industry, the balance of financial power and influence was moving away from the landed gentry into the hands of the meritocracy or 'nouveau riche'. They were even being awarded peerages and gaining a foothold on the social ladder.

'The richest of the traditional landed aristocracy, such as the Devonshires and the Westminsters, were, of course, so rich and had so many various forms of income, much of it from the colonies, that they could still afford to maintain their estates while remaining reasonably optimistic about their future prospects.'[9]

For those less blessed, 'selling off the family possessions, as the seventh and eighth Dukes of Marlborough did spectacularly in 1875, 1881 and 1886, was one way to keep afloat'[10]. The other way was to marry into American money.

This refinancing of old-world aristocracy with new-world money involved the simple expedient of selling British prestige to American heiresses. The most historically well publicised would be Lord Randolph Churchill's marriage to the American Jennie Jerome. While the Mitfords did not profit directly from American money, they certainly used their connections with the Churchills to their advantage.

Clementine (Airley), wife of Bertie Mitford, had a sister, Lady Blanche Hozier, otherwise known as 'Aunt Natty', who had a daughter also called Clementine who married Winston Churchill, or to be more precise, Bertie's wife's sister's daughter married him. Whichever way you put it, it was an extremely tenuous relationship but it did not prevent the Mitfords from exploiting Winston's political power to bail them out of various embarrassing and unpleasant situations. This would be particularly obvious in the case of Unity.

*   *   *

Having inherited the baronial Batsford House in 1886, with its large estate and considerable local responsibilities, which included accepting the roles of local magistrate and Lord Lieutenant of Gloucestershire, Bertie Mitford had to give up his post at the Board of Works. After a couple of years he also gave up his position as Member of Parliament for Stratford-upon-Avon.

During his first years at Batsford, 'Bertie threw himself with enthusiasm into country life and local pursuits, going rather little to London.'[11] In 1889, in an effort to afford him the opportunity of socialising with Edward VII and Wilhelm II of Germany, both keen yachtsmen, he also purchased a yacht and, despite having never served in the navy, was accepted as a member of the Royal Yacht Squadron at Cowes, on the Isle of Wight.

Bertie also retained an interest in gardening, though more in the monumental style than the herbaceous, and when the Prince of Wales was crowned Edward VII, he apparently 'made great use of Bertie as a gardening advisor for Windsor Castle, Sandringham and the other royal residences'. Years later, King George VI would inform Lord Dulverton that he was having trouble with polygonum (*Fallopia japonica*): 'Old Redesdale got my grandfather to plant it at Sandringham and we can't get rid of it.'[12]

Among the Cotswold gentry, Bertie was said to be 'well liked', if a bit 'full of himself'. It was also claimed that 'he was regarded with special respect, since he possessed in addition [to his perceived social standing] the glamour of a scholar and a traveller'.[13] However, the cost of achieving these social ambitions meant that he continually lived beyond his means.

Bertie was doubtless a gifted man of considerable intelligence, but unfortunately he lacked modesty and was prone to a bumptious demeanour and overtly formal manners. He was also in the habit of exaggerating his own achievements or getting others to exaggerate on his behalf. One of the Mitfords' favourite family myths was born during Cowes Week at The Royal Yacht Squadron when, in 1905, Bertie was invited to give a welcoming speech to a French naval

squadron. 'He spoke so beautifully (in French) that the French officers wept, and the Admiral, Caillard, said he could not speak more than
a few words in reply.' [14]

*   *   *

Early in 1885, Thomas Bowles made what was to become his most
successful publishing decision when he chose to start the first
weekly magazine 'for gentlewomen'. It was a success from the start,
particularly its small ads that concentrated on vacancies for cooks,
butlers and other domestic staff. *The Lady* is still owned by descendants of the Bowles family and run from the same offices in Bedford
Street, in London's Covent Garden.

Having established his new publication, Thomas Bowles also
decided to buy a yacht, but less for social effect than for the pure
adventure and 'edification' of his family, with whom he intended
embarking on an astonishingly ambitious extended cruise with
a crew of ten Aldeburgh fishermen, Tello the governess, a nurse,
a steward and a cook. In August 1888, they departed and for the
next twelve months the Bowles family home was Thomas' 200-ton
schooner, *Nereid*, named after the sea nymph in Greek mythology.

In the spring of 1889, after many adventures, they reached Beirut
and from there travelled to Jerusalem. Following a trip to the Wail-
ing Wall, the Mitford girls' maternal grandfather recorded in his log
a somewhat disturbing side to his character:

I don't see what the Jews have got to wail about. If they have been
expelled from Jerusalem, they are the rulers of London, Paris
and Berlin. If they are no longer governors of Palestine, they are
the tyrants of Europe and I cannot believe that they really hold
themselves to be worse off for the change. Nor shall I believe
it till I see the great house of Rothschild abandon London in
order to set up as bankers in Jerusalem; Baron de Hirsch leave
Paris in order to make a railway from Jerusalem to Jericho, with

a free refreshment bar at the place where the man fell among thieves; and all the Jewish controllers of the European Press, from Mr Levy Lawson downwards, cease printing startling intelligence in the West, and take to achieving the largest circulation in the world in Hebrew near the Gate of Damascus.

Thomas also displayed little of his reputed pro-Semitic 'sympathy' towards the less financially privileged Jewish refugees from Russia, writing, 'There is, I suppose, no human animal more utterly devoid of all dignity and nobility, none that bears an aspect at once so abject and so dangerous as the lower class of Russian Jews who have recently overrun the Holy City.' He talks of 'their pale womanly faces, rendered loathsome by a long, greasy curled lock in front of each ear; their narrow shoulders, bent carriage, filthy gabardines and furtive glances.'

These views, not uncommon at that time, serve as a reminder that Britain had already started playing her part in 'laying the foundations for inter-war racist and fascist thinking'.[15]

In 1899, when Adolf Hitler was still only 10 years old, the English-born Houston Stewart Chamberlain published *The Foundations of The Nineteenth Century*, which confirmed the author's belief that 'our' race was threatened by 'impurity', the worst agents of which were the Jews; as he put it, 'A mongrel is frequently very clever, but never reliable, morally he is always a weed.' Some twenty-five years later Hitler would draw upon Chamberlain's anti-Semitic writing for his own theory of race. But by then the English had already pre-empted both his and Oswald Mosley's use of racism as a political tool with the formation of The British Brothers League (BBL):

A British proto-fascist group that attempted to organise along paramilitary lines. The group was formed in 1902 in East London in response to the arrival of Jewish immigrants from Eastern Europe that had begun in 1880. The Aliens Act of 1905, which restricted immigration, was largely seen as a success for the BBL and, as a result, the movement, if not its aims, largely disappeared. [16]

Meanwhile, Austria would inherit the baton.

On Christmas day, some two years later, a Swastika flag would be flying for the first time over Werfenstein Castle, situated on the Danube near Linz, where a defrocked priest by the name of Jörg Lanz von Liebenfels had set up the headquarters of the newly formed Order of the New Templars. Funded by wealthy industrialists, he had bought the castle from where he planned to direct the creation of a 'heroic Aryan league that was to form the advance guard of the blond and blue-eyed master race'. He also promised 'to counter the socialist class struggle by a race struggle "to the hilt of the castration knife"' with a 'systematic program of breeding and extermination'. Apart from sterilisation, Lanz von Liebenfels promoted deportation to the 'ape jungle' and liquidation by forced labour or murder. He also launched *Ostara*, a magazine named after the German goddess of spring, from which he proclaimed a deranged and dangerous doctrine that included a 'heroic struggle between men he called Asings or Heldings and dwarfish, apelike creatures called Äfflings or Schrättlings'.

Having arrived in the Austrian capital in 1908, where he was rejected by The Vienna Academy of Arts for the second time, the young Hitler immersed himself in the music of Richard Wagner and became an avid reader of *Ostara* and the writing of Houston Stewart Chamberlain.

* * *

Having eventually reached Malta, via Alexandria, with his family, Thomas Bowles was reported to have received mail that informed him of urgent business matters that required his immediate return to England. This was thought to include an offer for the purchase of *Vanity Fair* that resulted in its sale for £20,000 to Arthur H. Evans at the end of March 1889, by which time Thomas had become, by anyone's standards, a very rich man.

Presumably because it was in need of a major refit following its lengthy sojourn, Thomas sold *Nereid* in 1889 and as if to illustrate his eccentricity he insisted on successfully fighting the next general election from his new yacht, *Hoyden* (the term for a woman of saucy, boisterous or carefree behaviour). This resulted in his being frequently depicted 'in *Punch* as "The Cap'en", in pirate dress with pistol and bandanna'.[17] It also resulted in his finally winning a parliamentary seat as Conservative member for King's Lynn in 1892.

Around this time yet another 'Mitfordesque' scandal arose, which by today's standards would probably have stopped Thomas Bowles' political career dead in its tracks. At some time during the cruise of the *Nereid*, Tello (Rita Stewart), the governess, had become pregnant and a son, John Stewart, was born to her not long after their return. There can be little doubt that Thomas was the father, for despite the fact that he never married her or even admitted his responsibility, he installed her in a house in London and gave her a job on *The Lady*, where after about three years she rose to the position of editor. She also found time to bear him three more sons while remaining 'on friendly terms not only with him but also with his children throughout their lives'.[18] However, neither she nor their four sons appear as part of Thomas Gibson Bowles' family trees! This was not an unusual situation at the time, either in England or Germany, where it was somewhat more extreme:

> It has frequently been demonstrated that the typical master of the Wilhelmine bourgeois household thought that a kind of right to sexual access went along with hiring a servant girl. He would often encourage his sons to have their first sexual experiences with the servant girls, when the boys were still too young to visit brothels. From the very beginning, therefore, relations within society created a tendency to equate the servant girl with the prostitute.[19]

Though it has to be said, a governess would have considered herself a considerable cut above a 'mere'[20] servant girl.

In the meantime Sydney, whose education had been limited to that imparted by the wayward Miss Stewart, and privileged to some rich and varied experience of life, was considered, at 14 years of age, 'old enough to start doing the housekeeping'. This arrangement, which also consisted of control of the household servants, apparently lasted for ten years, or until she left home in 1904 to marry David Mitford.

*   *   *

By now it had become obvious that neither of the Mitford grandfathers were quite what they seemed. Thomas, the pugnacious journalist and publisher, appeared to have been 'fortunately' illegitimate, while Bertie, the courtly and cultured landowner was, through inheritance, also undoubtedly fortunate! This same good fortune would continue to bless the Freeman-Mitfords, both financially and socially.

During the three years when they were in Parliament together, Bertie representing Stratford and Thomas King's Lynn, they 'were both on what would now be called the right of the Conservative Party'[21] and so perfectly qualified to develop in their offspring a sympathy with the fascist movement. But first the two families had to come together and it was politics that would enable this union.

The first visit of the Bowles family to Batsford took place in the winter of 1894/95. Bertie Mitford had apparently asked Thomas Bowles to come and speak for him at a political meeting, to which he had agreed. But there also appeared to be something distinctly non-political on the agenda: an informal but carefully stage-managed progeny 'presentation'.

Having been ushered into the library, the visitors were greeted by Bertie and Clementine. As Sydney recalled:

> Their daughters Frances and Iris were there as well, and, with his
> back to the fire, standing half on the fender, and wearing an old

velveteen coat such as keepers wore in those days, stood a wonderful figure of a young man. It was David, aged 17. So, when I
was 14 and he was 17, I fell in love with him. Certainly, I fell out
again, and we did not marry for nine years after that.

The meeting was obviously considered a success by the Bowles
family, 'for they went fairly often after that'.[22] Unfortunately, while
David's social pedigree and his 'handsome patrician features, tanned
skin and strikingly blue eyes' may have been viewed as appropriate
attributes for marriage to Sydney Bowles, some effort was required
to try and encourage the boy to amount to something beyond that
of amateur gamekeeper. It was obviously this parental pressure, rather
than his own motivation, that resulted in his attempting to pass the
written entrance examination to Sandhurst and subsequent ban-
ishment to a Ceylonese tea plantation, while Sydney continued to
manage her father's household and spend at least part of every long
summer aboard their yacht in Trouville.

With a love of the sea and the outdoor country life, it was perhaps
surprising that Sydney should 'grow up to be so tall, slim and good-
looking;'[23] 'some considered her a beauty, with her light brown hair,
blue eyes, regular features and slim figure.'[24]

Having not been totally convinced that 'young Mitford' might
develop into a suitable husband for his daughter, the decision was
made by Thomas to advertise her marital potential by preparing
Sydney for presentation at Court, a process that she found particularly tedious. This was evident by her reaction to the first party of
her season as a debutante at the Duke and Duchess of Devonshire's.
'The latter I thought too awful for words, dreadfully painted with a
hideous set grin on her face,' she later recalled.

Sydney was far happier in Scotland where the family and their
servants took up residence at Birsemhor Lodge in Aboyne. There
she learnt to shoot and to play golf and cricket. There were picnics, bicycle rides and long tiring walks up the misty, gorse-covered
mountains. All her life Sydney was said to have had a 'feeling' for

Scotland and its romantic scenery, though of course it would have been considered frightfully bad form not to display an appropriate enthusiasm for the Highlands. However, she soon developed an even greater enthusiasm for skating, and in particular for a Swedish skating instructor called Grenander. Sydney even daydreamed about him proposing to her: 'If he were English, and in every way a man of my own station, I know I would say yes.' She also fell 'passionately in love' with a somewhat notorious and very good-looking womaniser called Edward, known to his friends as Jimmy Meade. But his reputation went before him and marriage was considered quite out of the question, although it was said 'tears were streaming down her cheeks as she walked up the aisle to get married to David and that this was due to the fact that her heart still belonged to Jimmy Meade'.[25]

2

THE 'GOLDEN' YEARS

1904–18

Golden boys and girls all must
Like chimney sweeps
Come to dust
William Shakespeare

Sydney Bowles finally married David Freeman-Mitford in 1904, when she was 24 and he was 26. Her father, Thomas, lent them his yacht, *Hoyden*, and its captain and crew for their honeymoon cruise. Afterwards he gave David a job on *The Lady*, but with his limited academic abilities, let alone administrative knowledge, it is difficult to tell exactly what his employment might have entailed. The only record of any work was of his having rid the building of rats with the assistance of his tame mongoose (the Indian subcontinent's equivalent of a Jack Russell terrier), which he had brought back with him from Ceylon. Apart from the occasional foray into urban field sports, David admitted to being generally bored to death, yet he still continued diligently for ten years. Thomas also paid Sydney a small allowance.

One or other of their fathers, probably Thomas, must have also bought them a house in Graham Street, Islington, where, despite a lack of space and limited income, David and Sydney Mitford immediately started a family. Nancy arrived in 1904, followed by Pam in 1907, Tom in 1909, Diana in 1910 and Unity in 1914.

> With David's salary the couple had a joint income of around a thousand pounds a year and on this Sydney's meticulous household accounts reveal that they employed five female servants. In a house that Nancy described as 'minute', there was a cook, a parlour maid, a housemaid, a kitchen maid, a nanny and a nursemaid. Nancy once asked her mother, 'What did you do all day?' and received a reply to the effect, 'I lived for you all'.[1]

While it is highly unlikely that Sydney would have spent much time in the kitchen, her cook and kitchen-maid being responsible for the preparation of the family's food, both Jessica and Jonathan Guinness suggested Sydney had inherited her father's somewhat unusual dietary principles. They alleged these principles were in fact based on kosher dietary laws, whose adoption by Sydney had been based on her belief that Jews did not get cancer, while her father vehemently believed 'their diet had given them the necessary health to survive persecution through the centuries'. But the evidence to support their claim seemed to be based on Thomas' refusal to consume pork or shellfish, which Sydney continued to enforce in the Mitford household.

The consumption of either uncured pork or shellfish in the days before domestic refrigerators were readily available was considered far too risky for most English people to even consider. But that precaution hardly constituted a kosher diet. There was certainly never any evidence of the existence on their menu of such Jewish staples as chicken soup, latkes, chopped liver, matzos, gefilte fish or the like. Meanwhile, David never displayed any intention of being deprived of his smoked bacon and pork sausages.

A far more dangerous inheritance was that of Thomas' aversion to conventional medicine, which Sydney would also adopt. In broad terms they believed that the 'Good Body' supported by the afore-mentioned diet and plenty of fresh air was quite capable of over-coming illness without the introduction of medicines. However, if these principles had been adhered to without compromise, David would not have survived his injuries in the Boer War.

David's domestic requirements offered neither the staff nor his wife any particular challenge, apart from his three specific aversions. One was to a lack of punctuality. The second was sickness, while the third was the spilling of drinks and generally 'untidy' eating. His reaction to any of these misdemeanours could be extreme. Fortunately, he was a lifelong abstainer from alcohol, not on grounds of health or moral principle, or even the incendiary effect it could have had on his temper; he just never liked the taste.

He and his family certainly lived to a standard that today would be regarded as extremely comfortable; a standard considerably higher than either his responsibilities or his abilities warranted. Children continued to be born despite the fact that their first house was so small, but by 1914, just prior to the outbreak of war, they managed to move to a larger house on Victoria Road, Kensington, where Unity, their fifth child, was born.

> David would have been better prepared for what was in fact to be his future, if his own father had given him a house on his estate and sent him to be trained in agriculture or estate management. But he was the second son and there was no intention to leave him any land of his own.[2]

David's brother, educated at Eton and commissioned in the 10th Hussars, was unlikely to have ever intended to become seriously involved in farming.

All things considered David's – and thus the Mitfords' – future prospects seemed unlikely to amount to a great deal.

*   *   *

Like most fathers, David Mitford probably found his daughters more appealing than he would have done sons, while Sydney would undoubtedly have preferred a family of Mitford boys. But *six* daughters were too much, even for David, and had a profoundly negative effect on his well-being. Attempts to convince the readers of numerous tomes that, rather than being a bad-tempered, self-centred if entertaining man, he was in fact sensitive and affectionate, seem somewhat far-fetched. He may have been 'present at the births of all of his seven children, anticipating by many decades the vogue for paternal participation in childbirth',[3] but this was far more likely to have been the result of Sydney's giving birth to her children at home, where David was invariably present, than his insistence of being present at the actual delivery. Few midwives would have stood for such a thing. 'Whatever next?' she would have said. It is certainly unlikely that his favourite daughter, Nancy, could confirm with any degree of accuracy who was at her own arrival in 1904.

Favourite or not, Nancy liked to give the impression, particularly in her book *The Water Beetle*, that there was scant sensitivity or affection involved in her childhood, especially on the part of her mother: 'I was never hugged or kissed [by our mother] as a small child … She was very cold and sarky [sarcastic] with me. I don't reproach her for it, people have a perfect right to dislike their children.' Decca, as Jessica was known amongst family and friends, agreed, claiming, 'I guess it's that awful disapproving quality that I always hated about her.'

Jessica's condemnation was probably true as far as parental affection was concerned, for like most young children of their financial and social position, they spent more time with their nanny than their parents. In a letter dated 20 July 1952, Sydney denied Nancy's accusation. 'You were terribly spoilt as a little child, and by all. It was Puma's idea. She said you must never hear an angry word and you never did, but you used to get in tremendous rages, often shaming us in the street but the angry word was never allowed.' Puma, more often known as Pussy, was in fact David's eldest sister, Frances Kearsey.

Giving their aunt two nicknames could be considered unremarkable, particularly in a family dominated by children for over thirty years. But there was something about the Mitford habit of giving everyone juvenile nicknames that, after a while, became rather tedious. Especially when they had nothing else particularly remarkable to say about many of the people in question.

* * *

While the Mitfords were busy breeding girls, Bertie began to develop his fascist ideals and an interest in Houston Stewart Chamberlain and his anti-Semitic Social Darwinism. Even though Chamberlain was English, he wrote in German and became best known for his work of historical philosophy, *The Foundations of the Nineteenth Century*, published in the original German in 1899.

An ardent disciple of Wagner, Chamberlain eventually married the composer's daughter, Eva. During the First World War he adopted German nationality, following which his own countrymen were said to have come to regard him as being 'beyond the pale'. But this was probably more the result of propaganda than a true reflection of his English following, which remained loyal and sympathetic and included many of Bertie's contemporaries. Chamberlainstrasse in Bayreuth was named after him and still exists to this day.

According to Jonathan Guinness, an ex-chairman of the Monday Club (renowned for its promotion of extreme right-wing views concerning race and immigration), 'Chamberlain believed that culture was determined by racial character, that the races associated with the Indo-European or "Aryan" languages were the best in the world, and that of these races the Teutonic or Germanic people were pre-eminent.'

Probably as a result of his interest in Chamberlain, on a number of occasions Bertie attended the Bayreuth Festival, at the time effectively run by the composer's son, Siegfried. As a result, Bertie came to know the Wagner family well. He also accepted Wagner's claim that 'the music dramas of his maturity [were] not operas', but something on a higher creative and spiritual level. Bertie's descendants, Tom, Diana and Unity, and afterwards Diana's sons Jonathan, Alexander and Max, were also to become devotees of his music and friends of the composer's family. On numerous occasions they joined the annual pilgrimage to his house, *Wahnfried*, where, following the death of Wagner's wife, Cosima, their hostess was Siegfried's widow, Winifred. They were in no way discouraged – and in some cases appeared to have been positively *encouraged* – by Wagner's subsequent reputation as an anti-Semite.

*   *   *

In 1906 David Lloyd George, the British-born, Welsh-bred Liberal politician, joined the new Liberal cabinet of Sir Henry Campbell-Bannerman as President of the Board of Trade after a landslide victory at the general election. He would be largely responsible for what would prove to be the basis of the Welfare State but which was known at the time as the 'People's Budget'. The bill was initially rejected by the House of Lords because it angered the landed gentry, and Lloyd George would anger their lordships even further by announcing, in a language none of the aristocracy could understand, his intention to stand up for the common man at the expense of what he called 'The Dukes', who were predictably incandescent with rage and indignation, even more so when he translated his speech from Welsh into English.

With 10 million working men living in conditions of chronic destitution, and Russia and Poland having already entered the initial stages of armed revolution, it was hardly surprising that the English upper classes were feeling threatened. Death duties, land taxes and super tax would do little to improve their humour.

While their fathers were reacting to political and social events, David and Sydney were celebrating the arrival of what they doubtless hoped would be their first son, Tom's birth in 1909 having 'delighted' Sydney. However, a return to the Mitford form soon followed with the birth of Diana. It was due to Diana's beauty, already apparent when she was only months old, that one of the most important additions to the family arrived in the form of Laura Dicks.

After Sydney and the children had already worked their way through three nannies and advertised in *The Lady* for a fourth, Laura Dicks applied for the post.

> She was thin, pale, fine-featured, with curly reddish brown hair and a kindly expression. Sydney liked her on sight, but wondered, looking at her, if she was physically capable of coping with four children even though she was only thirty-nine. The same thing occurred independently to Laura. However, the sight of Diana as a baby decided her … 'Oh! What a lovely baby!'[4] she exclaimed and was accepted and signed on for life and immediately christened 'Blor'.

Dicks became in the process the best-known nanny in the country, apart from 'Lillibeth's' beloved 'Crawfie'.[5]

> Nancy, who admits, or to be more accurate proclaims, that she herself was vile to others, thinks she would have been much worse but for Blor: 'My mother's scoldings and my father's whippings had little effect, but Blor [who had a reputation for fairness and consideration for others] at least made me feel ashamed of myself'.

One wonders how children brought up under such a fine influence could develop such extreme fascist tendencies. Was it perhaps the 'whippings'?

As 'whippings', or 'thrashings', became less socially accept-able, their father's physical reaction to major and sometimes minor annoying misdemeanours would be increasingly denied by the family. Doubtless, nannies were also encouraged to raise a hand from time to time. Schoolteachers certainly were. But it was not only the English who fostered their parental responsibilities into the hands of English nannies and governesses; American historian Jonathan Petropoulos has spoken of Friedrich Karl von Hesse and Margaret using the services of 'a series of English governesses' to educate their children. Apparently this was the case with many German princes.

'Princess Margeret ("Peg") von Hessen-Darmstadt (née Geddes and born in Dublin) noted: "a great deal of English was spoken in the house as a result of the English nannies, who supervised all six brothers when they were children".'[6] It was this German influ-ence on the English accent that resulted in Oxford or Queen's English, its adoption in Victoria's Court and subsequent affecta-tion by the upper echelons of England's 'posh' society, exemplified by the Mitfords.

*   *   *

In 1911 the academic connection between the Mitfords, anti-Semitism and fascism was endorsed when the English translation of Houston Stewart Chamberlain's *The Foundation of the Nineteenth Century* appeared with a lengthy and toe-curlingly embarrassing introduction by their grandfather, Bertie Redesdale, which included such phrases as 'pages adorned with brilliant passages of the loftiest eloquence' and 'one of the masterpieces of the century'.

Far less embarrassing, but considerably more worrying, was Chamberlain's writing, which propounded such theories as, 'Physi-cally and mentally, the Aryans are pre-eminent among all peoples; for that reason they are by right … the lords of the world.'

In the book he not only promoted the Aryans, but more spe-cifically the German Aryans who he believed to be the only ones qualified to inherit the power and glory of ancient Greece and Rome. He also claimed that it was the Jews who had, since the first century, been preventing this inheritance from taking place.

Having denigrated the Jews both racially and religiously and analysed them physically, Chamberlain recommended that the Germans had the right and the responsibility to reduce the risk of Jewish contamination. Presumably by whatever process they saw fit to employ.

As the author David Pryce-Jones points out:

> The bogus apparatus of justified racial persecution was at hand, and the Nazis had only to pick it up from him … The association of Unity with [H. S.] Chamberlain through her grandfather won her a place by divine right [or so David believed] in the Nazi scheme of things. It was a source of wonder to Hitler and according to 'Gaby' Bentinck he referred to it often during conversations with Unity and others, as positive proof of the way that breeding and blood were the masters of destiny.

While it is not too difficult to appreciate the effect such a book may have had on Adolf Hitler, its appeal was not limited to political extremists or Germans, and when its English translation was published in 1911 it was roundly praised and received positive reviews in much of the British press. By 1938 it would have sold a quarter of a million copies.

As the English translation comprised 1,185 pages, it would also give a clear indication as to why its privileged readership were also known as the 'leisured classes'. George Bernard Shaw called it a 'historical masterpiece' and it has remained in print and enthusiastically read up to the present day.

So, there can be little doubt that the whole ghastly business had already started well before Hitler and the Nazis came to power and that the seeds had not just been sown in the Mitford family; they were sprouting in other, similar English families, and in some they were already well established.

*　　*　　*

In 1912 David Redesdale was said to have been persuaded by a chum at his club to purchase a gold mine in Canada consisting of claims totalling 40 acres on a new gold field in the Kirkland Lake district of northern Ontario. It was a remarkable undertaking. Just getting there and back, which they did on a number of occasions, would have presented considerable logistical and financial problems. According to Unity, as revealed many years later to Gaby Bentinck, the whole enterprise was in fact financed by Sydney's father, who was motivated by somewhat darker forces than mere fortune and adventure.

Having already displayed a belief in the extreme social and political ideas symbolised by the swastika flag, Bertie was all too easily persuaded to invest in this particular claim. The name of the local town in Ontario, Swastika, being an overpowering omen that they all doubtless believed would have a profound effect upon their fortunes and in their involvement in the creation of a master race. The fact that David and Sydney accepted Bertie's suggestion to call his granddaughter Valkyrie as a mark of reverence to Wagner, only serves to support the conjecture that even before her birth, Unity's future was pre-ordained; particularly in view of her parents' proud claim that she was conceived in Swastika.

*　　*　　*

With the birth of their fourth daughter it must have become obvious to both David and Sydney that they would eventually be faced with the expensive task of finding suitably wealthy and socially acceptable husbands for their daughters. It was the process of 'marketing' the girls at which Sydney would prove so adept. But first they had to make the then unavoidable investment in their participation in the social season as debutantes; the highlight of which would be their presentation at Court. This process served to announce their social position and marital eligibility. It also involved a huge amount of entertaining, dressmaking, hairdressing and travel; a process that all the girls pretended to hate. Meanwhile, they also invested in their son's education at prep school prior to the inevitable Eton and Oxford. All of which would have been quite impossible without considerable financial assistance. Traditionally, such funding would have been the responsibility of their grandparents.

It helped, of course, that all the girls were attractive; in the case of Diana outstandingly so. But from an early age, due to their father's difficulty with accepting visitors and their mother's refusal to allow them to mix with anyone or go anywhere that she considered of insufficient social status, they were obliged to develop an ability to amuse themselves at home or by visiting, or being visited by, relatives. Unfortunately this social self-sufficiency had a rather unpleasant side to it, usually hidden beneath a veneer of somewhat sadistic humour.

Jonathan Guinness talked of the family having been 'decent and sensitive' and 'sparklingly funny; but with the jokes came an intensity of passion in love and politics. Some find this disturbing.' This was not always as appealing as it sounds and needs a degree of translation, for the jokes were only funny if you were not the butt of what passed for sparkling fun and often took the form of quite cruel teasing:

> Much of the sisters' childhood was spent in fear of Nancy … her barbed teasing became second nature to Nancy and the ethos of the Mitford nursery … the only defence against it was laughter. Nothing was sacred, any outward display of feelings was to be mocked, everything became the subject of a joke or a tease ('We shrieked!').

The 'passion in love and politics' presumably referred to their often questionable sexual and political morality and, with the exception of Jessica, their subsequent commitment to fascism.

While the more theatrical members of society found all this quite irresistible, many potential suitors found the mixture more than somewhat challenging.

★   ★   ★

In 1914, *The Times* reported Britain's declaration of war against Germany. It sent cheering crowds surging through London to gather outside Buckingham Palace singing the national anthem. From there many headed to the recruitment centres, and from there, to war. This misplaced patriotism usually, though not always, vanished within moments of appreciating the full hideousness of it all, despite theatricals like Ernest Thesiger's attempting to make light of the situation by commenting with epicene languor, 'Oh, my dear, the noise! ... and the PEOPLE ...!'

The First World War had much to do with Germany's jealousy of the British Empire and Britain's jealousy of Germany's growing industrial power. It didn't help that Kaiser Wilhelm, who had never really grown up and still enjoyed nothing so much as playing soldiers, was quite round the bend. The outcome of this spectacularly dreadful and totally pointless game was the death and maiming of 37 million people, of whom a particularly high percentage came from the British and German privileged classes. This was largely due to the policy of sending young men into battle ahead of their troops armed only with a revolver, which was particularly ineffective against machine guns and mortars, or even the marginally more effective policy of giving rifles to the terrified troops who were forced to follow them.

It should be said that not all Englishmen were in too much of a hurry to get involved in such suicidal lunacy in the first place. In *Hurrah for the Blackshirts!* Martin Pugh reported that, 'The country still seemed a prey to fears ... that its young men were too corrupted by materialism and leisure to respond willingly to the call to arms', which resulted in the need for military conscription:

By the summer of 1915 the press was denouncing 'shirkers' for holding back, and young women had started distributing white feathers to men seen in public wearing civilian clothes. These were said to be the first symptoms of the post-war obsession with declining masculinity, the spread of effeminacy and the influence of homosexuality in Britain.

But regardless of whether their young men were 'AC or DC' and were pushed or jumped (i.e. whether they were conscripted or volunteered), the grand families of England and Germany were decimated.

Soon after the outbreak of hostilities, David Mitford rejoined the Northumberland Fusiliers, despite the fact that he was not obliged to do so. Largely as a result of the appalling casualties amongst the young officers, he was also finally given a commission, albeit as a lowly second lieutenant, logistics officer. While he would no doubt have preferred to have undertaken a more active combatant role, his position behind the lines probably saved his life. But once again David displayed considerable determination and courage and was even 'mentioned in dispatches' for his 'sterling work' in getting supplies through to his battalion during the Second Battle of Ypres. This activity also took a considerable toll on his health and he was subsequently rewarded with a move to Oxford as assistant provost marshal; involved in the somewhat less demanding task, for him, of recruitment.

All five of the Mitford brothers answered the call to arms but, ironically, in May 1915 it would be the failure of Clement, Bertie's chosen 'golden boy', to return that would eventually transport David Mitford from his lowly role as an office manager into his new role as Lord Redesdale, peer, member of the landed gentry, fascist and father of the Mitford girls.

The following year his father Bertie died. Apparently he had gone fishing, sat on wet grass, caught a feverish chill and died on 17 August. After which, his widow 'Clementine went to live at Redesdale Cottage in Northumberland, where her health improved'.

And, presumably not suffering from any surfeit of grief, she 'lived until 1932, and her descendants loved her in her mellow old age'.[7]

And so David, more by luck than judgement, inherited the title of Lord Redesdale and even a stately pile in the form of the vast, mock-Elizabethan Batsford House. It was a social elevation to which the family were said to have taken like ducks to water. People were soon encouraged to refer to them by their titled name, an imposition that was not appreciated by all, particularly the wife of novelist Richard Hughes, who remarked that, 'The Redesdales were terribly grand. Quite unapproachable!'

The estate was said to have been valued at some £33,000 in cash and shares. After tax and other bequests David was left with just under £17,000, which would represent a present-day monetary value of more than £600,000, while the land and properties in Gloucestershire, Oxfordshire and Northumberland would be worth seven or eight times that amount.

Despite their inherited wealth, the family liked to give the impression that their life was in no way exceptional and that they lived in a sort of genteel poverty. They even claimed that Sydney was obliged to raise cash by keeping bees. 'She managed the bee-hives herself with the help of the "redoubtable" Miss Mirams'[8], the children's governess, selling the resulting honey in London, presum-ably charging a Mitford premium. Many years later Debo would develop a similar strategy to assist in funding the Duke of Devon-shire's crumbling estate.

At this time it was fashionable for the privileged classes to claim poverty, or what they liked to think may have been a kind of genteel relative of such a thing, while in fact, they continued to live in very considerable comfort and enjoy many privileges.

Unfortunately, due to excessive debts and death duties, Batsford House, the arboretum and much of the land would need to be sold off, but the decision was made to delay the sale until after the end of the war. The Redesdales also decided to share the house with the children of Ronald Norman, brother of the governor of the

Bank of England, and his wife, Lady Florence, who wanted to get their four children out of London for the duration of the war. There was certainly enough space for half-a-dozen families, though it is quite likely that the arrangement was adopted to lessen the likelihood of the house being requisitioned by the army. The move from their undistinguished London home to a dramatically ostentatious country mansion also ensured that at least the first five Mitford children were assured of developing an appropriate degree of eminence, thus setting them on the right social path, particularly in the case of Unity.

According to David Pryce-Jones:

> A Hon ... then, Unity was from the age of two, but a rebel she was to become only by way of disobedience, for the deeper outlook of superiority and indifference to others which is at the base of every racial theory, anti-Semitism included, was natural to her elders, as it was to be to her.

There is also some anecdotal evidence to suggest that the Mitfords enjoyed a fairly relaxed lifestyle while they were in residence. 'When David was at home, the family played hide-and-seek all over the house, bringing all five staircases into use.'[9] Diana remembered 'the sound of footsteps thumping down the corridor, a distant scuffle and scream and Farve's triumphant roar when he caught someone.' One of the Norman children's few anecdotes concerned Diana's reaction to seeing their father reading a book. 'I've never heard of a man reading.' Apparently, 'she judged all men by reference to her own father.'[10] It was also another indication of the limitation of Lord Redesdale's academic abilities.

*   *   *

While they obviously enjoyed their time at Batsford, 'the classic years of the Mitford childhood'[11] only really started when they arrived at Asthall Manor, in the quintessential Oxfordshire village of Swinbrook, in 1919.

Even today it remains a quite remarkably original, picture-book English village where deer appear from lush green hedge-rows, hedgehogs scamper along the verges and ducks and ducklings paddle across the duck pond. In the words of Dame Edith Evans, *the* actress of that era, the village is 'a veritable haven of sylvan joy'.

In early summer, Swinbrook resembles a Rousseau-like green jungle through which the most beautiful Windrush trout stream runs; the heavy flow of the deep stream swirling the green river grass, like Ophelia's hair. The picturesque Swan Inn and cottage stands next to the stream. Inside are large, sepia pictures of the Mit-fords indulging in various rural activities in the company of assur-edly 'devoted' servants. A small sign reminds one that the inn is now the property of The Duchess of Devonshire, née Debo Mitford; or at least her trust.

But like so many things concerning the Mitford girls, everything is not quite what it seems; even in death. Some of the local residents seem unprepared to accept the reality of their inheritance: 'You can see their gravestones in the village churchyard. All except Unity of course. They wouldn't allow her to be buried there because of that business with Hitler.' But they did and she is. There, 'in pride of place' amidst her sisters' suitably weathered but simple Mitford family gravestones.

3

FASCISM AND FANTASY

1918–34

Spoil the child
Spare the rod
Open up the caviar
And say Thank God
Noel Coward

After the First World War it had soon became obvious that the extravagantly theatrical Batsford House and its surrounding Gloucestershire farmland was of little use to any owner lacking agricultural ambition or the desire to open his home to the public. With little of either, Lord Redesdale was faced with not only the aforementioned debts and inheritance tax but also the ever-increasing cost of maintaining the house. So, encouraged by a post-war boom in land prices, his financial advisers managed to convince him of the wisdom of selling both the house and its land. Thus, he could refill the family coffers while retaining his holdings in Oxfordshire. However, he would also have to move into a somewhat more practical house, though of course somewhere still befitting his recently 'ennobled' status.

Fortunately, just such a house had recently become vacant. More importantly, if the remaining profits from the sale were safely invested by the aforementioned financial advisers, the Mitfords could continue to live in considerable comfort with little risk of any of them ever having to seek gainful employment or involve themselves in any form of trade apart, perhaps, from their father's various financial investments; investments from which he would have been isolated by bank managers, stockbrokers and other 'financial servants'. He was also eventually persuaded to sell his Canadian mining interests, which was a great relief to his family who considered any form of manual labour to be quite unacceptable, for a man in his position.

Thus, Lord Redesdale remained free to indulge his two great passions in life: shooting and fishing, for which the Oxfordshire countryside was ideally suited and which, naturally, his fellow peers expected of him. But Lord Redesdale lived in an age when such indulgence was becoming increasingly threatened and even as a young child Jessica appreciated the anachronistic qualities of her father, saying, 'Farve, d'you realise that as well as being a sub-human you're a feudal remnant?' The latter observation was remarkably accurate if somewhat precocious, coming as it did from a 14-year-old girl, but considering the family's association with the Third Reich, the former part of the statement was cause for considerably greater concern; sub-human being the term used by the Nazis for those they considered unfit to be considered part of the human race.

Lord Redesdale was assisted in the enjoyment of his various sporting pastimes by his 'devoted' chauffeur, James Turner, who loved shooting as much as his master and enjoyed driving him to grand shoots; like most personal servants he was almost certainly an even greater snob than his master. Turner took an active role in ensuring that his master's prowess remained something of which to be proud. He caused some confusion by dressing in almost identical moleskin jacket and polished leather gaiters, which, so it was said at David's club, probably resulted in Lord Redesdale occasionally achieving questionable bird counts.

Asthall Manor, the beautiful, 'rambling and commodious'[1] Jacobean house, was – and still is – situated not in the village of Swinbrook at all, but 2 miles down river at Asthall, a fact that the Mitfords tended to gloss over, perhaps because they did not own the village as completely as those of Swinbrook and Widford. Those were the days when one could 'own' villages and their inhabitants as a result of tenancies or cottages 'tied' to jobs on the estate, but because David's tenants were obliged to paint their doors, gates and fences Redesdale blue, it was easy to distinguish exactly which properties formed part of his estate.

The manor actually adjoined one of his Lordship's farms, a situation that Redesdale never found easy to accept. He even endeavoured to advance its status with the addition of a ballroom, though there is little evidence of their having given a lot of balls. But David also enjoyed a lifelong enthusiasm for building, or at least the instructing of craftsmen to do so on his behalf, and the ballroom was a perfect excuse for such endeavour. Unfortunately, following Prince Albert's example and to the extreme detriment of some of England's finest architectural heritage, it was something in which many members of the aristocracy had dabbled for several years.

The manor was also situated next door to the village church, but due to the fact that David held no sway over the vicar's stipend and was thus unable to control the length or subject of his sermons, the family frequented the Swinbrook church. However, there is no evidence of any religious commitment beyond that which the family considered their social duty, apart, that is, from Unity's somewhat extreme spiritual development.

Diana insisted their father never intended to stay there long, always planning to build his own 'unattached' house on the hill above Swinbrook. But by the time his new house was finally built the children had come to realise how perfectly Asthall had fulfilled its role as the Mitford girls' family home.

If devotees of the girls had been invited to imagine such a thing, there can be little doubt they would all have described Asthall Manor.

*   *   *

While the Mitford family could be said to have profited both socially and financially from the First World War, the death of so many eligible young men also reduced the chances of the girls finding suitable husbands. As the next generation of British and German ruling classes were being slaughtered in the trenches, the Mitford girls were kept busy in the nursery and fields, developing what their mother hoped would be the advantageous appeal of their unique social character. The resulting, charmingly childlike qualities would stay with them for life. It was an English tradition amongst the privileged classes. Because they saw so little of their parents, who considered formal education for girls to be quite unnecessary, they relied on Nanny to adopt the role of surrogate mother; with whom the girls would share their lives until marriage. It was thus hardly surprising that they developed such things as their own nursery language and humour.

David and Sydney were not alone in believing that it was unnecessary to educate girls beyond reading, writing and basic arithmetic; the latter skill only deemed necessary in order for them to be even vaguely capable of keeping or checking household accounts. They were also expected to have a reasonable grasp of the French language and enough geography and history to prevent them appearing ignorant in polite society. Music, needlework and deportment were also included in their curriculum. The imparting of this knowledge was the responsibility of a governess, and/or private lessons in Oxford.

Sons, of course, who were packed off to boarding school as soon as possible, often from as early an age as 5 years old, had to rely on 'Matron' for surrogate maternal reassurance. The fact that

Tom was an intelligent and good-looking boy who was adored by both his parents may have contributed to his not being 'encouraged' to attend Lockers Park preparatory school until he was 9 years old. 'David's admiration helped Tom to become unusually self-confident', although there were also those who believed him to be more accurately described as 'supremely arrogant'[2].

This arrogance was doubtless encouraged by the fact that even from an early age Tom was better read than his father. Not a supreme challenge it has to be said; and it was a fact that Lord Redesdale rather graciously accepted. This became obvious when he sold Batsford in 1919 and sought his 10-year-old son's literary appreciation in advising him which of the inherited books they should leave and which should form the basis of their new library. 'It was Nancy and Tom who became generally well read, followed by Diana and "in some areas" Unity.'[3]

Sometimes it appeared that the children's influence on David was greater than his on them, even to the point where some of his field sports developed a distinctly 'nursery' quality. The biographer Mary Lovell recorded one splendid example:

> One of David's dogs was a bloodhound and the major participant in a favourite game they called 'child hunt' … The quarry, or the 'hares', as the participating children were called, were given a head start and would set off running across fields, laying as difficult a trail as possible by running in circles, through 'fouled' land such as fields containing sheep or cattle, and crossing and re-crossing streams. When they could run no more they would stop and sit down while they waited for the hound to find them. Invariably the hound would then jump all over them and lick their faces in recognition before 'poor old Farve' (puce in the face as a result of his exertions) caught up to reward the animal with pieces of raw meat.

While they all enjoyed the sport, it doubtless acted as a substitute for the more conventional form of pursuit, for while fully immersing himself in the life of a country gentleman, David did not ride to hounds. Having previously broken his pelvis in a frightful fall, he never got on a horse again. Instead, he bred shire horses. While riding was said to have remained an integral part of his children's lives, there remains remarkably little evidence of such; Pam proving the only exception.

*   *   *

Three or four times a year, when it is said they were old enough to appreciate it, the 'whole family' also used to visit Stratford-upon-Avon to see a Shakespeare play. It actually seems highly unlikely that David attended these performances, which were probably organised by a long-suffering governess. As the children giggled and joked their way through every performance it also seems unlikely that 'they came to know Shakespeare' on anything other than an anecdotal level. These occasional visits to Stratford, combined with free access to a library full of books chosen by a 10-year-old child, do little to validate the claim that 'the Mitford household was a cultured one'[4]. It was also not a unanimously held opinion. The writer John Atkins said that Nancy's childhood was 'as intellectually restricted as that of a slum child'.

What the Mitford girls were developing 'in spades' was a quite remarkable ability to entertain each other and those in their social circle by lambasting themselves and their social class in a manner and style that was unashamedly theatrical.

One of the essential elements of their mutual entertainment was the development of a distinctive way of speaking that was, despite their protestations, affected. It was not just the extreme 'Oxford accent' that so many of their contemporaries had also adopted; it was their use of words, phrases and exaggerated emphasis that was so unique. Their habit of adding importance and style to the most trivial of objects or occasions also proved immensely popular with their friends and acolytes. A particular favourite concerned toast.

'During the war Evelyn Waugh took Nancy to lunch at the Hyde Park Hotel; there was (Melba) toast on the table in little silver racks. "Oh!" she exclaimed in tones of rapture: "Toooooast!"[5] Waugh was so impressed that he subsequently included this anecdote in *Brideshead Revisited*.

Equally, the Mitfords developed a habit of gift-wrapping any request for even the simplest (in fact, *preferably* the simplest) favour in 'elaborate injunctions'. One was not to even *think* of carrying out the request if it gave one the *least* trouble. On completion there followed an equally ornate letter of appreciation.

Debo wrote to Diana shortly after Christmas 1943:

> Darling-Honks, Oh Honks oh Honks the gifts, I am completely overcome by their glory I can't think what to thank you for first. The underclothes Honks, the stockings, all the Honnish things for Em, well I must say I never saw such a parcel. The coupons Honks, you must have spent so many I can hardly bear to think of you going quite naked which is what you'll surely have to do …

Exaggerated nouns, verbs and adjectives as in '*lashings* of', 'simply *swathed* in' and '*quite* too divine' were also used a lot. By the 1920s 'everyone' was doing it. Noel Coward even used such words and phrases in his songs and they thus entered common usage, which was, of course, a total contradiction in terms and not what the purpose was at all.

As well as their style and manner of speech, during their early years of nursery life, like many of their contemporaries, the Mitford girls and Tom not only adopted the popular habit of awarding nicknames but also developed their own languages. Of course, Jonathan Guinness explains it quite sublimely:

> Boudledidge was the odder of them, shared between Unity and Decca; it had to be uttered while making a miserable, frowning and rather costive-looking grimace with the mouth pulled

sharply down to one side. Hopeless yearning was the keynote, together of course with deadly seriousness. The language itself was English with the vowels distorted, the consonants softened and extra syllables inserted, the word 'boudledidge' being itself derived on this system from 'pallish', the language of the pals or boudles. 'Dear old pals, jolly old pals,' the sisters would sing; or in Boudledidge 'Deedre oudle boud-d-d-dles, juddledy oudle boud-d-d-dles'.

The other language, Honnish, was the language of Decca and Debo. When overt snobbery became less socially acceptable, the girls denied that 'Hon' meant Honourable despite the fact that Nancy plainly confirms as much in *The Pursuit of Love*. Instead they claimed 'Hon' to have meant 'hen' and Honnish to be the official language of their Society of Hens. Based on Oxfordshire country dialect, it was more the colloquial nursery language of one-line whimsy than Boudledidge, and like much of the Mitford humour had a rather spiteful side to it. James Lee-Milne said of Nancy, 'There is a vein of callousness in her which almost amounts to cruelty ... All the Mitfords seemed to have it, even Tom!'

Kathleen Atkins, a Burford doctor's daughter and contemporary friend of Unity's, confirmed that even at such a young age, the girls were already advanced in the art of snobbery. There being no fun in being a snob if you don't have someone to patronise they chose to parody the household staff and local farm workers. Only Nancy would exploit the full creative and commercial potential in parodying her own ilk.

At this time and amongst people such as the Mitfords, this type of behaviour would have been considered quite acceptable and charmingly camp rather than socially precocious, and certainly not worthy of criticism. As Oscar Wilde wrote, 'It is absurd to divide people into good and bad. People are either charming or tedious.'

*   *   *

The development of nursery language did not stop even after childhood, while nicknames lasted for life in many and various forms. In 1915 Lady Londonderry, née Lady Frances Anne Vane-Tempest, wife of Lord (Charley) Londonderry, started The Ark, a nursery-flavoured club for her chums, including army chiefs and government ministers who believed fascism was preferable to communism. Their nursery tradition was upheld in the encouragement of members to adopt the use of epithets. Hence, 'John the Buck, Arthur the Albatross, Winston the Warlock (a cousin of Charley Londonderry's), Barrie the Bard, John Dory, Nancy the Gnat, Sam the Skate and Orpen the Ortolan were among those who turned up to drink champagne and eat canapés served by liveried footmen'[6], while millions continued to be slaughtered in the trenches of north-eastern France!

The Ark also illustrates the English addiction to clubs and social networking, often based on public schools. The use of relatives, no matter how distant, was another basis for such things. Lacking a school network (apart from Tom's), the Mitford girls were particularly diligent in extending their family tree.

The favourite relative (or the most socially valuable) was a great aunt called Lady Blanche Hozier, known as 'Aunt Natty'. She was Clementine Redesdale's sister and the mother of another Clementine, who was married to Winston Churchill.

According to Kathleen Atkins, the Mitford girls were also encouraged by their mother to exaggerate the intimacy of their relationships with people who in reality probably qualified socially as little more than acquaintances.

Jonathan Guinness, in his book, *The House of Mitford*, gave this habit yet more credence:

> They knew Winston Churchill, John F Kennedy and Hitler; were friends of Lytton Strachey, Evelyn Waugh and Maya Angelou; sat for Augustus John, Lucian Freud and Cecil Beaton; entertained the Queen, the Duchess of Windsor and Katherine Graham; were

guests of Lord Berners, Goebbels and Givenchy. They lived their lives in very different spheres, from the London of the Bright Young Things.

Sydney, with her media background, also became a skilled promoter of her daughters' social importance, using the letters pages of *The Times*, *Telegraph*, *Daily Express* and *Daily Mail* for keeping her daughters' names in print. This was usually achieved by leaking anonymous snippets of information to the social pages and then following up with indignant letters of denial on the letters page, in which she would outrageously flaunt her title, the names of illustrious friends, relatives and, of course, her daughters. By such means it was not long before her daughters had achieved what is known today as 'celebrity status'.

While still quite young, they also managed to create their own urban myths. The following example having been retold literally 'thousands' of times: 'Apparently at a dinner party, [Pam] was placed next to Lord Louis Mountbatten, who said to her, "I know who you are, you're one of the Mitford girls, aren't you?" "Yes, that's right," Pam replied kindly. "And you are …?"'[7]

*   *   *

The Mitford girls would also manage to gain a considerable literary reputation as authors, though Nancy was the only one to write fiction and even that is a debatable description. She wrote her first novel, *Highland Fling*, in 1931 when she was 27 years old and penned seven further novels which were thinly disguised satirical caricatures of the Mitford family, or people remarkably like them. The books proved highly popular and added immeasurably to the public's awareness of the Mitford girls, although they were not always received sympathetically by the other sisters, who were all, at one time or another, victims of Nancy's 'acerbic wit'.

But Nancy was perhaps best known for what many believed to have been her creation of the 'U' and 'Non-U' linguistic terms used by the English upper class to distinguish them from mere mortals. In reality the term was coined by the Linguistics Professor, Alan S.C. Ross. Nancy 'developed' it as an essay for Stephen Spender's *Encounter* magazine, 'unleashing a national debate about English class-consciousness and snobbery'[8]. Reprinted as *Noblesse Oblige: an Inquiry into the Identifiable Characteristics of the English Aristocracy* with contributions from Evelyn Waugh and John Betjeman, it helped promote Nancy as *the* guide for the socially ambitious and, by association, gave her considerable literary cachet.

Meanwhile, Jessica wrote a number of investigative non-fiction works. But even she couldn't resist returning to the Mitford family as the subject of her focus in the highly successful *Hons and Rebels*. Debo would subsequently write numerous guides to Chatsworth while the other sisters' literary skills were limited to their letters, which would have been demanded of them as soon as they could manage joined-up writing. The fact that they considered 12,000 of their letters worthy of retention is in itself a barometer of the Mitford family's estimate of their own importance, even beyond their lifetime. Some of the letters are undoubtedly fascinating as social evidence of a life of privilege but most revealed little more than the accuracy of Nancy's novels, with flashes of the Mitfords' often-attested 'wit' and 'literary brilliance'.

*   *   *

The Mitfords were not a military family and, as such, like many others in their social class, having bravely served their king and country, those of them that had been lucky enough to survive the Great War returned to limit their killing to fish, foul and the occasional stag. Notwithstanding their constant claims to being the victims of genteel poverty, the Mitfords remained substantially privileged, despite the fact that the winds of change were blowing ever stronger.

The working class were becoming increasingly grumpy and less prepared to 'know their place' and dedicate their lives to domestic and industrial servitude. The Russian Revolution and the assassination of Tsar Nicholas II and his family made the British aristocracy particularly nervous, though not sufficiently sympathetic to offer their royal cousins a safe haven. Some considered this a frightful waste; the Romanovs being so much more attractive and *imperial* than the Saxe-Coburg Gothas.

What far more of the 'upper crust' were concerned about was Prime Minister Austen Chamberlain's imposition in 1919 of 40 per cent death duties on estates worth £2 million or more, particularly in the knowledge that so much of the tax was going to pay for the war. However, with a bit of planning and forethought this did not have to present an insurmountable challenge, although many heirs preferred to just wallow in financial self-pity. It even became rather fashionable amongst those with more than adequate funds to wear clothes full of holes and hold up their trousers with old school ties. For those less fortunate members of the gentry who were forced to seek gainful employment there were still opportunities in the armed forces, Church or Foreign Service.

In Germany, a gentleman, or *Junker*, served as an officer and then joined the reserve. There was no choice. To be an officer in the German military before 1914 was to be one of Germany's rulers. There were only two classes: civilian and military. Journalist and author John Heygate reported that it was considered quite acceptable for officers to strike waiters in the same way they struck their men. They would take the last seat in the railway carriage while a civilian was expected to stand.

But with the war lost and the old German army disbanded, redundant officers were presented with the problem of what to do with themselves, while retaining even a modicum of self-respect. Many joined the Freikorps or private armies whose existence as 'eastern border patrols' was permitted by the allies. Organised by returning officers, their role was in fact to fight the German revolutionary working class. Recruited from a kind of rural petty bourgeoisie with semi–feudal traditions, they would also form the basis of the SA (*Sturmabteilung*) and assist in bringing the Nazis to power; by brutalising the opposition.

* * *

The German aristocracy had been made insecure not only by the rising tide of 'Reds and Bolshies' but also, originally, as a result of the unification of Germany in 1871. The upshot had not only been the First World War but also the 'neutering' of so many European aristocrats, many of whom had English relatives or chums. After the British had 'won the war' things got even worse.

In November 1918, when workers and soldiers had revolted and Emperor Wilhelm II, otherwise known as 'Kaiser Bill', had been forced to abdicate and subsequently flee, 'all twenty of the German monarchies were abolished, bringing down the centuries-old kingdoms, grand duchies, duchies, and principalities like a great house of playing-cards'.[9]

In June 1919, the Treaty of Versailles was finally signed and in July Germany was declared a republic; unofficially called the Weimar Republic, named after the city where the constitutional assembly took place.

'Overnight the aristocracy appeared to have outlived the social, political and economic functions it once possessed.' It had become an anachronism, and to add insult to injury:

> The German Republic had not only lost its Emperor, but also 13% of its territory and some 10% of its population, as well as all its colonies … Parliamentary democracy was considered un-German in right-wing circles … all over Germany, authority was disintegrating. Only the Bolsheviks [and the Freikorps] seemed to know where they were going.[10]

*   *   *

Released from the constricts of their courtly existence but exposed to a 'steady stream of economic and political crises, many princes struggled to reconcile themselves' with their loss of privilege and with the need for adaptation to the new order.

It was hardly surprising that the English aristocracy, even after five years of such an appalling war, which had at least been run by 'gentlemen', should start to develop a sympathy with their German counterparts and some of their more unpleasant political and social practices.

Anti-Semitism was 'rife throughout British society and across the political spectrum. Its best-known advocates were the writer and MP, Hilaire Belloc, and his friends, Cecil Chesterton and G.K. Chesterton'[11]. This could have been the result of needing someone for the upper echelons of society to blame for their financial ills, or the involvement of Jews in the rise of the left; or both. By the standards of the day there is even some doubt that Belloc and Chesterton were, by comparison, unusually anti-Semitic.

*   *   *

In Germany, anti-Semitism was enhanced by the 'stab-in-the-back' myth, the notion that the country 'had not been defeated on the field of battle but had been betrayed by the civilian leadership (dominated by Jews and socialists)'. Even aristocrats such as the Hessens 'came to believe that they, as a family, had fought valiantly for Germany but had nonetheless been victimised and suffered an unjust loss of status'.[12]

It was not only the aristocracy who felt betrayed. In 1914, while still an Austrian national, Adolf Hitler had enrolled in the 16th Bavarian Reserve Infantry Regiment to serve as a courier between the regimental staff and the front line. He soon gained the reputation for being a committed loner, who stood out amongst his fellow soldiers to the point where he was nicknamed 'The White Crow'. But they still listened, spellbound, to his social and political oratorical outbursts and remained deeply impressed by his apparent fearless bravery. Serving with distinction, Hitler won the Iron Cross; both Second and, finally, First Class, the latter normally only being awarded to officers. He considered the war 'the greatest and most unforgettable time of my earthly existence', convinced that his miraculous survival and apparent invulnerability had been ordained by a divine power in anticipation of his designated role as a supreme leader.

When the war ended and was followed by military and civil revolution, the fall of the Imperial House of Hohenzollern and the formation of the Weimar Republic, Hitler was distraught. Sweat streaming from his scarlet face, he screamed and shouted:

> And so it had all been in vain. In vain all the sacrifices and privations; in vain the hunger and thirst of months which were often endless; in vain the hours in which, with mortal fear clutching our hearts, we nevertheless did our duty; and in vain the death of the millions who died.

Meanwhile, the military doctor, Dr Forster, who had been treating him for the effects of a gas attack, wrote in his report that Hitler was 'a psychopath with hysterical symptoms'. These would not have been considered sufficiently unusual failings amongst surviving soldiers to have attracted undue attention.

Despite the fact that most people, both on the English and the German side, wanted nothing more than an end to the slaughter, Hitler was not alone in believing the Communists, Unions, workers and soldiers councils and the Jews were responsible for 'stabbing Germany in the back', or what became known as *Dolchstoßlegende*. The belief in the Jews' involvement had no doubt been enhanced one year earlier by the Russian Revolution and by the assumed Jewish responsibility in the form of Marx, Lenin and Trotsky.

In his book *Weimar Culture*, Walter Laqueur stated, 'Without the Jews there would have been no "Weimar culture". To this extent the claims of the anti-Semites, who detested that culture, were justified, for Jews were indeed in the forefront of every new, daring revolutionary movement.

'The period of the Weimar Republic was a uniquely creative period and it produced in many respects the first truly modern culture.'[13]

Few places and periods could match Berlin's equivalent of the Jazz Age. Its outposts in Dessau and Munich (home to Thomas Mann), or even Freiburg, Heidelberg and Marburg, had their sparkling brilliance and longer-term cultural and intellectual effects, but it was Berlin where the flame burnt brightest. This culturally explosive city was certainly lawless and amoral and while the armed conflict between left and right continued, and you could pay to watch people have sex with animals or murder your wife's lover, for many Berlin was irresistible.

If Unity and Diana had been ten years older, they would never have found the time to bother with fascism, the Third Reich or Hitler. They would have been far too busy immersing themselves in everything that was Berlin during the Weimar period.

The English loved it. Particularly the likes of Christopher Isherwood and Stephen Spender, though they obviously appreciated the city as much for its sexual mores as its creative and financial attractions. Homosexuality was still illegal in Britain, although it might have been overlooked if you were at one of the more expensive public schools, or if you were a lesbian. It was also illegal in Berlin but as at Eton, no one took any notice. Meanwhile the value of the pound increased spectacularly as the value of the mark fell. For five pounds you could buy the city and all the boys, and girls, in it. Unfortunately, the Mitfords didn't get there till after Hitler had come to power, by which time it was all over and the Weimar Republic had come to an end.

*   *   *

In 1920 the public first became aware of the existence of the aristocratic Oswald 'Tom' Mosley, who was to prove a profound political and sexual influence on Unity Mitford. At this point in time the society columns were more concerned with his marriage to Cynthia 'Cimmie' Curzon, second daughter of Lord Curzon of Kedleston and his first wife, the American heiress Victoria Leiter. 'Mosley clearly fell in love with the personable and intelligent young woman, [though] her father's position, and her own personal wealth (through trusts settled on her by her millionaire American grandfather), undoubtedly affected his decision to marry her.'[14]

At the time this source of wealth was not unusual. It was estimated that by 1914, 12 per cent of the baronetcy and 17 per cent of the peerage had some American connection, and that American money had enriched the British aristocracy by some £40 million.

Realising that for Tom, Cimmie's attraction was mainly financial, the remarkably hypocritical Lord Curzon needed some convincing to agree to the match. Nevertheless, the wedding was the social event of the year, attended by many branches of European royalty, including King George V and Queen Mary.

But while old Curzon may have been an annoyingly superior financial opportunist and womaniser, his suspicions proved remarkably accurate. Even prior to marrying Cimmie, Mosley had developed a reputation as a philanderer, and 'his marriage vows did not change what was a virtual obsession'.[15] During his marriage to Cimmie, Mosley had an extended affair with her younger sister, Lady Elizabeth Metcalfe, as well as their stepmother, Lady Grace Curzon, née Hinds, while it would not be too long before he was also having an affair with the 'delicious' young Diana Mitford while 'initiating' her younger sister.

The unwritten rules of the privileged society were that liaisons outside marriage were inevitable and accepted. While they may prove regrettable, such things were socially permissible provided they were conducted with discretion. Divorce, of course, was unthinkable and amounted to social suicide. None of this appeared to be of any consequence to Mosley who, rather like another chum of the Curzons, the immensely rich American bisexual political socialite, 'Chips' Channon, appeared to be self-obsessed to the point where he was quite incapable of even considering that the generally accepted moral and legal rules might also apply to him.

Chips was a source of considerable entertainment for those who found his boundless pretension (and subsequent incendiary diaries) amusing. As an opening gambit, when he first arrived in London from Chicago in 1918, he declared, 'I am in love with London already and feel that it is pregnant with my destiny.'

*   *   *

Like their British counterparts, the German nobility had suffered dreadfully during the First World War. One *Junker* family lost twenty-four fathers, sons and brothers, while the German aristocracy as a whole lost 22 per cent of their adult males. This was a devastating toll, especially for such a male-dominated caste.

Still suffering from the shock of waking up to find themselves living in a republican democracy, most of the *Kaiserreich* felt that both the world they had known – and indeed their very existence – was threatened. Regardless of the fact that many German 'commoners' remained deferential to the nobility, especially the princes, to all intents and purposes they were redundant. This made them susceptible to extravagant promises and in due course Hitler would, initially at least, experience little difficulty in convincing them that National Socialism offered them a real chance not only of survival, but also of regaining their power and glory. 'How otherwise would a mere corporal hope to recreate the German Empire?' he asked them.

On a more positive level, with the transition from monarchy to republic came a freedom from responsibility and the opportunity to indulge in the new opportunities for pleasure and excitement. Like many English of the same ilk, they developed a passion for adventurous pursuits such as flying, automobile and motorcycle racing, skiing, skating, riding, and rowing. They became addicted to speed and cars, boats, planes and even ashtrays were 'streamlined'. They developed [like Mosley] a belief in the concept of a new man or a man of action. An athletic, 'new breed' of independent young women such as the aviator Elly Beinhorn-Rosemeyer and auto adventurer Clärenore Stinnes also sprouted wings and celebrated their newfound freedom.

Oswald Mosley, fired by the same dynamic, named his 'new' political movement the New Party. Described as 'youthful, vigorous and aristocratic'[16], he attracted a number of 'well-bred' supporters, including Winston Churchill's son, Randolph, and Harold Nicolson, diplomat, author, profound anti-Semite, arch snob and husband of Vita Sackville-West. Churchill would, in turn, propose Mosley for membership of the Other Club – a dining club for men prominent in political life.

But the first country to create and bring to power a political party that would appeal to the 'new man' image, while placating Germany and Britain's privileged classes, was, in fact, Italy.

On 23 March 1919 Benito Mussolini founded the first fascist party, Fasci Italiani di Combattimento, promising to protect both the aristocracy and the working man's rights. The establishment of the new one-party state would be aided by armed squads of Blackshirts who aggressively convinced all opposition of the error of their ways. Much of the funding for Mussolini's political ambitions in fact came from the British government who had paid him large sums of money for his journalistic services as a propagandist during the war.

Within two years Fasci Italiani di Combattimento had expanded dramatically and become the National Fascist Party, resulting in 'Il Duce' being elected into the chamber of deputies. Following a somewhat theatrical March on Rome, Mussolini was handed the reigns of power by King Victor Emmanuel III, who had been persuaded that 'it was necessary to create a new aristocratic class based on

Fascist values'. Many English, such as Mosley and the Mitfords, were deeply impressed.

*   *   *

While both the British and German ruling classes were trying, respectively, to retain and re-establish their power, the Germans had one huge advantage in possessing, via the Freikorps, an active warrior class. It gave their burgeoning fascist movement an aggressive power base that the English aristocracy would, fortunately, have found impossibly difficult to emulate but which to the Mitfords would prove infinitely more attractive.

According to Klaus Theweleit, author of *Male Fantasies*, for many Germans the period between 1914 and 1945 was a continuous, almost uninterrupted war; in no small part because they made it so. 'They think the war is over. Shit! As long as we have lost, the war is not over.'[17]

*   *   *

In 1920, the birth of their sixth daughter put an end to the Redesdale's sixteen-year breeding program and their attempt to create 'a spare'. Had David known that he was looking at the future Duchess of Devonshire he may have been somewhat more welcoming than Mabel, the parlour maid, remembered: 'One look at His Lordship's face told me everything. It was another girl. His Lordship's face was like thunder. I don't think anyone looked at Miss Debo for three months.'

After such an unwelcoming reception it seems likely that the following description was perhaps somewhat exaggerated: 'Unencumbered by spite or malice, Deborah possessed a cheerfulness and buoyancy of spirits that never deserted her.'[18] However, it does seem that the future duchess certainly made a very good job of overcoming the difficulties of being unwanted and overshadowed.

Lord Redesdale was obviously having some difficulties accepting the fact that his wife had presented him with only one son and six daughters, two of whom were, as far as he was concerned, still at the 'screaming brat' stage. So, in 1921, in order to escape her husband's ill-humour, Sydney made the sensible decision of taking the children with nanny, cook, a lady's maid, a chambermaid, a car and driver to Dieppe for the summer, renting Aunt Natty's house for the duration.

Then, a financially fortuitous event took place, which while personally upsetting for Sydney, served to put her star back into the ascendancy. In 1921, while on holiday in Algeciras, Spanish Morocco, her father died. Following probate, his estate was discovered to be worth just under £60,000, which was a great deal of money for the time – it was almost twice the amount that Bertie Redesdale had left. Sydney inherited just under a quarter of it. Her father also left her a significant shareholding in *The Lady* magazine.

*　　*　　*

By now, a few of the more intelligent landowners, not that there were many, either in Germany or England, were beginning to realise that if they were going to stand any hope of retaining what was left of their estates, they had to press their sons to learn something of the mysteries of farming by attending agricultural college. There they could discover the then more profitable alternatives to stocking their land with game.

Despite the fact that the Cirencester 'Royal' Agricultural College was founded in 1845, and Munich's Landwirtschaftliche Hochschule in 1872, they did not become popular until they became socially acceptable to young members of the English and German nobility, or ex-nobility. In Germany, agriculture then became one of the most popular subjects of study for young aristocrats, particularly those who were to become Nazis.

Meanwhile, these same young Germans fortunate enough to have English or American friends – and often lovers – with ample dollars or sterling, which they were willing to use to pay for their hospitality, could and did enjoy fabulous financial advantages. It enabled both parties to indulge in the full extravagant decadence of the Weimar 'culture'.

Despite the inclement financial conditions in Germany, many grand country houses managed to survive the Weimar period in considerable if somewhat anachronistic style.

The presence of their English or American chums often provided the upper-class Germans with an excuse for organising extravagant social events complete with the donning of Hussar dress uniforms swathed in gold braid and death's head insignia; all memories of the horrors of military confrontation presumably overlooked.

In England, the new plutocrats had also been assisting the aristocracy's financial – if not their material – survival by continuing to buy their estates, a pattern that had commenced even before the war amongst nouveau-riche figures such as Lord Leverhulme the soap king, Lord Cowdray the banker and Sir James Buchanan the distiller. This new source of investment was of particular advantage in the case of David Redesdale's sale of Batsford House, about which few details were given by any of the Mitfords as they were doubtless deeply embarrassed by the fact that their fortunes were so enhanced by one Gilbert Alan Hamilton Wills, subsequently to become Lord Dulverton of Batsford, thus further disguising the fact that he was nothing more than common old Gilbert Wills, heir to the Wills tobacco fortune.

*   *   *

By 1922 Diana, then 12 years old, was apparently bored by her three younger sisters' eternal squabbling and joking in their private languages, playing with their animals, or 're-enacting their fantasy of being kidnapped by white slavers'[19] – a not entirely mythical, criminal band. They were notorious for their kidnapping of young girls, who they reputedly then sold into harems, as sexual slaves. Without a care in the world, the 'younger' Mitford girls were indeed said to have celebrated their attraction of the idea, especially Unity, now 8 years old, who apparently went out of her way to attract and appeal to any lurking white slavers. Jessica, 5, and Deborah, 2, were unlikely to have had any idea of what 'white slaving' entailed. Perhaps in the spirit of Noel Coward's 'Gentle Alice', Unity may possibly have gathered sufficient 'animal' knowledge to by now have had some rough idea where babies came from, though it is unlikely she would have been attracted by anything other than the thrill of the unknown. Only Nancy and Pam, aged 18 and 15 respectively, and possibly Diana, would have been likely to have experienced sufficient sexual awakening to have been attracted by the erotic nature of the adventure.

One thing was 'for sure'. By now the age differences amongst the girls was sufficient to guarantee a state of almost constant conflict. In a less privileged family the girls would have had little choice but to look after each other both in work and in play. But in the Mitford family, where none of them were expected to lift a finger to help themselves, let alone anyone else, there would have been little in the way of sisterly love and affection, let alone loyalty.

'Nancy was too sharp-tongued and sarcastic to be anyone's Favourite Sister for long', Decca noted. Diana was said to have resembled, '"a Vogue cover artist's conception of the goddess of the chase"[20] but despite being bored and rebellious' somehow managed to gain a reputation for being 'unfailingly kind to them'.[21] This seems highly unlikely, as she spent much of her time being bullied and teased by her sisters. It was the inevitable response to the adults' constant and shameless reminders of how much prettier Diana was than her siblings.

★　　★　　★

The year 1922 was to see the first in a seemingly endless series of annual London 'seasons', during which, as they reached marital age, Sydney launched her various daughters into society by presenting them at Court. First they had to survive a whole string of social events, from February till August, without disgracing themselves or their family by falling foul of the strict code of etiquette. It resembled nothing more than a marriage 'chase' by National Hunt rules. Each debutante's family was also expected to host their own, individual social function. So, during the season there would be a dinner or ball every night from Monday to Thursday. In those halcyon days when young men still addressed each other with the familiar prefix, 'I say', social status and financial security was often the result of 'breeding', and a 'good marriage' was every mother's goal. Newspapers encouraged the whole ghastly business by devoting considerable amounts of space to these 'society' activities.

Nancy was to be the first of the Mitford girls to be entered for this social steeplechase. While she described Sydney's function as that of chaperone, this was far from the full extent of her role.

The Court ruling was that the preferred person to present young women was the mother, who had herself already been presented. Failing this, a friend or relative would be acceptable. Thus, Sydney not only acted as presenter but, as the whole purpose of the fiendishly expensive and time-consuming process was to get her daughters married to young men with suitable financial and social credentials, also had to act as agent and promoter. Finally, in perhaps her most difficult role, particularly in the case of Diana, she did indeed have to act as chaperone, mainly to ensure the avoidance of what would have been a disastrous pregnancy, before a successful marriage had been achieved.

It was hardly surprising that she would have preferred to have had six boys or that she appeared to have cared so little about her one, rather attractive son's homosexual dalliances that began while he was still at Eton. Known rather coyly as 'the love that dares not speak its name', it was considered quite acceptable and certainly preferable to one's son getting one of one's friend's daughters pregnant.

'Tom had the rare good fortune to enjoy his preparatory school',[22] but not so much as Eton, which he entered in 1922. For, when not being whipped and kicked or taught the finer points of fagging, he was apparently proving 'above average in his schoolwork' and, more importantly, in what was politely referred to as his 'social interactions'[23]. One such recipient of this 'interactive' passion was a boy called Milton, who he assumed his mother knew nothing of. But having gossiped on the subject to Diana, it was not long before all his sisters were party to the most intimate details of his *affair de coeur*.

According to Jonathan Guinness, who also went to Eton, 'Once Tom brought a friend home to stay [presumably the aforementioned Milton]. The house was full, so Sydney asked if the friend would mind sharing with Tom. She was [or pretended to be] surprised when one after the other all her daughters filed out of the room, doubled up in mirth.' They considered the whole matter 'Killing!' or highly amusing, which it probably was if you were doing it at Eton, Winchester or similar public schools. Anywhere else it was of course considered a criminal offence, punishable, as in the case of Oscar Wilde some two decades earlier, by two years' hard labour.

★   ★   ★

Germany continued to suffer from almost constant left and right-wing civil, political and military upheaval, often involving extreme, organised violence. The country seemed to be permanently poised on the edge of civil war. But in 1922 the turmoil was eclipsed by the new threat of hyperinflation, which reached its peak in 1923 and would not be stabilised until 1924. While it brought incredible hardship into many people's lives, often wiping out lifetimes' worth of savings, it served Germany well insofar as forcing the allies to accept the restructuring of their reparation payments. Meanwhile, those with access to foreign currency could use the situation to pay off their personal debts, while industrialists such as Stinnes used dollars to buy up whole groups of bankrupt companies, for virtually nothing.

In 1922, Walter Rathenau, the Jewish businessman and German foreign minister, was assassinated by extreme right-wing, nationalist conspirators, who opposed his policy of abiding by the Treaty of Versailles. His murder illustrated the continuing antipathy towards the Weimar government by the anti-democratic, redundant nobility. New legislation sought to tackle this apathy:

> The government passed a law for the protection of the Republic, which included the so-called Emperor's clause. This gave the government 'the right to prevent members of the former ruling dynasties from entering Germany'. While this provision was not implemented in full, only the former Kaiser being prevented from setting foot in Germany, it had symbolic significance.[24]

Many, including Jonathan Petropoulos, saw it as 'part of the ongoing international decline of the feudal elite'.

The old ruling class continued their fight to restore the monarchy by somewhat ironically forming themselves into counter-revolutionary groups such as the Steel Helmet paramilitary organisation or the German Aristocrats' Association. Described by some as little more than a 'toffs union', some 28 per cent of the German aristocracy were members of the latter and openly supported the restoration of the Hohenzollern monarchy. Membership could be instantly revoked if one were discovered to be supporting the Weimar Republic, while Jews, who formed about 1.5 per cent of the nobility, were excluded altogether. This was done under an 'Aryan clause', which had been introduced in the early 1920s; more than ten years before Hitler came to power.

*   *   *

The chances of the British aristocracy ever playing a similar role to the Germans in assisting a fascist party to assume power, regardless of the strength of their motivation, would be hampered by the apparent inability of many members of that social stratum to concentrate for more than 24 hours on anything other than sleeping with someone else's husband, wife or mistress, and sometimes all three; as in the case of Lord 'Charley' Londonderry.

The social commentator Charles Jennings[25] saw little to admire in Londonderry's amoral philandering, his entertainment value as an endless source of gossip or his lacklustre political 'career', but could not resist writing about him with that grudging degree of admiration the English reserve for 'cads'.

The 7th Marquess of Londonderry's total assets were estimated to be worth in excess of £2.5 million. However, 'worth' may have been a misleading word:

> Like the latter-day Duke of Marlborough [Charley], was a walking compendium of deficiencies … slim, elegant, surgically well turned out and infected with the terrible restlessness of failure … He claimed never to have spent more than ten consecutive nights in the same place. He philandered constantly and pointlessly. He sired an illegitimate daughter, born six weeks after he married Edith. He ran off noisily with Consuelo Marlborough in 1905 … he then had a long and blowsy affair with the American-born Eloise, Countess of Ancaster … He reflexively made an attempt on Lady Diana Manners, shortly before she married Duff Cooper, in 1918. He was still at it well into the 1930s, with Olive Murray-Smith, daughter of Lord Burnham. It was infidelity on a pathological level.[26]

Hardly surprising that Winston Churchill described Londonderry as a 'half-wit'.

The social elite throughout Europe and America often felt exempt from traditional sexual restrictions and taboos. Many aristocrats firmly believed that morals were for the lower classes; something invented to enhance the social and political control of the ruling elite. Another theory, garnered from first-hand experience, was eventually proposed by Lady Diana Mosley, née Mitford, who agreed that 'upper-class Englishmen were constantly hopping into bed with each other's wives'. (Or vice versa, for there was no less enthusiasm amongst the wives, liberated by marriage from the telltale dangers of pregnancy. That was of course assuming they avoided such reckless behaviour as taking red-haired lovers.) 'I think it is because people had more leisure. Everybody had servants and people had nothing to think about except their lives and emotions and relationships. Nowadays, they simply haven't got time.'[27] This situation would have also applied to Unity, for without her family's inherited wealth she would never have had the time or the money to have pursued Hitler.

Londonderry's sexual diligence had not prevented him from realising a considerable degree of political success, though many believed it to have been the fulfilment of his wife's ambition, with which he shared fascist sympathies. Boosted by Edith's marathon and eye-wateringly expensive social courtship of Ramsay MacDonald, Charley rose all the way to the position of Air Minister, before being sacked by Stanley Baldwin. He then crowned his political career by publicly attempting to conciliate Hitler shortly before the outbreak of the Second World War.

★　　★　　★

While Germany and some in England were flirting with some form of right-wing authoritarian political system that would re-empower the nobility, Italy had stolen a march on everyone, literally!

The fact that no one put up any resistance to Mussolini's theatrical coup d'état did little to diminish the international publicity value it was awarded; a fact particularly appreciated by Martin Pugh, historian and author of *Hurrah for the Blackshirts!*

King Victor Emmanuel III continued to retain a central role in Mussolini's Italy which many conservatives, particularly in London, held up as proof 'that the central role played by the monarchy would soften the alien qualities of a fascist system'[28] while the same system would, in turn, protect both the monarchy and the aristocracy.

When Mussolini came to London, he attracted the 'admiring attention' of several newspapers, including the *Daily Mail* and *The Morning Post*.

'The second and most obvious explanation for the favourable reception of Italian fascism lay in the perceived threat of the Bolshevik Revolution … the Mussolini coup offered the first check to the forward march of this revolution'[29] (which so many feared was imminent).

Lord Rothermere, owner of the *Daily Mail*, was Mussolini's most ardent supporter, largely due to his fanatical anti-communist stance and, of course, the fact that he managed to install an authoritarian fascist government while, initially at least, retaining the monarchy in the form of Victor Emmanuel III. This gave Mussolini a quite spectacular appeal to many amongst the English privileged class, including Winston Churchill and the Mitfords.

★   ★   ★

Mussolini also made an extremely favourable impression on the androgynous, militaristic figure of Mrs Rotha Lintorn-Orman who, funded by her mother, decided to form the British Fascisti in 1923. Initially it confined itself to the violent stewarding of Conservative party meetings and canvassing for the party while pledging to 'smash the reds and the pinkos'. Later she changed the name to the British Fascists, after being accused of being in the pay of Il Duce.

One of the British Fascists' more telling or socially revealing policies was a call for a reduction in income tax, which they claimed would encourage the privileged classes to hire more servants, thus achieving a reduction in unemployment. They also wanted to award the House of Lords more power and, equally, to curtail the power of the trade unions. But the party lost a great deal of its momentum when the General Strike of 1926 failed to result in the 'British Bolshevik Revolution' that Lintorn-Orman and her supporters had pledged to fight (and which didn't stop them adopting a strongly anti-Semitic stance and becoming ardent supporters of Hitler and the Nazi Party).

The British Fascists attracted various members of the armed forces, the aristocracy, Members of Parliament and a number of frightfully well-bred women. Viscountess Downe (a lady-in-waiting to Queen Mary), Lady Sydenham, Lady Menzies, Baroness Zouche and Nesta Webster, author of *The Jewish Peril*, were all members. But working-class and middle-class 'toughs' were also recruited to engage with the Communists. They excused their violence by insisting that organised physical resistance was the only possible means of defence against 'such people'.

However, eventually the best-known – or certainly most publicised and entertaining – recruit of the National Fascists (an off-shoot of the British Fascists) was Valerie Arkell-Smith, a transvestite who spent many years masquerading as Sir Victor Barker and thereby dragging the organisation into ridicule and disrepute. She also served to fuel the attitude of the many activists in the Labour movement who regarded the organisation as too ridiculous to constitute a serious threat.

Had Lintorn-Orman been a more conventionally attractive and charismatic figure, the organisation may have flourished and metamorphosed into a fully developed political party – the ground certainly appeared to be sufficiently fertile – but the appearance of the party's founder led to some doubt concerning her gender.

She was in fact the daughter of General Sir John Arabin Lintorn-Simmons and the wife of Field Marshal Charles Orman; though one wonders what type of relationship he had with a woman of such masculine appearance, who was seldom out of a collar and tie. It was said that they used to sit up half the night studying foxhound breeding records and marvelling at the prolificacy of the great 'Tipperary Growler'.

It was ironic that despite the fact that the fascists opposed women's rights and feminist influence on politics, most of the British fascist organisations enjoyed a high level of female membership.

*　　*　　*

By now Sir Oswald Mosley realised that if he wished to assume the degree of political power that he believed he deserved, and which would enhance his sexual attraction, he was probably going to have to resort to a fairly spectacular gesture. So, in 1924, after a brief flirtation with the 'Asquithian' Liberals, he crossed the floor of the House to sit with the Labour Party.

It should have been obvious to even the most naïve politician that Mosley had absolutely no real interest in – or sympathy with – the Labour movement. Yet by 1927 he had reached the five-strong National Executive of the Labour Party; an extraordinary feat for a man from the other side of the class barrier who had been a party member for only three years. Indeed, while many believe Mosley to have been a deeply unpleasant man, one could certainly not accuse him of being unintelligent. Many women also found him quite irresistible. Mary Lovell, the Mitford family's biographer, described him as being, 'brilliant, gallant, confident, rich, darkly good-looking, over six feet tall and athletic'. What she fails to mention was that he was also unscrupulous, calculating, unethical, amoral and generally 'blessed' with all those other questionable qualities that were and still are mandatory for success in politics. He was also quite prepared to outrageously exploit what at the time was undoubtedly his greatest asset.

Largely as the result of Cimmie's charm and social skills, the Mosleys were now also close to the Labour party's leader, Ramsay MacDonald.

At the same time, according to Anne de Courcy, author of *Diana Mosley*, Diana Mitford was already developing an interest in politics.

One of her many admirers was Winston Churchill's son Randolph, whom Diana had known since he first came to stay at Asthall when he was 12. There was no evidence that Diana returned his admiration; she appeared far more interested in his father.

Her mother encouraged their acceptance of the Churchills' hospitality, while Tom and Diana were reputed to have 'loved these visits to Chartwell':

> One of the charms of staying with the Churchills was that the rule that children should be seen and not heard did not apply. Randolph was encouraged by his father to take part in intelligent conversation; Tom and Diana were treated as thinking beings ... Diana realised the fascination of politics. Here, as a 16-year-old, she heard discussion after discussion about the General Strike and the long-drawn-out stand by the miners which followed; it became, in consequence, the first major political event to impinge on her consciousness. Her sympathies were all with the miners.

In light of Diana's background and her future, this claim seems somewhat unlikely, as did her interest in politics at that age. With her celebrated physical attraction already well developed, its effect on both men and boys would have been of far greater consequence to her, as well as a great deal more entertaining. Winston, recognising her dangerous potential, took to calling her 'Dina-mite'.

James Lees-Milne wrote in his diary that Diana was the most beautiful adolescent he had ever seen: 'Divine is the word, for she was a goddess. More immaculate, more perfect, more celestial than Botticelli's sea-borne Venus'. The diary was of course kept and the degree of Diana's beauty repeated *ad tedium, ad nauseam*.

*   *   *

Unity, nick-named 'Bobo', was reputed to have been a sensitive child. It was a term that was often used for misunderstood, artistic children. In Unity's case, her family's lack of understanding of how to deal with her was reflected in her mother's assertion that as a small child she was introverted and also that she was:

> ... shy and easily upset. If anything was said at meals that she did not like or that caused her embarrassment she just slipped quietly off her chair and disappeared under the table until such time as she felt ready to face the world again. It was an understood thing that no one took any notice.

But as she grew up, Unity became more 'boisterous', her former behaviour having no doubt been due to the fact that like many highly intelligent, imaginative children she had created her own reality, fuelled by images she discovered in books and during visits to museums.

While still in her early teens Unity drew well and while illustrating her fantasies became fascinated by the work of Hieronymus Bosch (probably best known then, as now, for his triptych, *The Garden of Earthly Delights*, and numerous paintings of Purgatory featuring explicit sexual and violently gruesome images), Arnold Böcklin (whose work was as much admired by Hitler as it was by Marcel Duchamp) and Henri Rousseau, particularly his 'Valkyrie' painting, *La Guerre (War, or the Ride of Discord)*.

At the same time her taste in literature and poetry was also developing. She even began to display a 'rather precocious talent for rhyming'. But while some of her poetry was admitted by various members of the family to have been 'quite passable', the reason given for none of it having been quoted is, or appears to be, in itself rather revealing. 'Her bent was for the serious rather than, as Nancy's was, for the comic and serious juvenilia are not very quotable'.[30] Of course, this was still a time when being too brainy, especially for girls, was considered at best rather unseemly and positively off-putting to many potential suitors. So it would not have been something that one's parents would have wished to call attention to.

Meanwhile, Unity had also discovered William Blake, the graphic and poetic genius who consorted with angels on Peckham Rye. His engravings had given her the opportunity to freely indulge in the enjoyment of erotic imagery in the name of art, culture and even religion.

Considering her taste in art and some of her literary influences, it appears highly likely that Unity's poetry also contained a degree of explicit, sexual content. This is something that neither her parents nor her sisters would have been terribly keen to reveal, either subsequently or at the time.

The poet John Milton was also said to be, like Unity, of 'sensitive demeanour', though perhaps for somewhat different reasons that doubtless influenced his gaining the title of 'The Lady of Christ's College'.

Milton was also a powerful influence over Blake, who illustrated much of his writing. Unity was obsessed by his work, particularly *Paradise Lost* and its references to such elevated subjects as love, war and heroism and the battle between fallen angels and those still in heaven. It deals with the downfall of Adam and Eve, Satan and Jesus Christ, with much fire and anger, which in turn appealed to both Blake and Unity. The sin and heroism represented by copulating angels would have certainly appealed to her more than the purity and virtue promoted by the Christian Church. However, she was unlikely to have supported Oliver Cromwell, under whom Milton served as an administrator. English people of her elevated social position and doubtless royalist sympathies just didn't, though Hitler did. He would even advise Mosley to call his followers 'Ironsides' rather than blackshirts.

Unity's family appeared to oscillate between being somewhat embarrassed by her intellectual precocity and proud that she was indeed very different from the rest of her sisters. Sydney must certainly have been aware that her daughter's poetic tastes were very advanced for such a young girl and admitted, 'Keats, Shelley, Byron and Blake were her poets, especially Blake.'

Unity was an avid reader of equally impressive prose, including fiction by Huxley, Poe, the Brontë sisters and Waugh, the first and last of whom were of course Mitford literary collaborators. She was also known to have been extremely excited by Huxley's surreal, socially advanced novel *Chrome Yellow*, which was set among people from her stratum of society. Described by F. Scott Fitzgerald as 'too ironic to be called satire and too scornful to be called irony', it could be considered the English equivalent of *The Great Gatsby*.

The Mitford family would later maintain that Unity's taste in literature and art supported their claim that she was a 'quintessential romantic' or, when excusing her relationship with Adolf Hitler, 'a naive and easily led romantic'.[31] Up until now their various biographers also seem to have been quite prepared to accept this defence, despite the fact that her artistic choice was so emblematic of her role as a dangerously intelligent fantasist; as of course was Hitler, and it was this shared trait in their character that would inexorably draw them together.

Hitler was also impressed by the fact that the work of Milton and Blake contains many parallels with the Norse legends and occult elements that influenced the Nazi movement and Hitler's beloved Wagner.

Since William Blake did not agree with many of the Christian teachings, despite being reverential towards the Bible, he also invented a personal mythology or profound fantasy. In a mixture of Biblical and Greek mythology he used characters such as Urizen, Los and Orc as archetypes of human nature. He believed that Christianity advocated the repression of natural desires and inhibited earthly joy. Such things were regarded as evil. According to Blake, some of what we consider evil was in fact good. In one of his Prophetic Books, *The Marriage of Heaven and Hell* (*c.* 1790), he entertains the notion that existence requires an equal amount of good and evil. He defined good as 'the passion that obeys reason' and evil as 'the active springing from energy'.

Fascism would have appalled Blake for the same reason that he opposed orthodox Christianity. But that did not stop his words to the song *Jerusalem* becoming the battle hymn for the English patriots and fascists. He also appeared to believe that Jesus Christ had at one time visited Britain. This is reflected in the *Jerusalem* lyrics, 'And did those feet in ancient land, walk upon England's pastures green.'

His disagreement with the Christian Church was based on the fact that he believed it encouraged 'inactivity or stagnation, thus allowing life to become stale, static and eventually poisonous ... "Reason" will tell a person to stop before one finds out what one's limits are. In order to enjoy life to the fullest people should find out exactly what is more than enough.' It was a belief that was distinguished through his iconic quote, 'the path of excess leads to the palace of wisdom'.

In the family's post-war efforts to cover up Unity's sexual relationship with Adolf Hitler and his disciples, they inferred that her lack of physical attraction would have made such a thing quite out of the question.

'Unity was always rather big, which increased her shyness.'[32] Sydney also said she was 'very tall and very straight and she had two thick plaits of golden hair and a severe and serious expression'. Nancy, spiteful as ever, christened her 'Hideous', and Decca, somewhat more subtly, remembered her as 'a shaggy Viking or Little John'.

They also liked to give the impression that Unity was clumsy and physically inept. But she was an award-winning ice skater, an activity that requires considerable agility and physical co-ordination. It also tends to severely punish those lacking balance. But it was her height that everyone made most of.

In fact, Unity was very similar in height to Diana, as can be seen from photographs of them together. Unity also proved extremely attractive to Hitler and his SS officers, who greatly appreciated her Wagnerian 'Rhine Maiden' looks and athletic abilities.

According to John Betjeman, Unity possessed a highly developed sense of humour, 'that was often overlooked'. Though it may be difficult to accept, it was also a quality that she shared with Hitler.

One sometimes gets the impression that biographers' acceptance of the family's insistence that Unity lacked wit, intelligence and physical attraction is all part of their fear of being seen to be in any way condoning not just a fascist but a Nazi, especially a Mitford Nazi.

*   *   *

Far from being received as a redundant, defeated veteran at the end of the First World War, Hitler was rewarded with a post that could have been tailor-made for the assurance of his political future. He was recruited by the right-wing Political Department of the Reichswehr, a defence unit permitted under the terms of the Versailles Treaty to infiltrate and report on subversive political groups. In preparation for his duties, he was enrolled at Munich University to attend lectures on right-wing political history, economics and political theory.

The misleading inclusion of the word 'workers' in the name of any organisation was sufficient to ensure investigation and cause for Hitler to be instructed to attend a meeting of the fledgling Deutsche Arbeiterpartei (German Workers' Party or DAP), shortly to become the NSDAP, commonly known in English as the Nazi Party. It was in fact anti-communist, anti-Semitic and extremely right wing.

The DAP had originally been formed by the far-right politician Anton Drexler, and sponsored by the Thule Society. Claimed to have been formed as a 'Study Group for Germanic Antiquity' by Walter Nauhaus and his friend Karl Maria Willigut, the society had its roots in Ariosophy, the Germanic occult revival inspired by German paganism, romantic mysticism and extreme racism.

At one of the first meetings of the DAP that Hitler attended, he verbally assaulted a critic of one of the speakers with such authoritative ferocity that the man was forced to leave while the organisers, recognising the value of Hitler's 'mouth', offered him immediate membership. Appreciating the potential that such a small organisation could offer him, he accepted. Then, armed with his brilliantly effective theatrical oratory and a seemingly natural gift for political strategy and promotion, Hitler gradually assumed control; displaying no hesitation in encouraging the physical protection and assistance of the Reichswehr and Freikorps in brutally crushing all his opponents.

With a lust for power that left little time or motivation for the development of policies, he relied on developing the common fear of Jews and Communists to such a level of hysteria that thousands were soon fighting to pay to hear him speak. It still took him five years to gain what he felt was sufficient strength to challenge the state itself.

The 'March on the *Feldherrnhalle*' (otherwise known as the 'Beerhall Putsch') was in fact an attempted coup d'état led by Hitler in his role as leader of the Nazi Party, supported by General Erich Ludendorff, the First World War hero. It commenced on the evening of 8 November 1923 and collapsed in a hail of bullets fired by troops and police loyal to the Bavarian state on the following afternoon. That day marked the end of the first stage of Hitler's attempt to establish a new order in Germany: the 'Third Reich'.

In later years he stated that it had been a success, precisely because it had *not* succeeded. In 1933, Hitler claimed that if they had succeeded in taking over Germany at that time, it would have been a disaster as they would have been faced with a major problem in attempting to run a country with a 5-year-old Nazi Party totally lacking any experience in such things.

It would be ten more years before Hitler was invited to head a government, ultimately without a shot being fired. Adequate time, especially after the publication of *Mein Kampf*, for there to cease to be any confusion concerning his political and social intentions, particularly towards the Jews and the gypsies. But even as early as 1924 the Communists would be attracting 4 million voters; a great deal more than the Nazi Party.

*   *   *

It is very difficult to say exactly when 'The Mitford Girls' became an entity, but the decision to develop such a concept appears to have been taken in 1925, when their celebrity status had become sufficiently assured to consider it worth saving their letters.

The family had already been living at Asthall Manor for six years. Followers would be persuaded to consider them the classic years of the Mitford childhood; though for Nancy, now 21, Pam, 18, and even Tom, 16, it could hardly be considered childhood. It would also still be another five years before Nancy would write her first 'novel'; the first of several such books that so successfully established the family in the eyes of the public.

The books could not in fact be truthfully described as all her own work. Certainly her first novel, *Highland Fling*, was completed with considerable assistance from Evelyn Waugh, who also came up with the titles, and who knows what else, for two more of her books, *The Pursuit of Love* and *Voltaire in Love*.

Meanwhile, the Mitford myths continued to be developed; including the literary importance of the linen cupboard. 'It was at Swinbrook that the linen cupboard became a favourite resort because of its hot pipes'[33] and it was there that Nancy developed her literary skills, writing poems and stories for her siblings' entertainment. Or that is what was claimed, although she actually spent very little time at Swinbrook and even less in the linen cupboard. Nancy also had more interest in taunting her siblings than in entertaining them, and took particular delight in ridiculing the staff.

A typical story involved her impersonation of 'the governess in residence Miss Broadmoor's elocution, a tortured diction that passed for refined ("refained") speech: "*Ay* huff a löft, and öft/as ay lay on may eiderdown so soft/(tossing from sade to sade with may nasty cöff)/ay ayther think of the loft/, or of the w-h-h-h-heat in the tröff of the löf',", though some might say this was a bit rich coming from someone who pronounced "lost" and "gone" as "lorst" and "gorn".'

Physically attractive, with a sharp turn of phrase, good literary tastes, and an interest in modern art and fashion, Nancy should have been snapped up, yet she remained unmarried despite her parents' investment in a lavish season and presentation at Court. Pam would also be subjected to a social season and presentation but her love for the country ill-suited her to London life, let alone marriage.

Having spent some time in London and discovered that he was as attractive to girls as he was to boys, Tom had by now developed an even more unfortunate level of arrogance. This had become obvious even to his friends, though the more generous amongst them excused it as 'only the arrogance of youth'.

The planned 'presentation' of the 'stunningly beautiful'[34] Diana seemed quite irrelevant, as it had already become obvious that there would be no shortage of suitors, with or without a 'season' or a presentation at court.

Regardless of their age the girls were all still living at home, while Unity, Jessica and Deborah were the only ones young enough to have accurately qualified as children, though they all qualified to adopt the prefix of 'Honourable'. There was also little doubt that they had been brought up to believe in their social superiority, but despite the fact that Jessica later confirmed the girls' shortening of the word to 'hon' as in Hons and Rebels, their mother and Deborah would subsequently continue to insist that the word 'hon' was a secret family codeword for 'hen'.

Evelyn Waugh remained unconvinced: 'It was a great day for "Hons" when you and your merry sisters acquired that prefix of nobility. Hitherto it had been the most shadowy of titles, never spoken, and rarely written. You brought it to light, emphasised and aspirated and made a glory of it.'

Somewhat mysteriously, the Mitford girls, despite having all the necessary qualifications, seemed determined to distance themselves from being branded Bright Young Things (or BYTs). Mary Lovell detailed what was required to qualify as such a thing:

> [The] post-war generation of young people … erupted into
> Society determined to change the world [at least socially], for the

better now that the war to end all wars was over. Their background was upper class, of course, but talented gatecrashers, working-class émigrés like Noël Coward and Cecil Beaton were not unwelcome. Girls shingled their hair, wore slave bangles and cloche hats, and dressed in shapeless, waistless dresses designed to 'move' across an uncorseted body and display the lower legs, clad in silk stockings and high-heeled shoes. They smoked cigarettes in long holders and drank cocktails with names like 'Horse's Neck'. Their elders, the Edwardian generation who had fought a world war, and whose mores were still Victorian, were satisfyingly shocked.

The Mitfords were said to have regarded them as too frivolous, but it is more likely that they wanted to retain their exclusivity as the Mitford girls, rather than being lumped together with so many others under such a common generic term.

*　　*　　*

Two miles up the hill from Swinbrook village, the next Mitford home, the large, Teutonic grey, three-story, eighteen-bedroom structure of Swinbrook House would become known by locals as 'The Mitford Barracks'. It is claimed that David designed the house. Not an easy thing to do for a man with no architectural training and limited literacy, even if it was described rather inaccurately as 'An unremarkable, rather insipid square building in Cotswold stone, such as councillors might have erected between the wars as a cottage hospital, or dons as a modest extension to an Oxford college.'[35]

The house in fact bares an uncanny resemblance in style to the pre-war *völkisch* architecture, albeit English-influenced, to which Adolf Hitler was so partial! Rather mysteriously there is no remaining evidence of who actually built the house, let alone who really designed it; though Cubitt's, the royal builder with a base in Oxford, seems the most likely.

By 1926 David's dream house was in the final stages of building, and Asthall was to be sold. But as the new house was still not habitable, in the autumn Sydney took all the girls to Paris for three months accompanied by their nanny and Miss Bedell, the current governess, while David finalised the sale of Asthall Manor and organised the move to Swinbrook House.

Of his six daughters, four had still to 'come out' and all but one was likely to require further social investment to achieve successful marital status. Therefore it seemed sensible and perhaps even, in the end, economical to acquire a house large enough for substantial receptions located in an appropriately fashionable area that could enable the family to elevate its social standing. So, David purchased a large townhouse in Knightsbridge overlooking Hyde Park, at 26 Rutland Gate, a leafy London cul-de-sac, with a mews garage and flat to the rear. The Victorian house was distinguished by two tall white pillars guarding its entrance. David was also especially proud of the passenger lift that he had installed.

The rate of exchange made France very good value for the English, as it had been in Bertie's childhood. So Sydney arranged a long-term stay at a hotel in the centre of Paris, while the socially precocious Diana attended a small day school called Cours Fénelon in the Rue de la Pompe. 'Why doesn't one always live in hotels?' Nancy wrote from Paris. 'There are dozens of sweet little boys here (hall boys) perfect pets, I shall give them my chocs.'[36]

For the Christmas holidays of 1926/27 the family returned to the new house at Rutland Gate, which both Nancy and Diana also found perfectly charming.

Unfortunately the reaction to Swinbrook House, which had been David's dream for many years, was not as positive. 'We all thought the house monstrous,' said Diana. But their lack of enthusiasm did not prevent the house from receiving an enormous amount of literary attention. Particularly the legendary linen cupboard.

The building of Swinbrook House had undoubtedly been an extravagance, but the Mitfords appeared to continue to live well with plenty of staff, while David never failed to buy a new car every year.

Rutland Gate was far less of an extravagance as it was frequently let, which unfortunately rendered it unavailable for entertaining. When this happened the family usually retained the mews flat over the garage as a pied-à-terre, which they always referred to, with a great flash of inspiration, as 'The Garage'. It was also claimed that: 'Sydney was always a help with her methodical housekeeping, her shrewd poultry farming and her small but steady income from holding 19 per cent of *The Lady.*'

It happened that the family's arrival at Swinbrook coincided with major changes in the lives of all the 'children'. Nancy, already 24, left home to share a flat in London. Tom left Eton, and somewhat surprisingly, as someone for whom it would have been safe to assume that 'going up to Oxford' would have been a forgone conclusion, went to Vienna to study German and music. Two years after the move Diana married Bryan Guinness, and set up house with him in Wiltshire and London. Finally, Unity went to boarding school at the age of 14. So, only the two youngest, Decca and Debo, actually lived continuously at Swinbrook for any length of time.

In 1926 the Nazi Party was busy forming the Hitler Youth, while in London Lady Maud Cunard, who was busy adopting Diana Mitford as her new 'pet salon siren', was changing her own name to Emerald. For some, such as gossip columnist Patrick Balfour, this was a moment of high significance. Both he and (subsequently) Charles Jennings seemed to think that it meant that (the new) Lady *Emerald* Cunard was 'now so confident of her social powers that she could brashly re-christen herself in order to draw attention to her place at the very peak of the new wave of wealthy American imports'.[37] Of course, the name Maud, with its music-hall connotations, would have been considered a rather 'common' name at the time, which was perhaps brought to her attention. But then to the English, if not Maud, the name Emerald would have been considered even more so!

While fascism was taking hold in Europe, London (and thus England) remained obsessed with snobbery and social position; fuelled and encouraged by the injection of conspicuous wealth by new American hostesses. The English, who had long prided themselves on their ability to avoid being seduced by such vulgarity, finally gave in, encouraged in their susceptibility by the monarchy.

> Neither the money, nor the parties, the golden gifts [which Laura Corrigan, the American social mountaineer, famously presented to the social elite to encourage their attendance at her 'soirees' in what became an intensely competitive activity], the intrigues, the bad behaviour, nor the gradual annexation of London society by American wealth would have greatly mattered if it hadn't been for the Prince of Wales. It was when he began his affair with (the Swiss born, US national) Lady Furness at the end of 1926 that what had been seen as a mildly distressing, mildly amusing, social trend suddenly hardened into a crisis in the making.[38]

This crisis being the result of Lady Furness' replacement by the infinitely more dangerous Wallace Simpson, whose relationship with the prince would, of course, lead to his abdication.

However, apart from Diana's involvement in this social strata and the Mitfords' investment in court presentation, the family would become largely committed to fascism and casually indifferent to royalty.

*   *   *

The year 1926 also saw the General Strike, initiated by 1 million miners locked out by their employers for refusing to take a pay cut and work longer hours, and for generally having to cope with 'a land' that was anything but 'fit for heroes'; as had been promised. Many men who had returned from fighting in the Great War were unable to get work and, by 1926, 1,751,000 were unemployed.

In those days before the welfare state, without charity food parcels, soup kitchens and begging, many would have faced starvation. Men who had watched their brothers and friends being 'blown to buggery and fuckin' bits'[39] while fighting for king and country, talked of only being in work for two Christmases between 1918 and 1939. This situation wasn't limited to the working classes. Many supporters of the 2.5 million strikers were ex-officers who, once they had removed their uniforms, ceased to be heroes and were simply unemployed.

The strike came close to overthrowing the elected government of Stanley Baldwin, while failing to develop into the communist revolution and takeover of the country that had been predicted by the British Fascists. That did not stop intelligence reports claiming that the General Strike was financed by the Soviet Union to the tune of £380,000, or that the British Communist Party had been funded from the same source.

But what most unsettled the right, pushing many of them away from their loyalty to the monarchy, was the royal reaction. King George V took exception to suggestions that the strikers were communist 'revolutionaries' saying, 'Try living on their wages before you judge them.'

The Duke of Windsor's (claimed) comment on visiting mining villages in South Wales that 'something must be done' for the unemployed coal miners, was also often quoted as an example of his sympathy with the miners and read as being directly critical of the government. But the duke had, in fact, far greater sympathy with fascists than workers and what he actually said, when visiting an abandoned mine in 1936 was, 'These works brought all these people here. Something should be done to get them at work again.'

The Mitfords continued to pay scant regard for the royal family and, apart from Jessica, even less for the working class. One of Lady Redesdale's more 'killing' and telling remarks followed Jessica's accusation that her mother was a 'class enemy', to which she replied angrily, 'I am not an enemy of the working class! I think some of them are perfectly sweet!' Even from an early age, Unity made no such attempt to hide her disdain. Mary Ormsby-Gore told David Pryce-Jones, 'Unity also disliked the working class for being so powerful.'

★   ★   ★

> When Diana attended her first ball at Oxford's Radcliffe Infirmary, in the autumn of 1927, Clementine and Diana stayed at Swinbrook and went to the ball with the Mitfords. Next day Professor Lindemann rang Diana to see how many proposals she had received. It was his little joke, but Diana's beauty guaranteed that she would be a sensational debutante and although she was watched extra carefully by Sydney, she took London by storm in the following spring when she was presented to the King and Queen.

So wrote Mary Lovell; but Anne de Courcy, despite describing Lindemann as 'a brilliant older man' and 'dazzlingly erudite', revealed more sinister personal details than were contained in Lovell's social commentary. '[The German educated] Professor Lindemann (the Prof) was the first person Diana had heard abusing someone for being a Jew. His target was author Brian Howard, of whom it was apparently his chief complaint.' He also tried to persuade Diana to learn to speak German in order that she could appreciate Schopenhauer, the sexually provocative, pro-genetic engineering, anti-Semitic philosopher by whom Hitler claimed to have been influenced.

Lovell then speculated on the effect such criticism may have had upon Brian who, it was generally agreed, was not Jewish. It would scarcely have affected the brilliant writer, poet and legendary wit, for whom abuse was little more than cerebral stimulation and his Anglo-American birth right a delightful subject of endless inventive possibilities. Brian was far more interested in Nancy and her savage wit than Diana and her sexual attraction. He told Harold Acton that

she was a 'delicious creature, quite pyrotechnical my dear, and sometimes even profound and would you believe it, she's hidden among
the cabbages of the Cotswolds'.

Both Brian Howard and Harold Acton were part of a group of
Oxford aesthetes who were star players in what is now known as the
'Brideshead generation', all represented as thinly disguised charac-
ters in Waugh's – and subsequently Nancy's – 'novels'.

Nancy impressed these young men, many of whom were homosexual, with her highly affected manner of speaking, her irreverent,
if rather superficial, camp witticisms and her sense of the absurd.
But on one occasion when 'a neighbour of the Redesdales spot-
ted Nancy and Brian Howard walking together in Oxford without
a chaperone, David [who had been informed by the said neigh-
bour] was furious and roared at her that her reputation was ruined
and that as a result, no respectable man would marry her'[40]. In fact,
David got on rather well with Brian, and as he was doubtless fully
aware that he was, in the words of the time, 'a bugger' or 'a pansy',
must have also been aware that he presented no possible threat to his
daughter. Well, certainly no sexual threat at least.

Fortunately, with a country seat so close to Oxford equipped
with an ample supply of both comfort and servants, Nancy's new
'aesthete' friends were soon being invited to country-house weekends, with additional entertainment being supplied by the highly
inflammatory Lord Redesdale.

There was little doubt the Mitford girls were in awe of their
father, or that it was partly due to his being so strikingly handsome.
But it was his violent temper that they found most entertaining.
Debo particularly remembered his rages, '… sometimes about small
things like Gladys, Duchess of Marlborough, [who] was never asked
to the house again because she left a paper handkerchief on a hedge.'
David also turned one young man out of the house because a comb
fell out of his pocket. Both anecdotes, while considered scream-
ingly funny by the girls, were also manifestations of their father's
extreme snobbery.

But the motivation for his fury was often more political than social, giving far greater potential for discussion, even while his right-wing fascist views were often hidden behind a cloak of contrived blimpish pomposity after the outbreak of war:

> Farve's defence of the peerage and the hereditary system offered one of the more obvious butts for his children [and their guests], though the suggestion of his that the abolition of the House of Lords would 'undermine the foundations of Christianity' attracted the derision of the political scientist Prof. Harold Laski, no less.[41]

Laski, who had rejected his Jewish faith, was a professor at the London School of Economics and was a proponent of Karl Marx, who was, of course, also Jewish; a fact that would not have escaped comment in the Mitford household.

Even David Pryce-Jones, the most critical of the Mitford biographers, seemed quite prepared to describe Lord Redesdale as a 'poor lovable ogre of a father', though his description of Sydney as a 'blindly opinionated mother' seemed more realistic. He was also prepared to accept the Mitfords' claim that Unity's childhood could hardly have been expected to be anything less than 'out of the ordinary', though this was undoubtedly the result of the Mitfords girls' determination to develop a reputation as charmingly eccentric aristocrats. They would fail to appreciate Pryce-Jones' quite independently developed opinion that Unity was less of an 'innocent romantic' than was usually portrayed. However, his opinion was not as independent as he would perhaps have liked. An example of this was his submission to the Mitfords' insistence that he removed the claimed 'rumour that Unity had [at one time] performed a lewd act'.

The family was also quite happy to promote 'Rudbin's' (Joan Rodzianko, née Farrer) claim that, 'Uncle David was frightfully pleased to have such brilliant and clever daughters', or that he became 'mad about Unity'. But they (particularly the Duchess of Devonshire (Debo)) subsequently became very grumpy when Pryce-Jones quoted her conversation with Unity in his book. "'Oh Rudbin, they're Jews", she would say when I was in a fury at the way they were being treated. "They're just Jews and must be got rid of.'"

★   ★   ★

Lord Redesdale was delighted with the move to Swinbrook, despite everyone else hating the new house. Nancy christened it 'Swinebrook', while Jessica described it as having aspects of a medieval fortress. It was also while at Swinbrook that David adopted the habit of taking sudden – and what the family insisted were inexplicable – dislikes to individual daughters, doubtless the result of their individual attainment of that age when young girls' emotions become particularly vulnerable and manifest in what sometimes appears to be terminal sulking. The only exception to this prioritised belligerence was Unity. While it is quite possible that even as early as 1926, when Unity was still only 12 years old, their political sympathies had already begun to develop symbiotically, the one other passion she and her father shared was skating. Unity displayed sufficient talent and bravery to win a bronze medal, of which her father was 'frightfully proud'.

What was particularly surprising was that he was prepared to take part in an activity that required him to share the ice with members of the general public or 'commoners'. This was something he found much easier to endure during regular visits to fashionable, German-speaking resorts in Switzerland than at ice rinks in London and Oxford; though the family admitted to his having enjoyed partnering the German wife of one of the skating instructors.

Socially, Lord Redesdale had a particular aversion to sharing the company of anyone outside the family circle. But Nancy was prepared to brave her father's outbursts, along with his downright rudeness to her friends and anyone to whom he had not been formally introduced, by insisting on inviting them home for tea or dinner, and sometimes even to stay for the aforementioned weekends.

'If neighbours had to be tolerated, cousins were a given fact of life';[42] particularly if they were socially important. David was one of a family of nine and Sydney one of four, so there were lots of comings and goings between the Mitfords and their relatives.

Favourites among them were the Baileys, the Farrers, and, of course, the Churchills, though in truth cousin Winston had little time for the children, while their parents claimed never to have cared for Churchill's politics and 'late in life Lady Redesdale took to referring to him as "that wicked man"'.[43] That did not stop the girls taking advantage of their relationship and his political power, or Diana adopting his wife, Lady Clementine, as a role model of elegance and beauty.

With so many cousins, uncles and aunts there was never a shortage of gossip. This was something that Mary Lovell found to be of particular interest. 'Clementine's sister, Nellie Romilly, was regarded as permissive, her mother even more so. "Aunt Natty" Hozier's marriage was desperately unhappy and she was credited with at least nine lovers.' But Aunt Natty had been a favourite visitor to Batsford. 'As for Natty's daughter, naughty Nellie Romilly, it was whispered that her brother-in-law, Winston Churchill, fathered one of her two sons, Esmond.'

While Mrs Violet Hammersley was not related to the Redesdales, she was sufficiently close to qualify for a number of nicknames including, 'Mrs Ham', 'The Widow' and even the 'Wid'. The Hammersleys had lived in Lowndes Square, close to the Bowles family, and the two groups had also met in yachting days in the north of France. After the death of her husband, Arthur, in 1913, Mrs Hammersley lived between Tite Street, Chelsea, and Wilmington, in Totland Bay, on the Isle of Wight. She was referred to by David Pryce-Jones as 'a blue-stocking, a woman of letters in her own right, an enigmatic but persistent presence'. She appeared not to have been as taken in by the Mitford girls as many other friends of the family;

referring to them as 'the Horror Sisters'. However, her morbid fascination with the Redesdales' adoption of Nazi sympathies would no
doubt contribute to her finding herself unable to resist the opportunity of visiting Unity in Munich.

Being a member of the family did not, however, necessarily qualify one for Lord Redesdale's affections. As Jonathan Guinness wrote,
in one of his favourite anecdotes:

> Joan, [David's] sister, was married to Denis Farrer and had six
> children whom the Mitfords knew well; resulting in frequent
> mutual visits … of Joan's husband, David is supposed to have said:
> 'He'd be all right if he wasn't married to that ghastly woman'.
> [His friend replied] 'But I thought he was married to your sister'.
> 'He is,' assented David.

Unsurprisingly, as his daughters began to attract an increasing
number of visitors and their teasing became more intense, David
began to spend somewhat more time away from home in the peace
and quiet of his – and previously his father's – London club, believed
to be The Marlborough.

*   *   *

By now Tom had fallen in love with Austria, 'the land, the culture,
the music, the literature'[44], but most of all with Janos Almasy, a handsome Hungarian count to whom he had been introduced by a
mutual friend. Janos lived in an ancient Gothic castle called Schloss
Bernstein in Burgenland, where Tom was said to have stayed as a
paying guest, though it was some way from Vienna, where he was
also said to have been studying.

Back at the 'Hons Cupboard' in Swinbrook House, when the girls
talked about what they wanted to be when they were grown-ups,
Unity reportedly exclaimed, 'I'm going to Germany to meet Hitler',
while Decca insisted, 'I'm going to run away and be a Communist.'

Exactly where the influence came from to form such political ambitions at such a young age, if indeed Unity and Decca had done so (they were, respectively, still only 16 and 13 years old), seems to have been lost in the records of the development of the Mitford girls' 'saga'. As far as Unity was concerned, the only likely influences would have been Lord Redesdale or her brother, Tom. It may have been both.

While the Mitford girls were only too happy to bring to their public's attention their father's more eccentric diatribes, they remained predictably unwilling to mention the increasingly extreme, right-wing views that he aired during his rare speeches in the House of Lords. While many members of the House were sympathetic to his criticism of the government, it was becoming ever more obvious that Germany's fledgling fascists were more in tune with Lord Redesdale and his sympathisers' socio-political demands than the British government were.

Jonathan Guinness was insistent that 'the question above all which divided parents from children at that time was the question of Germany', and maintains the Mitford girls' stance that their father was violently against the Germans. While this may, or may not, have been the case during the First World War, soon afterwards Lord Redesdale's claimed traditional enemy, 'the filthy Hun', had certainly been replaced by the 'Bolshies' and 'Reds', while his admiration for the opposing Nazi Party would replace any ill-feeling or animosity that may have still existed towards Germans. His new-found enthusiastic commitment was manifest in his financial support for Tom's – and subsequently Unity's – residency in Austria and Germany; it was also obvious from his membership of the Anglo-German Fellowship, the anti-Semitic pro-fascist Right Club and the Link, a non-political organisation that encouraged Anglo-German friendship and attracted pro-Nazi sympathisers.

The family gave little in the way of explanation as to why and how Jessica's sympathy for communism might have developed when she was still only 14 years of age and living a life of considerable privilege. But in *Hons and Rebels* she claimed that it was the indictment of war and eloquent pleading for global disarmament contained in Beverley Nichol's book *Cry Havoc!* that introduced her, like many young people at the time, to left-wing ideals. Socialists (in England, if not in Germany) were the main champions of pacifism and from there it was only a short step to communism.

*   *   *

Pam may have been the least colourful of the Mitford girls, and having been born three years after Nancy, who claimed to have resented her from birth, became the prime victim of her vicious wit, but she was the first of the girls to become engaged; if not married.

A few months before Diana became engaged to Bryan Guinness in 1928, Pam accepted a proposal from a member of another brewing family – Oliver Watney, otherwise known as Togo, 'a tall, dark young man'[45] who had only proposed under pressure from his father who subsequently died of a heart attack. Togo's mother was less enthusiastic concerning the proposed marriage into the Mitford family, particularly regarding those 'sharp, noisy sisters', and sent him off on an extended cruise to reconsider the engagement. His trip had the desired effect and on his return he succumbed to his mother's wishes and called the whole thing off; much to the fury of the Mitfords who immediately initiated a character assassination. They encouraged him to be described as having a stoop and being 'rather deficient in vitality because he was plagued by chronic tuberculosis'[46], and suggested he may even have demanded the return of the engagement ring. Tom certainly had to drive round London returning all the wedding presents, which must have been awfully embarrassing. But any sympathy for Pam was lost when she subsequently admitted that she had never been in love with him in the first place. This rather supported the suspicion amongst Mitford critics that she, or more specifically Sydney, may only ever have been attracted by Watney's wealth. Though subsequently it came to light that there had almost certainly been sexual problems.

The whole 'ghastly business' was soon overshadowed by Diana's engagement to an even larger fortune in the form of Bryan Guinness, who Charlotte Mosley, with hopefully at least the merest trace of bad conscience, described as 'the sensitive and diffident elder son of Lord Moyne and heir to the brewing fortune. [He] was part of a group of Nancy's Oxford friends that had [now grown to include] Evelyn Waugh, John Betjeman, Roy Harrod, Harold Acton, James Lees-Milne, Henry Yorke and Robert Byron.' They were also said to be frightfully 'clever, talented, witty and artistic', or they certainly thought they were. According to Charlotte, these were 'young men whose interests represented everything that Diana aspired to'. What she did not say was that unfortunately none of them, including Bryan, who was so obviously desperately in love, would eventually prove capable of fulfilling Diana's emotional and sexual aspirations. But considering that he was heir to one of the largest fortunes in the country, her ready acceptance of his proposal of marriage was hardly surprising, regardless of the fact that she was, like her sister before her, so obviously not in love with Bryan. Or certainly not to the same degree that he was with her.

It has been claimed that Sydney responded by immediately refusing to sanction the wedding, insisting they waited two years; well, one year anyway! Apparently this was on the grounds that they were both much too young. All of which appeared highly unlikely, although there may have been other reasons for her reticence.

Granted, he was only 24 years old while Diana was only 18 and 'barely out of the schoolroom', but Sydney's main objection, so it was claimed, was centred on her observation that Bryan was 'so *frightfully* rich'. No one seemed prepared to swallow this story, preferring to believe suggestions that she may have found the source of their wealth and involvement in 'trade' to be unacceptable. For an arch snob like Sydney this seemed far more likely, and she certainly spent some time and effort trying to interest Diana in available young men of a somewhat grander lineage.

Bryan's mother, Lady Evelyn, was, by contrast, reputed to have been entirely on the side of Bryan and Diana getting married as soon as possible.

> Diana, accompanied by Nanny, was allowed to visit her future in-laws on the coast in Sussex, and when Bryan introduced her to his mother he broke the quite remarkable news: 'And she can cook, Mummy'. Lady Evelyn, a delightful eccentric who only ever spoke in whispers, was dumbfounded. 'I've never heard of such a thing. It's too clever ...' [soon] even the nursery staff at Bailiffscourt had taken up the refrain: 'To be able to cook – *too* wonderful'.[47]

So the date was fixed for 30 January 1929.

This did not prevent the besotted Randolph Churchill from trying to prevent their marriage by means of various warning letters. While he was doubtless motivated by jealousy, his warnings would prove both perceptive and remarkably accurate. As a result he remained quite unrepentant:

> You know I never told Bryan anything about you which anyone could possibly resent. The most I ever said was that though you were basically of a good disposition, you have no fundamental moral sense. In other words, though you rarely do wrong, you do not actually see anything WRONG in sin ... I do not think he is a character capable of retaining your affection.

According to Anne de Courcy:

> If Bryan had taken any note at all of Randolph's remarks about Diana's flightiness, he might have thought that the enquiry she now made was somewhat portentous coming from one who

professed herself so deeply in love. She asked him if he would
mind if she went out with other men after they were married.

He said that indeed he would mind. Presumably she accepted this
response, but Bryan can hardly have been reassured by the knowledge that his future wife would have preferred an open marriage.

Diana's biographer eventually revealed Randolph's and Bryan's
misgivings. One can only assume that Randolph had personal experience of Diana's promiscuity. It also seems likely that he was influenced by his father's less than generous opinion of Diana's morality.

Sydney meanwhile appeared all too aware of her daughter's
sexual mores, and that they were not limited to Diana. While quite
in keeping with 'flappers' and the Jazz Age, she must have known
how dangerous it could be to the public's perception of the Mitford
girls, whether married or single, if such things became known. Thus,
even within the family, their wilder excesses were played down.

Some years later, after a typically bacchanalian Chelsea Arts Ball
attended by Nancy, Diana, Pam and Unity, where cross-dressing,
excessive inebriation, nudity and vertical 'rumpy-pumpy' were
common practice, 'Muv' ordered Unity, specifically, 'You're not to
tell the children (Jessica and Deborah) what you've been doing.'

There was also reason to believe that both David and Sydney
may have been suffering from pangs of bad conscience concerning
Diana's virginal white wedding; having initially raised objections
to a church wedding. Their somewhat suspicious excuse was that
'Diana had largely lost her faith'. The normally unassertive Bryan
found this attitude quite extraordinary, which, of course, it was, and
vehemently opposed it in a letter to Diana: 'I insist on being married in a church because to do otherwise might be the death of my
whole family.' Poor Bryan may of course have been better advised
to question the real reason for the Mitfords' reluctance. But it was
not in his nature, so 'the usual announcement was sent to *The Times*
and the Mitfords moved en masse to London to prepare for the
wedding, and the reception that was to be held at the Guinnesses'

London house in Grosvenor Place'.[48] The newspapers referred to it as the 'wedding of the year' and gave it acres of coverage. Ironically, it was the year of the Wall Street Crash, which would result in up to 70 per cent unemployment, hunger marches, an armed police response and work camps containing 200,000 unemployed men that remained in operation until 1939.

★   ★   ★

By 1928 Nancy had managed to persuade her parents to allow her to attend the Slade School of Art in London, which also involved her moving away from the family's supportive cast of domestic servants. It should have come as no surprise that she lasted less than a month, the problem being essentially one of service rather than skill or application, as she explained in one of her letters. 'I wept … Oh, darling, but you should have seen it', Nancy drawled. 'After about a week I was knee-deep in underclothes. I literally had to wade through them. No-one to put them away.'

She 'also began submitting items of gossip to *Vogue* and *Harper's Bazaar*, and from this graduated to writing the occasional article. The first known to be published was "The Shooting Party, Some Hints for the Woman Guest", by the Hon. Nancy Mitford.'[49] And so the denied 'Hon' word became a marketing tool!

Meanwhile, Unity became the second Mitford girl to attempt any form of institutionalised education, when at her insistence she was finally, at 15 years of age, enrolled at boarding school. Her determination was largely the result of her desire to escape from the confines of Swinbrook. Her first port of call was St Margaret's in Bushey. It was a girls' school that had originally been created for the education of clergymen's daughters, who still formed a large proportion of the pupils. This strongly influenced the school's Christian commitment and consequently the staff were appalled when Unity refused to be confirmed, claiming she was an atheist.

St Margaret's had been chosen because so many of Unity's relatives and chums were there, including the Farrers and Rosemary and Clementine Mitford, the daughters of David's late brother, Clement. But while Unity was delighted to be free to enjoy their company, she resolutely refused to endear herself to the staff. Aunt Joan claimed Unity had only enrolled there 'to gain more ample room for wickedness and fresh fields to conquer'. Lady Onslow said, 'Once in a scripture lesson we had the passage about he who calls his brother a fool is in danger of hell fire. Bobo put her hand up and asked, "Supposing your brother *is* a fool?" "Put your hand down, Unity Mitford", was the answer.'

The awakening of Unity's sexual awareness was particularly evident in her graphic skills. 'Her talent was for drawing. She drew naked figures in her rough notebook, an Adam and an Eve, and you can guess what they were doing.'[50]

But they were not Adam and Eve. They were copulating 'fallen angels' and when an observant horrified schoolmistress noticed them she screamed, 'Mitford! What is the meaning of this filth?' According to Kathleen Atkins, the Burford doctor's daughter, Unity replied, 'It's not filth. They are fallen angels from Blake's *Paradise Lost*.' Her lacrosse-playing school friends were suitably impressed by the mistress' total inability to know how to react. The school authorities were also deeply suspicious of her ability to recite long passages of Blake and Milton from memory.

* * *

The social season that heralded the Wall Street Crash in 1929 and the worldwide Great Depression of 1929–32 that followed was arguably the most hectic ever known in London, demonstrating that for some the crash was of little consequence.

So it was with Bryan's father, Walter Guinness, who supplied Bryan with sufficient funds to buy a country house of his own. His choice was Biddesden House, a substantial country seat near Andover in Wiltshire that Diana, soon known in the press as a society beauty, partygoer and hostess, would turn into a veritable bastion of social decadence. Regular visitors became known as 'The Biddesden Gang' and included, amongst others, John Betjeman, Harold Acton, John Sutro, Brian Howard, Cecil Beaton, Robert Byron, Mark Ogilvie-Grant, Christopher Sykes, James Lees-Milne, the Heskeths and all three Sitwells. Encouraged by the smell of money and promiscuity, Raymond Mortimer was soon a regular visitor. One of the best critics of his generation, like Evelyn Waugh he had also become an unofficial proofreader and literary adviser to Nancy.

Waugh's *Vile Bodies* provided the gang's maxim and was even dedicated 'With love to Bryan and Diana Guinness'. In a letter to a friend, the author described his novel as, 'A welter of sex and snobbery, written simply in the hope of selling some copies.'

Waugh was said to be, in a wholly platonic way, 'of course', a little in love with Diana. Maybe with Bryan as well! He saw the Guinness' continually, especially after his own marriage broke up in July 1929, following which all three of them went to Berlin to witness the legendary nightlife. Brian Howard was one of those who encouraged them to take what he considered a pilgrimage. 'It is the gayest town in Europe,' he told Diana, though she needed little encouragement. Perhaps he thought the delights of Berlin could drag Bryan out of the closet. Perhaps they did!

It would not be long before Unity, whose relationship with Diana was growing closer, would also be dragged into her social maelstrom, though Cecil Beaton acutely observed, 'Unity was not *really* a member of the Biddesden gang … She would not talk to people, only to herself.' But Brian Howard was one of the few people capable of understanding Unity's world and why she was there. Her relationship with her sister was largely based on her fascination with the intelligence of many of Diana's friends, and her amorality, particularly concerning her sexual mores.

★   ★   ★

Bryan and Diana's long honeymoon had taken them south towards Sicily where she first set eyes on the azure Mediterranean, cloudless sky, Greek and Roman temples, almond blossom and olive groves: 'It seemed to me a mystery why anyone who is not obliged to do so by work should choose to live anywhere else.'

The young couple actually spent the first part of their honeymoon in Paris, staying at the Guinness family's apartment at 12 rue de Poitiers. When they returned, it was to their new house in Buckingham Street which, with their excellent cook and full revenue of staff, quickly became a Mecca both for the Oxford coterie, who only had to pick up the telephone to be invited round by Diana, and for new friends such as Lotte Lenya, Peter Quennell and the Sitwells. John Betjeman even wrote a little ditty about it:

> I too could be arty,
> I too could get on.
> With Sickert, the Guinnesses, Gertler and John.

The reference to 'getting on' gives an indication that the whole process may not have been as guileless and indolent as originally thought and involved, at least on a literary level, a great deal of mutual promotion.

Bryan soon became disenchanted with his new wife's extravagant social decadence while Anne de Courcy described her as 'the central star, the flame round which they all gathered and, increasingly, the shrine at which they worshipped. Impeccably dressed, beautiful, funny, warm and flatteringly attentive, she fascinated them all.'

This social hothouse inevitably led to a considerable degree of tension, not least that which resulted from Evelyn Waugh's lack of loyalty:

Once in Diana's company, Waugh was dazzled. For Nancy, this repetition of a familiar phenomenon must have been galling. Against the fact of Diana's beauty, Nancy's own wit, sparkle and considerable attractiveness, her years of friendship with Waugh, counted little. Without intention or coquetry, in fact, without even trying, her sister moved to the centre of Waugh's life.[51]

Apparently Waugh was soon spending most of his time with Diana at her house on Buckingham Street. In the mornings, presumably when Bryan had left for the day, he would 'sit on her bed, chatting, while she read or wrote her letters or telephoned'. He would then 'accompany her on walks, drives or shopping, lunch with her and often return for dinner in the evening with both Guinness's'.[52] Diana was said to have found him an 'enchanting companion' and, who knows, possibly lover. They would certainly come to share political affiliations through their belief in fascism.

With almost as many servants as friends, there was certainly little reason for Diana to do any work, or invest effort in anything other than her relentless pursuit of pleasure. Mary Lovell told a wonderful anecdote concerning her attempts to achieve something as undemanding as keeping account of people to whom she may have owed money, having abandoned the tiresome habit of carrying any of her own. 'When Bryan's eccentric mother, Lady Evelyn, discovered Diana bookkeeping she was horrified: "How barbarous of Bryan," she whispered'. Diana never again kept anything that could, by any stretch of the imagination, be considered as 'accounts', or did anything a servant could not do for her; until after her divorce.

*   *   *

Having betrayed his Conservative background and developed a close relationship with Ramsay MacDonald, Oswald Mosley became extremely disillusioned after Labour won the 1929 general election and he was awarded nothing more than the position of Chancellor of the Duchy of Lancaster. For a man with the ambition, and many said the promise, to lead the country, it was a bitter pill. So, disillusioned by the Conservatives, Labour and Liberals, he had decided to create his own political party.

But as Mosley's New Party became more radical and turned increasingly towards fascist policies, many previous supporters defected, while Lord Redesdale's interest increased. This was especially true following Mosley's visit to Benito Mussolini's Italy in 1931, after which he returned inspired and determined to dominate Britain's various fascist movements and ultimately lead them into battle.

Arnold Leese was yet another somewhat eccentric fascist who attempted to start his own political party, the Imperial Fascist League, in 1928. Motivated by his understandable aversion to kashrut, the Jewish laws dictating the slaughtering of animals, Leese, a veterinarian by training, was a particular expert on the diseases of camels. Perhaps as a result of his love of animals, his aversion quickly grew into hysterical anti-Semitism and a perceived Jewish threat to the British Empire. His anti-Semitism was so extreme that he would later accuse Mosley of being a 'kosher fascist' in charge of the 'British Jewnion of Fascists'.

The league was also strongly influenced by Mussolini and included black-shirted legions, violent street battles and a fasces as its symbol. But eventually, as the movement started to be more influenced by Hitler, they adopted the swastika superimposed on a Union Jack. Initially Leese, who had been a member of the British Fascists, was elected a councillor in Stamford, Lincolnshire, along with fellow fascist Henry Simpson. In his autobiography, Leese wrote, "We were the first constitutionally elected Fascists in England."

It often seems to have been the English inability to take life entirely seriously that undermined their fascist ambitions. It was certainly difficult to believe that any man who titled his autobiography, *Out of Step: Events in the Two Lives of an Anti-Jewish Camel Doctor*, lacked a sense of humour. Thankfully, he also lacked Mosley's sex appeal, wealth and 'breeding', which attracted so many, including Lord Redesdale and his daughters, to Mosley's political party; though not all for the same reasons.

4

DANCING ON THE EDGE ...

1930–34

Transcendenta! Transcendenta!
We shall dance a mad cadenza!
Jack Kerouac

While unemployment in Britain rose and the global financial situation headed towards the abyss, the Mitfords and their ilk continued to dance on the edge of the volcano:

Brian Howard blithely threw a party at St George's Swimming Baths at which guests were asked to bring a bottle and a bathing-suit: a black orchestra provided the music and a 'bathwater cocktail' was served ... the Hon. Stephen Tennant had a party for which the guests had to dress as shepherds [from a Watteau painting].[1]

Clubs, gay, straight, and those in between, continued to open and close. Fashionable people used the Embassy Club in Old Bond Street 'to get drunk with an element of decorum'[2]. After that there was always Rosa Lewis' Cavendish Hotel, a house halfway between the fantasy of nightclubs and the reality of dawn. There were also drugs available from a dealer called Brilliant Chang, who specialised in cocaine, or 'happy powder', and from Harrods, where one could purchase all manner of chemical stimulants.

Some people, such as Charles Jennings, at least attempted to give such decadence a degree of justification: 'People might scoff at London Society and its conventions, its artificiality, and its apparent devotion to pleasure as the main object in life; but there it was: it represented the elite of the governing classes of the British Empire.'

Jennings also realised that the social order was in a far more serious state of flux than the Mitford girls and many members of the privileged classes were prepared to admit:

> Mabell, Countess of Airlie, Mistress of the Bedchamber to Queen Mary and quintessential Establishment figure ... [quoted] in her memoirs a letter written to her by her brother, the 6th Earl of Arran: 'The days of family pedigrees are over ... They are clinging to the past and will not realise that an old family only remains such as long as it continues to own the family house and landed property ... I turn nostalgically to those halcyon years with delight and remember how much I enjoyed them. Yet I understand that even were I able to afford to live again as I did then it would be impossible owing to the march of democracy. To live that life demanded that domestic servants should be slaves and contented with their slavery. It was only by slavery that the old regime could be carried on'.[3]

In Germany, particularly in Berlin, there was more than just a change in social order. It seemed as if the whole culture of a nation was changing under the Weimar Republic, a transition graphically recorded by John Heygate:

> Whatever aspect of the town's nightlife one chose to explore, sexual, sadistic, or the combination of the two that have always

flourished in a military-minded nation, one came up against the same fact: Berlin was rotten … Germany had gone coituscrazy … The Imperial Capital of Germany had become the European market of bodies … The Empire of Flesh'.

Berlin attracted as many as 2 million tourists annually during the best economic times of the Weimar Republic. It was the most popular urban tourist attraction in Germany and a magnet for foreign travellers. Nearly 40,000 American visitors were reported in Berlin hotels and inns in 1930.

But there were shadows moving across Germany that were far more sinister than Berlin's taste for hedonism. Highly decorated First World War veteran and legendary nationalistic German writer Ernst Jünger elevated war, giving it the status of a quasi-religious, life-affirming art form, asking, 'What could be more sacred than a man doing battle?' He claimed war elevated the soldier's life, isolated from normal humanity, into a mystical experience. Jünger criticised the fragile and unstable democracy of the Weimar Republic, stating that he 'hated the democracy like the plague'. He rejected the liberal values of liberty, security, ease and comfort and sought instead the measure of man in his capacity to withstand pain and sacrifice.

While the English could still quite easily be motivated to take part in military action using such incentives as 'heroism' and 'duty to king and country', the feeling was that the German type of extreme warrior worship and the elevation of ritualised violence to a mystical level had largely lost its appeal in England after the Crusades. But the popularity of Blake's poetry and imagery, which reflected remarkably similar sentiments to the Germans, if more directly related to Christianity as opposed to the Norse gods, indicated that such beliefs held much greater influence in England than would subsequently be admitted. While *Jerusalem* remained the most popular nationalistic anthem classic, *A War Song to Englishmen* reflected the English propensity for giving the terrors of war God's blessing.

The arrows of Almighty God are drawn!
Angels of Death stand in the louring heavens!
Thousands of souls must seek the realms of light,
And walk together on the clouds of heaven!
Prepare, prepare!

Soldiers, prepare! Our cause is Heavens cause;
Soldiers, prepare! Be worthy of our cause;
Prepare to meet our fathers in the sky;
Prepare, O troops, that are to fall to-day!
Prepare, prepare!

Unity Mitford shared such convictions. But in 1930 she was still a strong-willed, sexually aware 16-year-old girl searching for her Jerusalem and an altar on which to sacrifice herself.

*   *   *

While Unity searched for her altar, Hitler continued his relentless rise to power. In part he achieved this by his continued courting of the German nobility, sustaining their belief that he intended to reinstate the Hohenzollern monarchy. The proof of his success was that 'between a third and half of the princes eligible to do so joined his Nazi Party [and] among the 312 families from the old aristocracy there were 3,592 individuals who joined'.

But the party's gaining of 107 seats in the Reichstag, after winning nearly 6.5 million votes in the German elections of September 1930, came as a surprise not only to Hitler's enemies, but also to the Nazis themselves. At the time, party membership in the whole of Germany only amounted to some 100,000. Walter Laqueur claimed, 'The only reason that could be given was that the vote for Hitler and his party was at that stage a demonstration against the existing state of affairs rather than a vote in favour of any specific political program ... The growth of the Nazis on one hand and the advance of the Communists on the other were both the result of the economic crisis (that had started on Wall Street).' With 6 million unemployed it was hardly surprising that the Communists outnumbered the Nazis, and they should have never been defeated. But they had one major disadvantage. In the street fighting which became a daily feature of German politics in 1930–32, the Communists still lacked the military support of the Freikorps.

In 1930, Ernst von Salomon's novel *Die Geächteten* (*The Outlaws*) was published, which drew on his experience as a member of the Freikorps fighting against the Bolsheviks in Latvia. He left little doubt that another war was inevitable, and that for many the horror would be gloriously limitless:

> We smashed our way into startled crowds, raging and shooting and beating and hunting. We drove the Latvians across the fields like frightened hares; we set fire to their houses; buckled their telegraph poles, pulverised their bridges. We hurled the corpses into wells and threw hand grenades after them. Anything that came within our grasp was decimated; we burned whatever we could. We have seen red, and our hearts were emptied of human feelings. At every stage of our journey the earth groaned under the weight of our destruction. Where there had been houses, there was now only rubble and ashes, smouldering woodpiles, ulcers festering on naked terrain. Giant smoke plumes marked our passage across the landscape. We had built a funeral pyre to burn dead matter; but more than this, we burned our hopes and longings, codes of civil conduct, the laws and values of civilisation, the whole burden of fusty verbiage we carried, our belief in the things and ideas of a time that had rejected us. We withdrew, swaggering, intoxicated, and booty-laden.

For Hitler, to achieve his ambition of total power over the Germanic 'master race' by such savage means was a fantasy he aimed to realise, and which he believed to be his destiny. A destiny that Unity Mitford, still only 16 years old, could not wait to share.

*   *   *

After the end of the Michaelmas term in 1930, it was made clear that Unity would not be welcome back at St Margaret's School. Sydney was reported to have said, 'I visited the headmistress, who explained to me that many girls left school at 16 and Unity could well be one of them.'

While this may have been true, her alleged statement fails to address the reason 'why' the headmistress was recommending that Unity leave after only one year. The reason seems quite likely to have been encapsulated in Jonathan Guinness' version of the episode and to have involved Lord Redesdale and his daughters' unabashed socio-political opinions:

> This puts paid to the legend, told to Pryce-Jones by more than one of his informants, that it was David who visited the headmistress and that in the course of the interview he was grossly and personally offensive. This was always improbable; David could be irascible, but he was never ill-bred.

It does not seem to have occurred to Jonathan that the concept that human behaviour was dependent on breeding, rather than parental and peer group influence and education, has chilling connotations. But it was something that many of the British middle and upper classes firmly believed in. Only some time after the war did it become generally unacceptable to voice such opinions.

*   *   *

In the summer of 1930 Bryan and Diana visited Tom, who was said to have 'just begun reading law at Berlin University'[4], presumably intending at one time to settle and practice there. According to Diana it was the first time she heard the word 'Nazi' used to describe those in favour of fascism. "'Do you take sides?'" Diana asked. "Oh no," [Tom] replied. "It's their own affair. But if I were a German, I suppose I would be a Nazi".' Apparently there were only two choices, fascism or communism, and the latter was of course totally unacceptable.

In 1928 the Nationalist Socialist Lawyers' League had been formed. It was the first special organisation by means of which the NSDAP (National Sozialistische Deutsche Arbeiter Partei) gained a foothold in public life, and probably said more about the character of lawyers than Nazis. They were not the only professional body to choose to accept the abandonment of human rights, morality and ethics. By 1933, for example, German doctors had abandoned the Hippocratic oath and were actively participating in the euthanising of both mental and physical cripples in pursuit of the Nazi policy of eugenics.

In 1934 the Gestapo (Geheime Staatspolizei) or 'Secret State Police' was established, under the control of Heinrich Himmler. His right-hand man, Werner Best, declared, 'As long as the police (and the judiciary) carries out the will of the leadership, it is acting legally.' In 1935 a law was passed officially permitting the Gestapo to act without judicial oversight. At its height, it had 45,000 members. It also controlled the camps and the extermination of the Jews.

Meanwhile, any form of intelligent, independent thought was actively discouraged: 'Intellectuals, however patriotic, were socially not quite acceptable in a conservative world still dominated by Junkers, generals and captains of industry. They were quite out of place amongst the Nazi elite.'[5]

* * *

Sydney was insisting that she was totally unconcerned by politics and that her main worry was her daughters' moral welfare, or more specifically Unity's and Jessica's obsession with 'matters risqué or mildly improper'. She claimed that the girls '[still] thought a lot about the White Slave Trade, always expecting to be whisked off to Buenos Aires'. Actually, 'hoping' may be a more accurate description of what was obviously now more of an erotic fantasy than a fear. Particularly in the case of Unity, for who sex was already a reality.

Although Decca claimed that it was her interest in politics that stimulated Unity's, it appears that the 16-year-old Unity, who was of course three years older than Decca, had already become interested in proto-fascist literature in 1930; three years before Decca had displayed any interest in politics. David Pryce-Jones came across a book Unity had signed and dated in 1930. It was a copy of *Jew Süss*, Lion Feuchtwanger's novel about an eighteenth-century Jewish financial-adventurer. Because of its stereotypical Jewish characters, it was used in Germany to encourage anti-Semitism.

As far as Jessica's commitment to Communism was concerned there were one or two contradictions, particularly in her choice of Julius Caesar as a role model. Unity's choice of Joan of Arc, arguably the ultimate female spiritual fantasist, made a great deal more sense. Jessica also revealed that Unity's political sympathies were more than likely to have been affected not only by her cultural and literary influences but also by her father: 'When Bobo was 16, my father's feelings for her shifted from total loathing to adoration.'

Jessica's credibility as a 'lefty' would also have been particularly difficult to establish, due in part to her accent, which simply screamed privilege. And the manner in which they said things could be as equally revealing as their accent. The Mitford girls were renowned for the manner of their speech but despite it handicapping any serious credibility as a communist, Decca appeared to make no attempt to change it. Journalist Philip Toynbee recalled her once asking a burly working man, 'Could you be absolutely sweet and tell us where we can get some delicious tea?'

The Mitford voice was often said to be affected because of its drawl and exaggerated emphasis' which of course it was. It certainly wasn't accidental. One was taught to speak in that manner to establish one's superiority over commoners, assisted of course by those wonderfully arrogant and patronising prefixes, such as 'My good man'. Then there was the emphasis. Writer and critic Lytton Strachey's voice had more than enough of the Lady Bracknell 'bray', but it was this that established his social superiority. '"What *is* coconut matting", Lytton had said, "Is it *really* made of coconut?"'

Meanwhile, the age gap between the girls and their eldest sister must have seemed immense, while her total disdain for them would have made any influence, political or otherwise, highly unlikely. By 1930 Nancy was 26 years old; dark-haired, with green eyes, which were later reputedly 'described by Evelyn Waugh, John Betjeman and sister Decca as triangular in shape'. But despite such attractive physical attributes, as she grew older her character if anything grew even more 'grievous'. '"The Queen of Teasers", or "a cosmic teaser" as her sister Decca would describe her.'[6]

'She once upset us,' Debo recalled, 'by saying to Unity, Decca and me, "Do you realise that the middle of your names are nit, sick and bore?"'

David Pryce-Jones was under no illusion concerning Nancy's corrosive character, nor Evelyn Waugh's caustic encouragement: 'The cruelty of the Waugh/Mitford novels has often been caught, but the weak child's need to jeer before being jeered at is there too.' Neither was Mary Lovell: 'Nancy called Debo "Nine" until she married, saying it was her mental age.' Her sisters were very generous to describe all this as 'teasing', but it was obviously more than that. More than once Nancy was described as a 'prize bitch', and not only towards her siblings.

It is difficult to believe that *The Lady* magazine hired Nancy to write articles for five guineas a week without a modicum of nepotistic influence. For it was an extremely cost-effective means of promoting both her first novel and 'Brand Mitford' to the ideal class of reader and, even more so, to those who thought they were.

The magazine also presented an opportunity for somewhat less honest financial advancement. Apparently Gladys, her mother's maid and a particularly gifted seamstress, was also responsible for making clothes for Nancy on the understanding that she paid for the material. Without announcement Nancy then sold the clothes for a handsome profit to a doctor's wife, whom she had discovered via a classified advertisement in the magazine. Jonathan Guinness thought it far more important to mention that Sydney, rather than Gladys, was kept in the dark concerning such exploitation.

*   *   *

By now Unity was beginning to develop her own persona as a young woman rather than a juvenile, and was not without her admirers. John Betjeman said:

> When I knew Unity she was just out of school. I always used to call her Unity Valkyrie, by both names. She was a joyful version of Miss Pam; she spoke like them all, she used all those phrases of theirs. Unity Valkyrie was funny, she had a lot of humour which doesn't come out in the accounts of her.

But out of all the Mitford girls, Diana was far and away the most attractive, blessed with the additional allure of Bryan Guinness' fortune. The combination proved an irresistible flame of attraction for London's 'tout le monde'. Their attraction was even further enhanced by the purchase of 96 Cheyne Walk, Whistler's old house in Chelsea. Even to Unity, who began to visit the house regularly while Diana and Bryan were busy becoming 'the acknowledged leaders of London Society'. Rich, young, intelligent and beautiful, there was hardly a ball or party to which Guinnesses were not invited. Diana was either entertaining or being entertained. She also lunched with Bryan every day, usually at the Savoy, close to the Inns of Court where he was working. He obviously found time to work quite diligently, admittedly an unfamiliar pastime for the Mitfords, for in 1930 he was finally called to the bar. He didn't need to work of course, but having failed to complete his studies at Oxford, there was probably a degree of self-respect involved.

Bryan certainly preferred the languid weekends when they escaped from London and drove down to Biddesden where, apart from entertaining the usual house-guests, he could escape the constant round of parties and balls and spend his time writing, riding and generally 'pottering about'. Diana also gave every appearance of enjoying the time she spent alone with Bryan, her new baby and her beautiful house. Everyone appeared content. But it was not to last.

That autumn, the Guinnesses made 'the annual pilgrimage to Venice. It had become a customary event in their circle'[7]. A circle which included Oswald Mosley who, considering his ambitions, would have been better advised to have stayed at home and attended to politics. This might also have been the first time that Mosley and Diana met and possibly the start of their affair. Meanwhile, the Mitfords, in an effort to minimise the duration of Diana's promiscuous relationship, claimed it did not start until 1932, when Barbara St John Hutchinson invited both to her twenty-first birthday party and seated them next to each other. The sexual electricity apparently did the rest. But while many women obviously found him quite irresistible, many men, including Jamie Gladstone, Daisy Fellowes' grandson, found him to be 'deeply unpleasant'. James Lees-Milne said:

He was in those days a man of overweening egotism. He did not know the meaning of humility ... he was overbearing and over-confident. He brooked no argument, would accept no advice. He had in him the stuff of which zealots are made ... he was madly in love with his own words.

*   *   *

By the beginning of February 1931, the plans for Mosley's New Party were well advanced. It advocated a national policy to meet the economic crisis that the Depression had brought, with particular reference to unemployment. 'They favoured granting wide-ranging powers to the government, with only general control by Parliament and creating a five member Cabinet without specific portfolio'[8]; edging towards totalitarianism. It was soon discovered that the Prince of Wales looked on the New Party with considerable favour.

'On 4 February Cimmie, lunching with Harold Nicolson at Boulestin, secured his promise to join; neither of them saw anything incongruous in discussing the miseries of the "working man" in an elegant and expensive setting ...'[9] Nicolson was convinced that Mosley would some day become Prime Minister, and the New Party leader also received the encouragement of George Bernard Shaw (who always professed, somewhat contradictorily, to be a committed socialist) and the financial backing of Sir William Morris (later Lord Nuffield), who was sufficiently sympathetic to Mosley's political aims and ambitions to contribute £50,000, which in those days was a very considerable amount of money.

The New Party's journal, *Action*, was used to recruit a number of young upper-class intellectuals. They also recruited a body of stewards, or what were to become known as 'Mosley's Biff Boys', whose role was to combat communist violence. Effectively it was a paramilitary force, trained in martial arts by Peter Cheyney, the legendary detective novel writer. They were of little assistance in preventing the collapse of the New Party at the 1931 election when it failed to gain a single seat. But Mosley did not give up. This time he made the decision to follow a path closer to his true convictions and in 1932, having once again visited Rome to see fascism in action, he set about absorbing the remnants of the New Party into his newly formed British Union of Fascists with evangelical zeal, having, in the style of Adolf Hitler, also awarded himself the title of 'Leader'.

Meanwhile, the Nazis continued their policy of seducing the aristocracy, Hermann Göring personally making two visits to the exiled Kaiser Wilhelm II in Doorn, Holland, in January 1931 and May 1932, where he was living courtesy of the Bentinck family, the

Dutch aristocratic family into which Unity's German friend, Gaby Thyssen, would marry. As Carin Göring recalled, 'The Kaiser has probably never heard anybody express an opinion other than his own, and it was a bit too much for him sometimes. Göring expressed support for the restoration of the monarchy, while the Kaiser wanted more – "the restoration of the entire princely brotherhood".'

> Later, the Nazi government provided the Kaiser with an annual subvention. This came about as a result of an agreement signed by Göring in his capacity as Prussian Minister President and a representative of the House of Hohenzollern, Friedrich von Berg, which was signed in late summer 1933: from then on, 'the Kaiser, the Crown Prince and the remaining Prussian princes received a substantial annual allowance from the Prussian state'.[10]

It was said that, as a condition of this arrangement, the Hohenzollern pledged never to publicly criticise Hitler or the Nazis.

*　　*　　*

The Redesdales gave Unity another chance to enjoy some semblance of formal education when, at the beginning of the winter term of 1931, they sent her to Queen's College in London's Harley Street, a school designed to encourage an interest in the arts rather than academia. Unfortunately, while this suited Unity, Sydney was not socially equipped to deal with the college's somewhat informal attitudes:

> I asked my mother if I could have some girls to tea the following Saturday. 'To tea? Oh no, darling, of course not. If you have them to tea they'll invite you to tea with them, and you wouldn't be able to go. You see, I don't know any of their mothers'.

London's art galleries gave Unity the opportunity to immerse herself in Blake's fantasies, while the recently opened Queens Ice

Rink in Bayswater allowed her to indulge her passion for skating and flirting. But Unity's intellectual and sexual development made it increasingly difficult for her to accept the restrictions involved in being a schoolgirl, with or without her mother's support. This was also evident in her blossoming physical appearance. As Dora Carrington noted, '... the little sisters were astonishingly beautiful and another of sixteen (Unity) was very marvellous or Grecian'.

Though it was claimed that Tom had read Law at Berlin University and he was indeed called to the Bar at the Inner Temple, there is no record of his having passed any bar exams or undertaken any kind of formal pupillage. This was in the days when qualifying as a barrister was an even vaguer process than it is today and positions could be, and often were, dependent upon 'funding'. Despite not being individually named as a practising barrister at 4 Paper Buildings, he apparently still managed to practise his profession 'quietly and competently' if not with a great deal of diligence. Tom preferred spending extended periods of time in Austria with his friend Janos Almasy at his schloss in Bernstein and his neighbours, the Erdödys, at Kohfidisch. They consisted of two young countesses, 'one known as Baby and the other, somewhat confusingly, as Jimmy'[11]. Diana remained convinced that her brother was also, 'at one time rather in love with Baby Erdödy'. As well as introducing Unity to Janos, Tom also took Bryan Guinness to Bernstein in August 1931.

That summer, Diana, still only 21 years old, was already pregnant with her second son, Desmond, born in September 1931. Sydney and the three youngest Mitford girls stayed at Biddesden to keep her company while Tom and Bryan, who were obviously under no pressure to work (or in Bryan's case, to stay with his wife), idled away the summer with their Austrian chums.

By November, Harold Nicolson, who was said to have been attracted by the virile and manly youths of the better classes, had joined the New Party but refused to give his support to the British Union of Fascists, claiming that his old friend Mosley's ideals were no longer worthy of his support. 'He believes in fascism. I don't.

I loathe it.' So it was somewhat puzzling why he should have agreed to accompany Mosley on a visit to the two fascist leaders, Hitler and Mussolini, in early January 1932. Given his journalistic experience and political ambitions, it seems highly likely that he was persuaded by the SIS (Secret Intelligence Service or MI6) to accompany Mosley. 'In the last issue of *Action*, published on 31 December 1931, they explained that they were going in order to study "new political forces born of crisis, conducted by youth and inspired by completely new ideas of economic and political organisation".'[12]

With the value of the pound collapsing and unemployment running at 22 per cent there were certainly plenty of people in positions of power and influence who believed that the parliamentary system was running out of options. 'It was this situation that made 1932 such a propitious time to mount a fascist challenge to conventional politics.'[13]

In Germany conditions were even more fertile. 'By 1932 there were 60,000 unemployed academics, [and] most students had no prospect of finding work. Theatres and opera houses closed. Three quarters of all musicians became unemployed. Writers' incomes collapsed, [while] painters and sculptors couldn't sell their work.'[14] It was the end of the Weimar's golden creative age and signified a bad time for everyone, except those who had kept their money in healthier currencies or invested in tangible assets such as gold, cognac or art. The practising of various occult sciences, such as theosophy, increased, while mystics such as Gurdjieff and Ouspensky found themselves in greater demand than ever before.

Meanwhile, not everyone was entirely convinced by Mosley's role as a fascist leader, probably because he spent so little time actively attempting to achieve such a position. But at least he dedicated a small part of the summer recess to composing his 40,000-word manifesto, *The Greater Britain*, though much of it was written well 'South of Calais' an expression in common usage to the accompaniment of plopping tennis balls and throbbing diving boards, while white-gloved waiters refreshed his drink. Mosley displayed considerable determination to avoid abandoning his hedonistic life-style; 'even Mussolini criticised him for spending too much of the summer on the Riviera and in Venice. "It's not a place for serious reformers to linger in villas or grand hotels for more than a few days," he told Lord Lymington.'[15]

*   *   *

In Germany's elections in July 1932, the National Socialists won 230 of the 608 seats in the Reichstag. But even this limited success had only been achieved after ten years of considerable effort. After the abortive putsch in 1923 and the short term banning of the SA, the Nazis soon resumed their brutalisation of all opposition despite the fact that Hitler had decided to concentrate on gaining power by political means rather than armed insurrection. This was successful largely as a result of his decision to leave the administration in the hands of Philip Bouhler, Franz Xaver Schwarz and Max Amann, while he concentrated on increasing the party's membership and developing his personality cult by use of theatrically staged rallies and his gift for aggressively coercive oratory. The political satirist Kurt Tucholsky stated, 'The man doesn't exist; he is only the noise he makes.' But it worked; the proof, if any were needed, came when Hitler's plane was delayed and a crowd of 40,000 enthusiastically waited several hours for him to arrive; shortly before the sun rose.

Despite the fact that Goebbels had a lot to do with the writing of his speeches, Hitler, in his own words, strove to achieve 'an encroachment upon man's freedom of will'. He was, without doubt 'a shrewd psychologist and a superb stage manager'[16], who drew his energy and much of his sexual fulfilment from the crowd.

In 1932 the government was becoming increasingly nervous about the size and power of the 2.9 million strong SA and banned them yet again. But Hitler soon persuaded the chancellor to lift the ban and their armed conflict with the Communists rapidly progressed to the point where it could have more accurately been described as a civil war.

The aristocratic Chancellor von Papen, having launched an unconstitutional coup against the 'leftist' Prussian government, arrested the chiefs of the Berlin police and appointed himself as their replacement. With dictatorial power, an emergency decree and the support of the army, he declared a military state of emergency. Konrad Heiden, the journalist and author stated, 'This was the last gasp of the crumbling, unwanted and now surrendered freedom of the Weimar Republic.'

It would be von Papen who would also persuade President Paul von Hindenburg to appoint Hitler as chancellor in the mistaken belief that he could control him, thus opening the (albeit unbelievably complicated) political route to the door through which the Führer needed to pass in order to gain full dictatorial power.

After thirteen years of freedom, the party was over; Germany was no longer democratically ruled and would not be again for another sixteen years. At least by 1932 the Depression had come to an end, which may have distracted people's attention from the fact that Hitler, sensing that power was within his grasp, had established a Berlin headquarters at the Kaiserhof hotel. There was little evidence to support the subsequent claim that 'Hitler staying in the Kaiserhof caused the same "fear and terror" in Berlin that the cry "Hannibal ante Portas" once did for ancient Rome.'[17]

Despite increasing censorship and trials, there was still as much freedom of expression in Germany in 1932 as in most other European countries. There were also plenty of opponents of Nazism. They just were not very effective, or not as effective as the Nazis' propaganda. In England, despite his commitment to fascism and authoritarianism, Mosley remained friends with Randolph Churchill and other upper-class grandees, while many members of London society would soon be far more interested in what was going on with the Prince of Wales and Wallis Simpson than who was, or was not, running the country.

Back in Germany, Hitler and his high command continued their successful courting of the redundant aristocracy, who were reacting with predictable enthusiasm and commitment to the fascists' return of at least some degree of their military power. Prince Philipp von Hessen claimed to have been informed at the end of 1932 that Hitler had awarded him an honorary rank in the SA. Other princes were also 'invited' to accept fascist military power. Furthermore, Heinrich Himmler, head of the SS, Hitler's elite personal guard, and the chief of the SA, Ernst Röhm, were said to have particularly favoured the policy of appointing princes as commanders, in the knowledge that they would inspire loyalty and deference.

'Himmler, while holding ambivalent views about aristocrats, conceived his order as "a new knighthood" and liked to surround himself with nobles. The Reichsführer-SS conceived his order as a *Blutadel* (blood nobility) and drew upon the resources and traditions of the aristocracy.'[18] He also displayed considerably greater commitment to mysticism, occult sciences and the more extreme racial theories than other members of the Nazi leadership.

SS Brigadeführer Karl Maria Wiligut was Himmler's personal spiritual adviser. Wiligut claimed to follow an Irminic religion based on a German deity called Irmin. He also claimed to worship a Germanic god called Krist, who he insisted the Christians had used as the basis for Jesus Christ. According to Wiligut, Germanic culture and history could be traced back to 228,000 BC. At that time there were apparently three suns and Earth was inhabited by giants, dwarfs and other mystical creatures. In the 1920s he developed paranoia and became convinced that his family was the victim of a continuing persecution of Irminists conducted by the Catholic Church, Jews and Freemasons. He blamed the same people for the loss of the First World War and the downfall of the Habsburg Empire.

One of the more outrageous mystic sciences encouraged by Himmler was the *Welteislehre* (WEL for short), the cosmological 'World Ice Theory' of the Austrian Hans Hörbiger, who was convinced all cosmic process was based on ice; a theory he came to by means of a vision rather than scientific research. His followers also wanted, presumably with his encouragement, to cleanse the world of all Jewish science.

* * *

Mosley and Nicolson arrived in Rome on the evening of 1 January 1932 for another audience with Mussolini. There, they were met by author and Oxford acolyte Christopher Hobhouse and installed in the most luxurious suite at the Excelsior Hotel, which Mosley firmly believed befitted his social status and political position. It was a political position that Hitler had already criticised as lacking 'harshness, provocation and violence'; elements that were already becoming part of British fascism, even while, at that time, Mosley seemed more impressed by the milder Italian model.

It was actually far more likely that a man with so little political integrity – but so obsessed with women and his own appearance – would simply have found the fascist uniforms and women in Italy more appealing. Despite Martin Pugh's insistence to the contrary, it would have been of no possible consequence to Mosley that Mussolini suppressed the Mafia, drained the Pontine Marshes or made Italy's trains run on time.

The Mitfords were always more impressed with the German version of fascism, both socially and ideologically. There was certainly never any indication, even historically, of any reticence concerning Nazi racial policies or even their appalling realisation. It was also somewhat ironic that the empowerment of women and liberalisation of attitudes during the Weimar period should have enabled Pam, Diana and Unity to live in and travel around greater Germany with such ease and independence.

Mosley's audience with Mussolini hardened his resolve to emulate the European fascists. But Harold Nicolson, wrote in his diary for 18 January that Mosley "does not want to do anything at present. What he would like would be to lie low till the autumn, write a book, then rope in Winston Churchill, Lloyd George, Rothermere and if possible Beaverbrook, into a League of Youth. Then launch an autumn campaign"', from which the British Union of Fascists would rise from the ashes of the New Party; a party that had proved so dramatically ineffectual during the most recent elections.

That year, 'Irene Curzon, Mosley's sister-in-law, who was frightfully well connected and enjoyed numerous adulterous affairs with wealthy members of the Melton Mowbray hunt, organised a fundraising ball and helped to persuade figures such as Lord Rothermere to contribute to the BUF coffers, with whose leader it appeared highly likely she had also slept.'[19]

In *The Greater Britain*, published through the BUF Press in 1932, Mosley 'unashamedly advocated totalitarian government: freedom for the individual but within complete state control; a democratically elected government headed by an authoritarian leader ... unlike Hitler's *Mein Kampf*, in which Jews are specifically mentioned as the enemy of the people, Mosley's book made no reference to Jews.'[20] It would be nice to think that Baroness Curzon's sexual relationship with the legendary pianist Arthur Rubinstein may have obliged the opportunistic Mosley to temper his public encouragement of anti-Semitism. Unfortunately, any selflessness in this regard was not to last, but for the time being it caused the Nazi Julius Streicher to accuse Mosley of being 'the tool of the Jews' in his magazine, *Der Stürmer*.

*　　*　　*

Despite ever-increasing independence and time spent at school, Unity was still very much tied to Swinbrook, her parents, her sister Jessica and perhaps, most surprisingly, for those not familiar with the aristocracy's reliance on surrogate mothers, Nanny:

> Boud [Unity] and I [Jessica] both avoided the company of the Grown-Ups at this time as much as we could. At Swinbrook,

we lived in the D.F.D. except for mealtimes. We divided it down the middle, and Boud decorated her side with Fascist insignia of all kinds – the Italian 'fasces', a bundle of sticks bound with rope; photographs of Mussolini framed in passe-partout; photographs of Mosley trying to look like Mussolini; the new German swastika, a record collection of Nazi and Italian youth songs. My side was fixed up with my Communist library, a small bust of Lenin purchased for a shilling in a second-hand shop, a file of Daily Workers. Sometimes we would build barricades with chairs and stage pitched battles, throwing books and records until Nanny came to tell us to stop the noise.

This version of their political leanings is rather typical of the Mitfords' habit of hiding anything that could subsequently be considered embarrassing behind a smokescreen of nursery humour. Rather surprisingly, some of the best examples were included in Jessica's *Hons and Rebels*:

Although Boud's interest in Fascism had at first been kept a secret from the grown-ups, it soon leaked out. She begged to be allowed to go to Germany … Boud wouldn't be teased about her devotion to the Nazis. She was completely and utterly sold on them. The Nazi salute – 'Heil Hitler!' with hand upraised – became her standard greeting to every-one, family, friends, the astonished postmistress in Swinbrook village. Her collection of Nazi trophies and paraphernalia now overflowed our little sitting-room – bundles of Streicher's anti-Semitic paper, *Der Stürmer*; an autographed copy of *Mein Kampf*; the works of Houston Stewart Chamberlain, a 19th century forerunner of Fascist ideologists; albums of photographs of Nazi leaders.

Jessica made no attempt to explain exactly where Unity might have obtained such things. It certainly would not have been at Swinbrook post office, and seems highly unlikely that they could have entered the house without her parents' knowledge, with or without Nanny's assistance.

Jessica also claimed:

> My parents at first looked on Boud's newfound interest as rather a joke. Conservative opinion of Hitler at that time ranged from out-right disapproval of him as a dangerous, lower-class demagogue to a grudging sympathy for his aims and methods – after all, had he not decisively crushed the German Communist Party and destroyed the labour unions in a surprisingly short time? Thus the words 'that feller Hitler' on the lips of countless English squires could be expressed equally in tones of derision or of admiration. Indeed, with Hitler's rise to power the concept of 'filthy huns' had mysteriously been completely discarded.

This statement would prove unsurprisingly accurate, particularly when Unity and Diana subsequently begged the 'Revereds' (parents) to go with them to Germany and see for themselves what life was like under a fascist dictatorship, where euthanasia and racial and political cleansing were already operating. Obviously, they did not have to beg too hard:

> 'Farve is really one of Nature's Fascists. He'd simply love the Führer', they insisted. Before long they would prevail and Muv and Farve would be given a royal time in Germany. They would be lent a chauffeur-driven Mercedes-Benz, shown all the gaudy trappings of the new regime and they return full of praise for what they had seen. [21]

This response would owe more to Unity's relationship with Hitler than Diana's, Hitler never having much time for Mosley.

★   ★   ★

Unity was undoubtedly attractive, albeit in that delightfully English sort of way, though most Mitford biographers seem determined to denigrate her with such comments as, 'Someone said that looking at her was like looking at Diana in a slightly distorted mirror.'[22]

Mary Lovell claimed Unity 'felt awkward about her appearance' and had endured a full complement of sisterly taunts about her size, but her character and behaviour made her what Decca called a *sui generis* [unique] personality. However, aware that her information came largely from Unity's sisters, presumably Lovell must also have known that Hitler declared *both* Unity and Diana to be 'perfect specimens of Aryan womanhood'. His appreciation of their physical qualities was manifest in a Ziegler painting of four nude models bearing remarkable similarity to the Mitford girls, that hung over the fireplace in the Führer Room at the Brown House.

The fact that Hitler would come to consider Unity and Diana equally attractive would have been a welcome relief for Unity, for whom the constant reference to Diana as the beauty of the family must have been wearing. But in bidding for attention, Unity was certainly more than capable of rivalling her sister.

According to Kathleen Atkins, Unity did indeed have a magnificent body. When she was 16 she had overheard two men using this word to describe what they thought she must look like naked, and realised she thought so too. She took to repeating the word 'magnificent' over and over again to herself, as a sexual mantra.

Unity still thought a lot about William Blake, and also thought a lot about sex, and often both – the former encouraging the latter. Kathleen remembered Unity showing her a notebook, on the front of which, underneath her drawing of the copulating angels, she had written, 'excess is sex spelt backwards', for she now firmly believed that what Blake had really meant was that the path of sex leads to the Palace of Wisdom, but spelt sex backwards so only those who talked to angels would understand.

She also continued to read Milton, and learnt quite a lot about sex and the power of her imagination from more contemporary writers whose illicit work was circulated by various girlfriends, one of whose brothers had returned from Italy with a copy of *Lady Chatterley's Lover*, which with the aid of an Italian/English dictionary caused considerable excitement.

While Nancy enjoyed teasing, Unity liked to shock, though in her teenage years her behaviour sometimes seemed more Dadalike than truly shocking. Her releasing of a white rat at a 'deb' ball is typical of the type of story that the Mitfords considered suitable for inclusion as part of their charmingly eccentric family saga, while less socially acceptable behaviour has remained buried. Kathleen Atkins, who grew up in the small town of Burford, next door to Swinbrook, delighted in recounting how Unity successfully shocked post office customers by raising her skirt to illustrate her preference for wearing no knickers. This may also have been the same 'lewd sex act' that Pryce-Jones was 'obliged' by the family to remove from his book.

While the decision by Unity's family and many of her friends to establish her lack of physical attraction appeared to have been motivated by their post-war determination to dispel rumours of any sexual activity between Unity and either Hitler or his SS officers, others had more personal reasons to establish her lack of attraction.

Elizabeth Powell, later to become Lady Glenconnor, remained quite determined to support the myth of Unity's 'exceptional height'; doubtless aware that it would have been a considerable handicap in the competitive business of finding a suitable match. 'I also came out in January 1932. I made friends with Unity at Queen Charlotte's Ball. We were both nearly six feet tall, bringing up the back of that procession with the cake, rebellious girls in white, it was ghastly.' In fact, it was more than likely that they were stuck at the back due to their propensity for bad behaviour.

The political animosity that developed between Jessica and her sister equipped the former with more than sufficient motivation for commenting, 'Boud had grown from a giant-sized schoolgirl into a huge and rather alarming debutante.'

The social media remained less easily convinced however. The *Daily Express* on 2 June 1932 was quoted as saying, 'I thought that the prettiest girl at Epsom was Hon Unity Mitford.' No mention was made of her exceptional height. As is obvious from photographs, Unity was very little, if any, taller than either Nancy or Diana.

The following week *Tatler*, by coincidence, featured 'a full-page portrait of Hitler as man-about-town, with the curious information [which they obviously considered relevant], that he had refused to look the camera in the eye'.

> On 10 March 1932, the *Daily Express* featured a large photograph of Unity, to explain among other things that 'she will find it difficult to retain her obvious clear-eyed freshness throughout the season, which year by year seems to become for debutantes more of an endurance test than a period of social delights'.[23]

The William Hickey column was in fact written by Tom Driberg, who was not actually very interested in girls, but his colleagues on the *Evening Standard*'s 'Londoner's Diary' backed him up by printing another photograph of Unity on the same day.

The 'obvious clear-eyed freshness' of the girls may have had other, more exotic, reasons for *not* fading; reasons that mothers would of course strongly deny, particularly in the case of Unity Mitford. But such things were quite obviously far more common than could possibly be admitted. Georgia Sitwell even admitted, 'Of course I went to bed with Tom [Mosley]. We all did, and then felt bad about it afterwards.'

God knows how many girls Oswald Mosley had slept with during the many seasons prior to his twelve years of marriage to Cimmie. And marriage did little to curtail his sexual extravagance; during his years with Cimmie he became involved with some three-dozen different women. He even invested in a property that was strictly reserved for such activities. He claimed that his flat in Ebury Street was essential for his work, but that would hardly have been a justifiable reason for his insistence that it remained off-limits to his wife. There can be little doubt that such time-consuming sexual activity was a major factor in Mosley's failure to fulfil his political ambitions. Thus, the girls who slept with Oswald Mosley could be seen to have contributed to England's avoidance of submitting to fascism.

But despite her mother's best efforts and the sexual opportunities on offer, Unity was still proving unresponsive to the whole process of 'coming-out'. Sydney was so concerned that she even persuaded David's sister, Joan, who had as little interest in the social season as Unity, to bring out her daughter Rudbin at the same time in order to try and encourage Unity's motivation; but to little effect.

The London season opened with a ball at Buckingham Palace (in May) at which debutantes were presented to the king and queen. Unity would have been required to walk up to the royal couple, curtsey twice and retreat backwards gracefully. Unity would have considered such a ritual and the following three months of non-stop social events as a perfect butt for her humour and an opportunity for generally outrageous behaviour.

★　　★　　★

To celebrate Diana's twenty-second birthday in June 1932, the Guinnesses held a grand party at their house on Cheyne Walk. She was then said to be:

> 'At the height of her beauty', having been painted by half a dozen leading portrait artists and her face, which had become virtually an icon for the era with its classical planes, carefully composed, so as not to encourage wrinkles, appeared in newspaper Society columns regularly. She was the woman who apparently had everything: youth, riches, a happy marriage, a charming [and incredibly wealthy] husband who worshipped her and [by now] two healthy children.[24]

139

Not to mention a highly skilled and experienced fascist lover who lacked any degree of loyalty and refused to appreciate even the concept, let alone the reality, of monogamy.

According to Diana:

> We invited everyone we knew, young and old, poor and rich, clever and silly. It was a warm night and the garden looked twice its real size with the trees lit from beneath. A few things about this party dwell in my memory: myself managing to propel Augustus John, rather the worse for wear, out of the house into a taxi; Winston Churchill inveighing against a large picture by Stanley Spencer of Cookham war memorial which hung on the staircase, and Eddie Marsh defending it against his onslaught. I wore a pale grey dress of chiffon and tulle and all the diamonds I could lay my hands on. We danced until day broke, a pink and orange sunrise which gilded the river.

It was said to be 'the party of the year'. It was also the first time that Oswald Mosley had been to the Guinnesses' Cheyne Walk residence, but his affair with Diana was already established. Despite the fact that Diana quite obviously shared many of Mosley's more unpleasant character traits, as a result of her wealth and beauty most social observers seemed quite determined to excuse, or even justify her behaviour. 'Diana genuinely cared for Bryan and was mindful of how she could wound him. But when she compared what she felt for Mosley with her affection for Bryan it was as the sun to a candle … nine months later Diana petitioned for divorce.'[25]

By then, Diana was, according to De Courcy:

> … in the grip of a physical passion so strong that it blinded her to everything else. She knew that Mosley was a philanderer, but she did not care. Gentle seeming; amusing and affectionate as Diana was, she was also completely ruthless. She took not the slightest notice of Bryan's objections to her lunching with Mosley even

when he took the painful step of writing her a letter forbidding it. She was very fond of Bryan but she was not going to let loyalty to him, the effect on their two children should the marriage be threatened, or the devastation she might cause, stand in her way.

By now it must have become undeniably obvious to everyone who knew Diana that she was totally amoral and quite appallingly selfish – qualities the Churchills had recognised and the unfortunate Bryan had chosen to ignore.

According to Jonathan Guinness, 'Mosley was a married man with children; Diana had no thought of breaking up his home.' Had she not insisted on a divorce, this statement might have been more believable; though, once again, quite how Guinness could possibly have known with any degree of accuracy, or Diana made such a claim, remains a mystery. 'But she herself must be free of ties, to love him as she could but above all to serve him, to serve his cause of Fascism which, he convinced her, was the only way to save the country.'

Although Mosley had only recently formed the British Union of Fascists and it was claimed, 'she fell simultaneously for his ideas and for his person', it seems somewhat more likely that Diana's prime source of motivation was sexual. Certainly, it was an activity at which Mosley could claim a considerably greater degree of success than politics.

Mosley's avowed love for both his wife and Diana did not prevent him from also having an affair with Lady Alexandra Metcalfe. Known as 'Baba', she was the wife of the (apparently consenting) Prince of Wales' equerry and close friend, Major Edward 'Fruity' Metcalfe. She justified her behaviour as a presumably pleasurable, if unsuccessful, attempt to keep Mosley away from 'the Horror', as she and her sister Lady Ravensdale called Diana. But Diana had already told Celia Keppel (subsequently Celia McKenna), 'I'm in love with the Leader and I want to leave Bryan.'

Cynics insisted Diana had only been in love with Bryan's money, so that when he 'suddenly developed a [active] sympathy with those who wrote to the newspapers criticizing their "disgraceful flaunting of wealth and privilege in the face of growing unemployment and real poverty"[26], he became imminently less attractive.

However, it was claimed, possibly by Sydney, that Diana had written, 'it was not necessary to have a particularly awakened social conscience to see that "Something must be done"'. Unfortunately, this remark was identical to that inaccurately claimed to have been made by the Prince of Wales, which made it difficult to believe that Diana was expressing genuine concern, so much as appeasing Mitford critics. Certainly, there had been no previous evidence that either she or her chums had displayed any concern for the appalling living conditions endured by millions of unemployed, whose attitude towards the privileged classes would hardly have been improved by the space devoted to society extravagance by the newspapers.

In the same summer of 1932, Mosley attended yet another ball at Biddesden, this time held by Diana to celebrate the end of Unity and Rudbin's debutante season. There Unity met Mosley for the first time, and, according to Lovell, 'she too, fell under his "mesmeric" influence … he became her ideal of a political leader – indeed she referred to him thereafter as "The Leader"'. Kathleen Atkins claimed that Unity, who was desperate to lose her virginity, willingly fell under his influence on the billiard table in the early hours of the morning. Knowing Mosley's predilection for sisters, it seems highly likely. There were even indications that Diana may have encouraged his 'covering' of her sister. Certainly, from that night on, the relationship between the two sisters became much closer; as did Unity's relationship with Mosley. Her experience would no doubt have added momentum to Unity's increasing emersion in fascism and her pledge to devote herself 'body and soul' to the Führer.

*　　*　　*

Leaving their babies at home with their nannies, Diana and Bryan decided to spend the summer touring southern Europe.

The Mosleys had apparently made similar plans. Within a matter of weeks the four of them were all together on the Venice Lido. It was hardly surprising that the shimmering summer days and velvety nights of their stay in Venice would inflame Mosley and Diana's ardour. Perhaps flaunting the intimacy of their relationship enhanced the thrill of their passion for each other. They certainly lost all sense of discretion and seemed quite determined to contradict Diana's intention to avoid wounding either Bryan or Cimmie, to whom it was soon painfully and embarrassingly obvious that Diana and 'Tom' Mosley were having an extremely physical affair. Cimmie apparently spent a great deal of time crying, while Bryan seemed quite unable to accept the truth of the situation.

On 1 October 1932, having finally returned from his lengthy European sojourn, Mosley, looking 'tanned and healthy' and more than usually pleased with himself, 'formally launched the British Union of Fascists with a flag-unfurling ceremony in its offices ... in Great George Street. This was followed a fortnight later by the first public meeting, in Trafalgar Square.'[27] There was something rather sad about the long-suffering, devoted Cimmie being there by his side, as supportive as ever. Particularly if, as Martin Pugh has claimed, she actually had an aversion to fascism.

Meanwhile, Diana, having ignored her family and friends' pleas to reconsider her relationship with Mosley, broke the news to the devastated Bryan that she was leaving him. Lords Redesdale and Moyne (Bryan's father) went together to see Mosley, but as Mary Lovell rather unsympathetically put it, 'Mosley refused to be lectured or intimidated into giving Diana up.'

In a last ditch attempt at reconciliation, Bryan agreed to go away to Switzerland for three weeks, to give her some time for reflection. But when he returned home to Cheyne Walk in mid-January 1933 Diana moved out. The marriage was over.

Diana had taken a lease, presumably paid for with her husband's money, on what she referred to as 'a small house of her own' at 2 Eaton Square. By her standards it may have indeed been small, but it was big enough to house her, her two children, a cook, a nanny, a parlour maid and a lady's maid. It was also situated just minutes away from what the press would refer to as 'Mosley's love-nest'.

★   ★   ★

In February 1933 Unity pressurised her parents into funding her enrolment at the Art School of the London County Council in Vincent Square, where she had little difficulty convincing the school that she had sufficient talent to justify her studies. Unfortunately, her promise was never fulfilled as she only stayed until Easter, before leaving to pursue her career as a fascist; a sacrifice she would share with Adolf Hitler. However, during her brief time at Vincent Square, Unity enjoyed art school, particularly the sexual freedom it offered her.

While she was there, Unity persuaded Diana to lend her the Eatonry (Diana's house in Eaton Square) for 'an orgy'. It was hardly the activity of a shy young romantic virgin but her family and friends managed to give the story of Unity's introduction to group sex a veneer of innocence, by encouraging her friend Rosemary Peto's report that 'everyone had been sick and there had been lots of "necking"'. In order to protect her own reputation, Rosemary also swore blind that she had not actually been there and only 'heard about it afterwards'.

Apart from orgies and the white slave trade, another subject 'beloved' by the Mitfords was incest. Whether Tom 'did it' and with which, if not all, of the sisters he may have 'done it' with was a favourite topic of conversation amongst their chums.

Around this time Unity had also been introduced to Gerald Cuthbert, 'a conspicuously good-looking man', who was also 'intelligent, musical' and, 'until her departure for the grand passions of Nazi Germany',[28] her lover. In a rather dramatic understatement, David Pryce-Jones suggested Unity had a 'foible' for Cuthbert, while both he and Gerald's sister, Vida, remained insistent that Gerald had never returned Unity's affection; though it must have been obvious to Vida that it was not his 'affection' that interested Unity and that their relationship could not, with any degree of accuracy, be described as a 'foible'. However, Vida did admit that Unity and Gerald enjoyed attending boxing and wrestling matches and that Unity was very partial to fine young men, especially when they were in some way involved with physical violence. Certainly, neither she nor Pryce-Jones were prepared to admit that it was more than likely Gerald Cuthbert who introduced Unity to sadomasochism.

Rosemary Peto said that she used to meet Unity quite often 'at [General] Sir Ian and Lady Hamilton's'. Sir Ian had unfortunately been involved in the costly Gallipoli campaign, the equally ill-fated Afghan War of 1878–80 and the disastrous Battle of Majuba Hill in 1881. But he had frightfully good manners and was terribly grand. The Hamiltons also 'had a house in Hyde Park Gardens and gave enormous luncheon parties for twenty or thirty people'[29]. It was at one such luncheon that Unity and Rosemary fell out, in a big way. Rosemary later recalled:

Bobo was wearing a swastika in her buttonhole. The Nazis had just done something particularly horrible, and I said, 'It's shocking that you are wearing that.' She answered, 'If you had any sense you'd be wearing it too.' She later boasted that it was such fun to have supper with Streicher, as he'd have the Jews in after the meal, they'd be brought up from the cellar and be made to eat grass to entertain the guests.

It was highly unlikely that Unity ever witnessed such a thing, but equally it was obvious that she would have liked to.

Far from considering Unity's swastika – or presumably her attitude towards Jews – abhorrent, the Hamiltons were to become great admirers of Adolf Hitler and were all for making a deal with the Führer, who subsequently received them personally, to show his appreciation that an English general of the First World War championed him as a lover of peace.

*   *   *

While the Nazi Party was gaining strength, so were the Communists. General Kurt von Schleicher had already replaced von Papen as Chancellor in November 1932 but to little effect. As the result of von Papen's suggestion and increasing pressure from businessmen, industrialists, particularly the Thyssens, and international (American) bankers, Hindenburg was persuaded to appoint Hitler as a replacement for Schleicher as chancellor. In order to limit his power, it was also suggested that Hitler lead a coalition government, contained within a framework of conservative cabinet ministers, with von Papen as vice-chancellor and controlling mediator. After numerous meetings and countless concessions and covert deals, Hitler was sworn in as chancellor on 30 January 1933. The wooden horse had finally entered the city of Troy and the lunatic had at last taken over the asylum.

On the night of 27 February 1933, the Reichstag went up in flames. A young Dutchman, Marinus van der Lubbe, was charged with arson and, after unsuccessfully trying to have him executed on the spot, Göring blamed the Communists. Hitler said, 'This is a God-given signal … there is nothing that shall stop us now crushing this murder pest with an iron fist.' The next day he persuaded Hindenburg to sign a decree, 'for the protection of the people and the state'. This decree, known as The Enabling Act, suspended all legal defence of personal liberty, freedom of speech, press and the right of assembly. Hitler had, in one move, assumed the full dictatorial powers for which he believed the gods had chosen him. Aged 44, he had only been actively involved in politics for fourteen years.

Almost immediately violence increased; groups of storm troopers roamed the streets, armed with revolvers and pieces of lead pipe, looking for Communists to kill and Jews to beat, or for other

Jews they could force to do the beating for them. A bonfire was lit outside Berlin University onto which books considered to be 'un-German' were thrown. Plans were drawn up for the sterilisation of 'imperfect Germans', while Jews and socialists were rounded up and herded into concentration camps.

The Enabling Act was the most significant law to be introduced during the Third Reich. The number of people arrested in Prussia alone within the first two weeks of its inception was estimated to have been more than 10,000. Goebbels declared, 'Now it is a joy to live!'

While the Nazis managed to finally overcome all political opposition, during the final elections they only achieved a majority of votes in Bavaria and Württemberg. Overall, despite massive promotion and violent coercion, they still barely managed to win 43.9 per cent of the vote. It was only with the support of the Social Democrats and the Centre party that they gained the majority of seats needed to take power; though by this time the Nazis would have taken control by force rather than accept political defeat. From now on Germany was to be a one-party state.

By April, taxi drivers in Berlin were complaining that the Jewish boycotts introduced by the Nazis had hit them hard, as Jews were good customers; the use of taxis being considered an unnecessary extravagance by most gentiles. But other than that, the order to boycott Jews and Jewish businesses had little effect. Most Germans ignored the directive, and so more extreme measures had to be introduced. Meanwhile, Christopher Isherwood and his friends left Berlin for Amsterdam, while Brian Howard, who was convinced of the horror that would result from Hitler and the Nazis' rise to power, remained in Germany. 'In 1931 I began reviewing for the *New Statesman* and went to Bavaria. There I became influenced by the (Thomas) Mann family's (and Andre Gide) loathing of Hitler and I devoted myself to writing anti-Hitler articles in the English press.'

In Brian Howard's interview with Hitler's press chief, Dr Hanfstaengl, published in April 1933 in the *New Statesman*, Hanfstaengl told him, 'Everything will be alright when we have turned the Jews out of Europe and the niggers out of France.'

*   *   *

Hitler had a grudging admiration for Britain and due to his Austro-Hungarian birthright was particularly envious of her empire. But he was also all too aware that it was a country built on battle honours that enjoyed a degree of kinship with the Austrian and German aristocracy but needed little encouragement to get into a fight, particularly when her empire was threatened. He knew that the British ruling classes were sympathetic towards his aggressive determination to annihilate the Communists and were also unlikely to waste a great deal of effort opposing his treatment of the Jews. His policy was to lull them into a false sense of security, for as long as he could. To this end, 'Hitler sent his chief party ideologue Alfred Rosenberg to London in May 1933, to clear up 'certain misconceptions that existed abroad in regard to recent events in Germany'.[30]

The Imperial Fascist League (IFL) was the organisation of British fascists most closely linked to the German Nazis in the early 1930s, largely due to their anti-Semitic policies, which were more extreme than Mosley had yet to adopt despite the fact that he undoubtedly shared the prejudices of his class and his era towards Jews.

The similarity of the BUF's policy to that of Mussolini's party was probably not unconnected to its continued acceptance of funding from the Italian organisation. Their only unique 'quality' was Mosley's encouragement of an extensive female participation, something both the Italian and German fascists, who professed to enjoy a reputation for extreme patriarchal attitudes, had effectively suppressed.

This BUF policy appeared to reflect its leader's sexual preference for aristocratic women. They included Lady Esther Makgill, ex-suffragette Mary Richardson, Viscountess Downe, Lady Clare Annesley, Lady Howard of Effingham and Lady Pearson. Lady Maud, Mosley's mother, also became a member.

The Prince of Wales, whose indulgence in women, or to be more accurate one particular woman, would seriously damage his monarchic future, shared many of the attitudes commonly held by the privileged classes at that time. These included a deep-seated fear of communism, a love of France but an antipathy towards the French and an enthusiasm for Anglo-German friendship. He was reported to have said of the Nazi dictatorship to the former Austrian ambassador Count Mensdorff, 'Of course it is the only thing to do. We will have to come to it as we are in great danger from the Communists too', and to Louis Ferdinand of Prussia, 'Dictators are very popular these days and we might want one in England before long.' He was believed to have considered Mosley a suitable candidate for such a role. Fortunately for England, before long the prince would have more pressing matters to deal with.

Around the end of January 1934, Lady Furness, the close and personal friend of the Prince of Wales, 'made her ruinous mistake'[31] by choosing to return to America to visit her sister. According to Charles Jennings, Wallis Simpson said to her:

> 'Oh, Thelma, the little man is going to be so lonely'. Thelma's answer was, 'You look after him for me while I'm away. See that he does not get into any mischief' ... Convention usually has it that the unsuspecting Thelma boarded her ship ... and returned to England to find, to her horror, that Wallis had turned predator and thieved the Prince.

*   *   *

The Nazis, who by now were all too aware that Berlin had become their international shop window, cracked down heavily on the city's more salacious nightlife. However, they soon liberalised many of the restrictions when they realised the detrimental effect they were having on their foreign exchange and shifted media attention away from Berlin by choosing Nuremberg, the unofficial Bavarian capital of the Holy Roman Empire, as the spiritual home of Hitler's master race and celebratory centre of the Third Reich. Hitler chose to develop Nuremberg as the host city for his spectacular annual rallies and he planned stadiums, a Congress Hall and a vast, open-air assembly area on open ground around the Luitpoldhain and the Zeppelinwiese. The first Nazi Party Rally took place in Nuremberg in 1927; the next was held in 1929; and it then occurred annually from 1933 till 1938.

There, in the Teutonic spirit of the Middle Ages, the Nazis created awe-inspiring military equivalents of Busby Berkeley's musicals. These highly theatrical events were enthusiastically reported in the British press by Mr Ward Price of the *Daily Mail* who, according to David Pryce-Jones, became 'as favoured by the Führer as was formerly Sefton Delmer of the [*Daily*] *Express*; first man inside the Reichstag after the burning'.

Hitler understood the power of excess, the religious excess reflected as much in the pyramids as in Chartres Cathedral. Christian peasant worshippers did not need such a building in which to pray. It was designed to awe them into subservience and obedience in the same way that Wagner's music was created with sufficient excessive power to 'force' people to believe in the creator's genius.

Hitler was also aware that the monumental excess reflected in Wagner's music and his theatrical party rallies were needed to transcend the Nazi movement from a political party into a religious movement and thence to mass hysteria and an orgy of violence.

Less enthusiastically reported by Sefton Delmer was the opening of the Dachau concentration camp on the outskirts of Munich, and the subsequent, genocidal policy which would result in the death of not only 6 million Jews but also 2.5 million non-Jewish Poles, 1.5 million Romany, 13.7 million Russian civilians, 275,000 mentally and physically disabled, 50,000 homosexuals and 2,600 Catholic priests.

★   ★   ★

In April 1933, Mosley paid his second visit to Mussolini and on his return wrote in the *Blackshirt* that 'fascism was the greatest creed that Western civilisation has ever given to the world ... destined to become the universal movement of the Twentieth Century'. It was not an unusual opinion. Winston Churchill had already said to Il Duce, 'If I had been an Italian I am sure I would have been wholeheartedly with you from start to finish in your triumphant struggle against the bestial appetites and perversions of Leninism.'

By now everyone seemed to be in full knowledge of Mosley's affair with Diana, including his wife Cimmie who was not taking it at all well. Diana's lack of emotional commitment, meanwhile, was somewhat at odds with those who had insisted that her relationship with Mosley was based on some celestial level of love. 'The fact that Mosley was so busy in a variety of ways,' Diana wrote, 'was one of his great attractions for me. I wanted more freedom than Bryan was prepared to give me.' She would probably have preferred to remain in the position of being one of Mosley's mistresses, but it was not to be.

In early May Cimmie was rushed into hospital with a burst appendix. Mosley apparently displayed his concern by visiting her in hospital in order to check on the successful outcome of her operation, before going for lunch at the Eatonry with Diana and Unity. But, 'Next day, Lady Cynthia developed peritonitis and her condition worsened.'[32]

The doctors' opinion was that if she fought hard, she might win through, but on '15 May she died at the age of 33, "without", her surgeon announced, "both mentally or physically ever lifting a finger to live"'[33]. It then came to be known that Mosley had walked out after a row before Cimmie was taken ill, and had gone to stay with Diana.

After his wife's death, Mosley was said to have thrown himself into building up the BUF. Not that he had a lot of spare time for either political development or grieving for his dearly departed wife, since he continued his affairs with Diana and 'Baba' Metcalfe, wife of the consenting 'Fruity' Metcalfe and his late wife's younger sister, with whom he went touring in Europe, presumably to assist him in overcoming his grief! So, it must have been a welcome diversion for Diana to receive her invitation from Putzi Hanfstaengl to visit Germany, while rather conveniently Nanny would take the children, one of whom was still only one year old, to the Isle of Wight.

★   ★   ★

Following months of refusing to communicate with Diana, it was claimed that her forthcoming divorce and the tragic death of Mosley's wife had weakened the Redesdales' opposition and a conciliatory meeting with their daughter was arranged in the country. There, Diana spent most of the weekend sitting in the garden with Unity, talking about Mosley and the BUF and how quickly she could become a member.

Considering how keen the party should have been to recruit new members, particularly those of Unity's newsworthiness, it was difficult to believe that there really was the necessity to make such a song and dance about it, unless of course the rank and file, who had been so desperately fond of Cimmie, felt that Diana could be by some degree held responsible for her death and in their eyes one Mitford was no better than another. This does in fact appear to have been the case, and to avoid any confrontations Mosley tried to keep Unity happy by personally awarding her membership.

While Mosley was attempting to limit the minor fallout from his appallingly selfish behaviour, Bryan Guinness was being subjected to the public embarrassment of a divorce in which he had to pretend to be the guilty party by spending the night at a seedy Brighton hotel with a young lady who was paid to pretend to have sex with the gentleman concerned, while one of the hotel's chambermaids was 'rewarded' for confirming that they had. When, of course, they hadn't.

Meanwhile, Diana gained her *decree nisi* and was said to have claimed minimal alimony. This apparently amounted to a 'mere'

£2,500 a year but it was still sufficient to afford her the services of two or three servants, elegant clothes and a car, unaffected by time or future marital status; unless of course, such things were considered 'expenses' and thus an additional cost to Bryan's estate. There would also have been generous trusts put in place for the children and their education.

Due to the fact that divorce was considered a disgrace, regardless whose fault it was but particularly for the woman involved, Diana was largely cut off from the grander side of society, particularly the older generation by whom she was now considered to be undesirable. 'Quite apart from their hatred of divorce, there was an intense disapproval of her behaviour; pity and sympathy for their contemporaries the Redesdales and shock that anyone should abandon a marriage [especially one that included such vast wealth] quite so quickly and for quite such a "shop-soiled" Lothario.' However, the divorce had remarkably little effect on the 'legion' of friends of her own age, who 'remained steadfast'[34].

Mosley unofficially awarded Unity membership of the British Union of Fascists by the simple expedient of arriving at Diana's on 14 June 1933, greeting Unity with 'his customary straight-from-the-shoulder salute' and the words 'Hallo Fascist,'[35] before removing a party emblem from his coat and presenting it to her. But he also advised her not to wear it when she went to HQ to officially enrol; a warning which Unity predictably ignored.

As Pryce-Jones describes it, much to her dismay she was refused membership, not only for 'flaunting a high party emblem', but also for being 'so disregarding of the Leader's instructions, so damaging his interests ...'

'Complete misery, utter despair ... the future of the fascist party, of the Leader himself, seemed in jeopardy.' Unity was distraught. '"I was so excited", that dream of the future, crumbled to ruins.' It is difficult to believe that they made it so difficult, and a total contradiction in terms. In a fascist party, the leader should of course be capable of overruling everyone. Probably, as with all English clubs, there would have been a membership committee, who would have become extremely grumpy were they to discover that they had been circumvented, even by the leader! Unity successfully persevered and eventually managed to enrol at the Oxford HQ, but it was hardly surprising that she would come to prefer Hitler's German fascism, where she was welcomed with open arms, at least by their leader, who had little time for committees.

★   ★   ★

Pryce-Jones wrote that around this time Unity and Diana started going to the Women's League of Health and Beauty together, in Great Portland Place, at least twice a week. The league was apparently remarkably similar to the Werk, Glaube und Schönheit organisation in Nazi Germany, which used exercise routines based on the German Sachsengruss (Saxon Greeting) movement. The two sisters would then return to Eaton Square, where they would often spend the night with Mosley.

By now the Redesdales had grown to accept their daughters' relationship with Mosley, and had even been drawn into the movement themselves. 'Mosley was hoping to proselytise personally among the rich and grand, trusting in the autumn rallies to cater to the masses.'[36]

'A dead set was made at such eminent men as Lord Nuffield and Lord Rothermere.' Small dinners and gatherings were organised to recruit suitable members.[37] 'One such meeting was held at the house of Sir Oswald's mother in Eaton Square. Unity took along Mary Ormsby-Gore and Anthony Rumbold.'[38]

'Sir Anthony Rumbold's father was ambassador in Berlin from 1928 to 1933, and his despatches had spelled out the Nazi menace more unambiguously than the Foreign Office liked.'[39] The young Anthony, in response to Unity and Jessica's demands to know if he was a fascist or a communist, replied, 'Neither, I'm a democrat.' 'How wet!' they brayed in unison. But that did not prevent him from accepting their invitation to a BUF rally at the Albert Hall, where Mosley was to hold forth. "'The Leader's going to make a speech", they said, "Do come.""[40]

According to David Pryce-Jones, 'The mass meetings attracted conservative-minded people as well as the temperamentally discontented, while in the person of Lord Rothermere, the party had a press lord and his papers at their service for a while, which could well have been crucial.'

* * *

Diana's separation from Bryan was causing huge social and family tensions, but supported by a more than adequate allowance, she appeared quite prepared 'to sacrifice her social position'. She was more concerned by her brother Tom's disapproval than her parents' alienation, manifest in their refusal to allow her younger sisters, Jessica and Deborah, visiting rights. Only Nancy supported Diana's choice; probably to delight in the annoyance it caused.

Meanwhile Unity, largely free of parental supervision, was able to call on her sister whenever she liked. There she met Mosley again. This time she was encouraged to appreciate his politics rather than his sexuality; with equal success. Having been raised as a fascist, the only puzzle to Unity was why all people like her were not fascists. Which many of her family and friends indeed were.

For Diana, who at the time was cut off from most of her family, Unity's enthusiastic support was immensely reassuring. But while the two sisters had been seduced both sexually and politically by Mosley, they were all too aware that he and his fascist party paled into insignificance compared with the German original. But before they could get to Germany to experience the real thing, a real Nazi arrived in London.

Dr Ernst Hanfstaengl, known to his friends as Putzi, was one of Hitler's earliest supporters. A huge, square-jawed, good-humoured Bavarian, who was Harvard educated and a gifted pianist,

Hanfstaengl introduced Hitler to Munich society and assisted him in polishing his image. There were those amongst the top echelons of the party, Goebbels in particular, who were jealous of his relationship with the Führer, referring to him as Hitler's 'court jester'. Much to Hitler's amusement he responded by referring to Goebbels as the 'little Rigoletto'. Goebbels was not the first to be mislead by Putzi's somewhat 'agricultural' physical appearance, which was at odds with his sharp intellect and middle-class background.

Putzi also enjoyed a degree of wealth from his family's Munich-based art gallery and publishing business, while their New York branch enabled him to raise invaluable American dollars during the period of Germany's hyperinflation. These comparatively small contributions kept the fledgling Nazi movement alive during the crises and even financed the purchase of a newspaper. It had also been Putzi who sheltered Hitler at his house in Uffing, near Munich, after the failure of his 1923 putsch. 'After Hitler's arrest he continued to support him throughout the two years of imprisonment that followed, during which Hitler wrote *Mein Kampf*.'[41]

When Hitler came to power it was Putzi, armed with his many influential English and American friends and a fluent grasp of their language, whom Hitler chose to place in charge of his party's foreign press bureau. His objective was to counter the horrifying revelations concerning the Reich that were beginning to appear in the international press. On his return to Harvard, Putzi was met with considerable aggression from Jewish and anti-Nazi student groups, while his financial contribution to the university's funds was refused. No such protests took place when he visited London in the spring of 1933 with his friend, William Randolph Hearst. 'I was on good terms with the Guinnesses and met Unity through them in London.'[42]

This, then, was the curious man whom Diana found at the house of Mrs Richard Guinness, wife of a distant cousin of Bryan's … he issued a challenge: those present should come to Germany and see for themselves what lies the newspapers were telling. To Diana, in particular, he made an offer that, if she came, he would introduce her to Hitler. Diana made up her mind to go; and go she did, in the summer, to Munich. As they now shared political ambitions and had become 'thick as thieves' she took Unity with her.

It was an invitation that would subsequently prove life threatening for Putzi. One also had to question what he thought he had to prove to two committed fascist anti-Semites.

The Mitford girls claimed to have gone as 'ordinary' visitors, which of course they were not and would not have been considered as such, under any circumstances. First, they apparently took to 'sightseeing round Bavaria with Nigel Birch and Lord Hinchingbrooke'[43], who presumably were also fascists or potential fascist sympathisers, with whom they chose not to have seen any signs of distress, nor obvious fear amongst the German people. Eventually they made contact with Putzi, though the meeting with Hitler failed to materialise. However, Putzi did take them to the theatrical Nuremberg Party Congress, also in Bavaria, which in 1933 was renamed the Party Day of Victory, though it was in fact a four-day celebration of the Nazis' accession to power with its choreographed cast of thousands. There they could both see and hear the effect the Führer had on his hysterical German public.

The 1933 rally began on 31 August, 400,000 party members having been collected by special trains. The SA, the SS and the Hitler Youth were all represented. One thousand chosen guests, including 'The Mitford Girls' (they did not all have to be present to be headlined as such), filled the main grandstand.

Diana was ecstatic. 'A feeling of excited triumph was in the air, and when Hitler appeared an almost electric shock passed through the multitude ... there were almost no foreigners; later on the diplomats and assorted guests came, but not in 1933. By a strange chance, Unity … and I witnessed this demonstration of hope in a nation that had known collective despair.'

Unity was no less enraptured. 'The first moment I saw him I knew there was no one I would rather meet.' It was typical of the Mitfords' – and particularly Sydney's – already skilful use of the press that this remark would appear in the pages of London's *Evening Standard* so soon after the event; a forewarning of a story that was going to fascinate the media for the next seventy-five years and beyond.

Diana and Unity weren't the only visitors to be so impressed. Many young Englishmen visiting Germany at that time were equally enthralled and moved to support Hitler's regime, though later, when it became socially and politically unacceptable, some, lacking the courage of their convictions, changed their minds and thereafter claimed to despise the Nazi movement. Nigel Nicholson was one such previously avid supporter, as was *The Times* correspondent, Michael Burn.

The official Nazi congress brochure published a photograph of the English delegation, with Unity in a tweed suit and black shirt, her gauntleted hand in salute. Almost next to her was William Joyce, who later wrote:

> In 1933, I joined Sir Oswald Mosley's new movement, the BUF. I became one of the leading political speakers and writers of that movement; for three years I was Mosley's propaganda chief. These were marvellous times and I shall never forget them. I used all my influence in the movement to give the party a strongly anti-Semitic direction – and I may say that I succeeded in that direction.

Jonathan Guinness seemed to think that in comparison to the intensity of the girls' experience at the party congress, it would have seemed 'pedantic' to worry about 'the tribulations of a few Jews'. Certainly, he was correct in doubting whether either Diana or Unity 'gave them a thought', while the girls came to regard stories of Nazi atrocities against any member of the human race as either unimportant and exceptional episodes or as downright lies. Later, it also became 'fashionable' amongst the right-wing middle and upper classes to justify the Holocaust by saying that 'Joe Stalin did far worse' and that 'he had admitted as much to Churchill'. Unity went one step further by developing an oft-voiced enthusiasm for ethnic cleansing, particularly in the case of Jews who she, in agreement with the Nazis, considered 'sub-human'.

Once the rally was over, the English delegation went home and Diana went to Rome, while Unity, in no doubt where her destiny lay, travelled the short distance to Munich, to discuss plans with Baroness Laroche for enrolment in her finishing school in the spring of the following year.

The Mitfords subsequently insisted that when David and Sydney found out that Diana had taken Unity to the Nuremberg *Parteitag* (party rally), they were furious. Judging from their political beliefs and enthusiasm for Hitler and the Nazis, this seems highly improbable.

In the autumn of 1933, Sydney had arranged for Jessica and her cousin, Idden, to spend the customary year at a Swiss, French or German finishing school. In this case she chose Paris. There they could brush up their French and hopefully develop at least a degree of sophistication before undertaking their 'coming-out' year back in London.

Unity had refused to attend such a school and her mother, in full knowledge that it would have been a total waste of money, made no attempt to force her. But in 1934, having unsuccessfully completed her social season, she wanted to go to Germany; not to be finished, but to learn to speak German, so that she would be prepared for her planned meeting with Adolf Hitler.

Given their own fascist sympathies, persuading the Redesdales to agree probably took a great deal less effort than has been claimed. Minimal organisation was needed as Unity had already enrolled at Baroness Laroche's establishment at 121 Königinstrasse in Munich. Apparently, Mary St Clair-Erskine, sister of Hamish, and other

English girls of 'the right sort' from families known to Sydney, had also attended the Baroness' school, which would have reassured her. The letter that Lord Redesdale was said to have written to Diana after her visit to Nuremberg with Unity thus seemed contradictory to Sydney's decision:

> I suppose you know without being told how absolutely horrified Muv and I were to think of you and Bobo accepting any form of hospitality from people we regard as a murderous gang of pests. That you should associate yourself with such people is a source of utter misery to both of us – but of course, beyond telling you this (which you already know) we can do nothing. What we can do, and what we intend to do, is to try and keep Bobo out of it all.

Whenever, and by whom, this letter was written cannot alter the fact that the Lord and Lady Redesdale financed Unity's six-year Munich 'campaign', which included her relationship with Hitler and the Nazis, without any other surviving indication of protest. Indeed, David and Sydney Redesdale would still be visiting the same 'murderous gang of pests' at the Nuremberg Party Rally in 1938! Both Kathleen Atkins and Baroness Gaby Bentinck were led to believe, by Unity, that Sydney had even had ambitions of a marriage between her daughter and the Führer. It would certainly have justified their major investment in her courtship.

* * *

Despite Nancy's independent spirit, she was nearly 30 years old before she accepted an offer from Diana of a room at the Eatonry and finally left home. There, despite her teasing, she adopted the political beliefs of her sisters. She also formed a 'suitable' relationship with Peter Rodd, son of Lord Rennell, which resulted in their engagement and marriage.

The *Evening Standard* of 19 July wrote, 'She is 29 and Mr Rodd is 26. Peter Rodd was educated at Wellington and Balliol. He left Wellington at the age of 16, having reached the top of the school.' He had also worked as a German correspondent for *The Times*, until he was sacked.

Peter Rodd was claimed to have been the prototype for Evelyn Waugh's fictional character, the brilliant but disreputable 'free-booter-in-chief', Basil Seal, though others claimed the 'unsavoury' Basil Murray to have been equally well qualified. His sister-in-law, Lady Rennell, described him as being both 'wild' and 'beautiful'.

The fact that she spent three years engaged to a homosexual seems to signify that all may not have been well in Nancy's emotional life; or her sex life, for that matter. Perhaps it had been little more than a convenient social arrangement for both of them and a means by which she could avoid her parents' constant pressure to marry.

Peter Rodd was also a fascist sympathiser. Apparently he had been influenced by the BUF's declared intentions of helping both the poor and the unemployed. Though quite what experience, let alone concern, either Peter or Nancy might have had for either poverty or unemployment is somewhat of a mystery. But they bought black shirts, 'fervently embraced fascist dogma and attended meetings, clapping enthusiastically'.[44] There was little evidence that the BUF had any long-term effect on either Peter or Nancy's concern for the less privileged and she remained a 'screaming snob' from birth to death.

They married in November 1933 and went to live at Strand-on-the-Green where they gained some limited personal experience of being poor. For while Lord Redesdale gave Nancy a small allowance, Peter's inability to earn as much money from his freelance journalism as he could spend on drink put a severe strain on Nancy's finances, even when bolstered by royalties, causing them considerable difficulty to live in anything like the manner that they had both come to expect.

By 1934 Nancy had nearly completed her third novel, *Wigs on the Green*. Once again it was based on the family, but with their enthusiasm for fascism hidden behind a thin veil of satire. Aware that the book would infuriate Unity and Diana, Nancy allowed them to see a pre-publication proof, which is said to have resulted in her being forced to remove three chapters concerning her comical portrayal of Mosley, thinly disguised as Captain Jack. Not only was publication delayed but it remained the source of a life-long 'pique' between Nancy and Diana.

With the eventual publication of *Wigs on the Green* in 1935, Nancy would have three novels in print, all based on the family. With the continuing support of Evelyn Waugh and his 'press pals', Nancy had succeeded in establishing the Mitford girls as a 'brand'. The irony of this achievement was that the more Nancy had satirised her family's most unattractive social traits, the more engaging the brand became.

By the time Nancy's book was published, the development of anti-Semitism as part of the BUF's policy had lost any element of humour, particularly now that people like the Mitfords were no longer under any illusion as to what the Nazis were already doing to the Jews and anyone else that Hitler and his cohorts considered a threat to their creation of a Nordic race of 'supermen'.

Diana justified her growing anti-Semitism by claiming, 'One felt the City was feathering its nest while three million unemployed were starved', later adding, 'You can have no conception of how totally divided the "two nations" were then.' But there was still no evidence that either she or Unity had any concept of what life was like for the 'other nation', of what being 'unemployed' felt like, or even that they knew anyone who did. Presumably it was Mosley who had instilled in her this justificatory theory.

Most of the Mitford family also still shared a strong predilection for Germany which, combined with their fascist beliefs, encouraged them to overlook or justify the Nazis' use of political violence, racial cleansing and eugenics in re-establishing the economy and defeating communism. In an attempt to justify their behaviour, years later Nancy wrote a letter to Evelyn Waugh, in which she claimed, 'but we were younger and high-spirited then and didn't know about Buchenwald'. But they were certainly aware of Dachau and they knew what Hitler's intentions were, and they displayed considerable enthusiasm. He did not put his policies into practice overnight. After eight years of warning what he intended to do, he spent a further eleven years doing it. Kristallnacht alone should have been enough to halt the family's relationship with Adolf Hitler.

In the spring of 1934, perhaps in response to Diana's encouragement of the continuation of their 'open relationship' and concern that he may have lost control of the situation, Mosley rented a house north of Grasse, in southern France, where they stayed for 'a month or so', once again epitomising his lack of political commitment.

At the end of 1934, with Mosley's encouragement, Diana returned to Munich to learn to speak German and socialise with leading Nazis. Unity had been in Germany since the spring of that year, attending Madame Laroche's finishing school. She had yet to be introduced to Hitler, but her determination to meet 'the greatest man of all time'[45] had in no way diminished her resolve. Meanwhile, she continued her language studies.

It has been said that 'No one could have foreseen the tragedy that resulted from the Redesdales' decision to allow Unity to go to Germany'[46]; though even when she started to tell all and sundry of her determination to shoot herself if there was a war between Britain and Germany, the Redesdales continued to finance her stay.

1 Unity reading to Decca (Jessica), 1923. *(Topfoto)*

2 Mary Ormsby-Gore and Unity Mitford. Photo by Bassano, 1932.
(Author's collection)

3 The Hon. Unity
Valkyrie Mitford.
(Getty Images)

4 Unity and Diana amongst their 'storms'. *(Author's collection)*

5 Hitler relaxing with friends. *(Topfoto)*

6 Hitler addressing 100,000 Nazis at Nuremberg in 1935. *(Topfoto)*

7 Painting by Adolf Ziegler in Hitler's apartment. *(Author's collection)*

8 Unity with Lady Redesdale and Doctor Fritz-Randolph of the German Embassy at a Christmas Party given by the Anglo-German Fellowship at Victoria Hall in Bloomsbury, London. *(Getty Images)*

9 Unity with Diana and her two sons. *(Getty Images)*

10 Unity at Nuremberg rally in 1935. *(Topfoto)*

11 Janos Almasy.
(Alexander Almásy)

12 'Creation of Eve' by William Blake. (*Author's collection*)

13 Hitler and Unity. (*Author's collection*)

14 Unity returning to England from Germany in January 1940 following her suicide attempt. *(Getty Images)*

15 Nancy, Unity and Diana laid to rest in the Swinbrook churchyard. *(Wikimedia Commons)*

5

BAVARIAN RHAPSODY

1934–36

Somewhere between fear and sex is passion.
Somewhere between God and the Devil.

Jeanette Winterson

On 30 June 1934 the Nazi Party exploded in an orgy of brutal political cleansing that became known as the Night of the Long Knives. Hitler had decided that mass assassinations were the only way to solve what he was persuaded to believe was a planned coup against him by the SA, its leader Ernst Röhm and other political opponents who were dragged from their beds and without any form of trial were either immediately or subsequently executed.

The SA was the Nazi Party's original, largely working-class paramilitary organisation which, after Hitler had gained dictatorial power over Germany, became redundant. But with 3 million armed members, dangerously sympathetic to the party's socialist roots, with ambitions to take over the existing army, they could indeed have been considered a threat, even while there was no evidence of any planned coup. They were superseded by the more middle-class SS, which had no political agenda and owed its allegiance to the Führer alone.

Unity, who was quite obviously determined to immerse herself in a mystical celebration of ritualised violence, could not have arrived in Germany at a better time. The mood was perfectly reflected in Leni Riefenstahl's *Triumph of the Will* and Ernst Jünger's *Kampf als inneres Erlebnis* (*Combat as an internal experience*): 'Death, where is thy sting / Hell, where is thy victory?' It sounded like a quote from William Blake, but is in fact from Corinthians.

*   *   *

Of all the Mitford girls, only Jessica would rebel against fascism. But to adopt socialist and even communist ideals she would need considerable support and encouragement to stand up against the political and social steamroller that was her family. Even Mrs Hammersley was ridiculing her as a 'ballroom communist, a cut below a parlour pink'. Her saviour arrived in the form of Esmond Romilly who, far from being a shop-floor socialist from a working-class background, was in fact her so-called 'social equal'. They were even related and between them would manage to gain almost as many column inches as Unity.

Decca had admired her second cousin Esmond from an early age. He was Aunt Natty's grandchild, son of Clementine Churchill's sister, Nellie. He possessed all the steadfast determination that young sons of the upper classes were supposed to have in order to run the Empire. He was, however, in rebellion against the whole status quo. They were made for each other.

Jonathan Guinness obviously found it frightfully difficult to tell his story, for while politically he was quite obviously a 'pinko' radical, Romilly was Winston Churchill's nephew and as such was, at least socially, an expression in common usage at the time, 'straight out of the top drawer'. So, he referred to him with patronising endearment as 'perverse, zany' and 'rather splendid'[1].

Jessica liked to give the impression that she was shipped off to Paris with cousin Idden for her 'finishing year' as much to keep her away from such goings-on as to brush up her French at the Sorbonne. Though one would have to admit that while, some time later, her mother may have come to appreciate Esmond's ability to publicise her daughter, such a 'young radical', particularly of a communist persuasion, would not have been the type of person she had in mind as a potential husband for Jessica, regardless of whether he was related to Winston Churchill.

*   *   *

It was Jessica who had insisted that 'Unity went to live in Germany with full parental approval', despite other members of the family's insistence that their parents had reacted with 'fury and distress' to the news of Unity's visit to Germany with Diana the previous year. Jessica had also pointed out that their mother had not only accompanied her to Paris where she was returning to complete her 'finishing year', but had then continued on to Munich with Unity, to 'settle her in' to Madame Laroche's.

The Baroness Laroche, whom Diana, if not Unity, rather diplomatically remembered as being, 'a charming woman', instilled in her girls some limited veneer of sophistication and cultural knowledge, while providing them with comfortable accommodation, or *pension complète*. She also joined them for lunch and dinner, at which the food was said to have been delightful and all conversation was conducted in German.

Most of her fellow students, who were a year or two younger than Unity, were being given a degree of European finish prior to 'coming out'. But due to the somewhat relaxed supervision, a number of them celebrated their lack of parental control by indulging in relationships with virile young SS officers, despite Madame Laroche's known dislike of Nazis. However, it was unlikely that Madame Laroche would have ever discussed such things, politics not being considered 'quite the thing' as a subject for polite conversation amongst her girls. Fortunately for Unity, Fräulein Baum, who taught the girls to speak German and supervised their evening entertainment, was very pro-Nazi.

Unity was doubtless in heaven and quite convinced that her fantasies were about to become reality, even though it would be some time before she would actually meet the Führer; which was just as well as she had first to learn to speak his language. This she achieved remarkably quickly, once again demonstrating that she was a great deal more intelligent than the rest of her family cared to admit.

Unity soon made useful friends in Munich. One in particular was Erna Hanfstaengl, who was a year or so older than her brother Putzi and who frequently referred to herself in the third person as Miss Hanfstaengl. She introduced Unity to the upper echelons of Munich society; mainly professional people but also those in business and the arts. The closest of these friends were said to have included her cousin Eberhard Hanfstaengl, the director general of the Pinakothek art gallery; Arno Rechberg, a chemical manufacturer; an eminent surgeon called Sauerbruch; Baroness Redwitz; the writer Bobby Shrenk; and the Bruckmanns, a publishing family from which Frau Bruckmann, the Princess Cantacuzeno, became a fanatical devotee of Hitler. Unity was also particularly attached to Pinky Obermeyer, the 'sharp tongued' German equivalent of Brian Howard.

Pryce-Jones wrote of Erna's obvious pride in her relationship with Unity:

On and off Unity lived with me practically the whole Nazi time. Her clothes were left in her room at Solln a well-to-do area in the South of Munich, with her books and photographs. In the winter she would come to Uffing (a fashionable town on the shores of Lake Staffelsee in the Bavarian Alps). Every summer, at least until 1939, she was my guest ... Before the war, Randolph Churchill came there 3 or 4 times. He introduced Selfton

Delmer (the *Sunday Express* correspondent) to me and he was on the best of terms with Unity. I told her that she looked like his sister, and she answered, 'You know my grandmother was a very naughty woman.'

It was Sefton who would describe Unity as, 'probably the only foreign woman in Germany to enjoy Hitler's acquaintance. Twenty years old, pretty with shining blue eyes and flaxen hair, she seemed … to embody the Hitler ideal of a Nordic woman'.

Erna claimed that such remarks did nothing to increase Unity's popularity amongst the Nazi elite. 'I know how deeply hated she was by the party. Jealousy of course. She was more prominent than some German leaders and they could not forgive that. Frau Himmler came into my shop and in the course of conversation she remarked on "that good-for-nothing Unity".'

This questionable opinion was largely the result of somewhat understandable sour grapes and spite on the part of Erna, whose brother Putzi would eventually pay dearly for his friendship with Unity.

Unity took up anti-Semitism as breezily as everything else, talking about Jews with her usual exaggeration; she wanted to have them all burnt. "Burn the Jews, that's the thing for them", she would say, it was the fashion to chatter on like that … her education [background] forced these attitudes on her.

But Erna Hanfstaengl's revelations only served to illustrate how little she really knew of Unity's relationship with Hitler: 'Only her education as a lady was perfect and that appealed to Hitler, she didn't make love to him or fall on her knees and make an exhibition of herself as other women did.'

★　　★　　★

While developing various friendships in Munich, Unity also soon started to make regular visits to her brother Tom's bisexual friend and lover, Janos Almasy, in his castle on the Austro-Hungarian border at Bernstein, over which the swastika flag was already flying. According to John Heygate, 'By the end of 1933, there was a large and vigorous Nazi Party in Austria, demanding to be free of Vienna, the Catholic Church and Mussolini.'

Janos was also a friend of Gaby Bentinck, née Thyssen, whose father Heinrich owned the infamous neighbouring Castle Rechnitz and, with his brother Fritz Thyssen, contributed considerable funds towards Hitler's rise to power. Gaby, who, like her sister, Margit Batthyany (who was later involved in a major Jewish atrocity), also gained notoriety for her sexual exploits, described Janos as, 'An astrologer and necromancer in the Wallenstein tradition, rather sinister-looking but invited everywhere, dashingly Nazi and Unity's bosom friend.' She would later form a friendship with Unity and also enjoy encouraging her to go into intimate details of her adventures; particularly those involving Janos.

Apparently, he shared Hitler's obsession with the occult; an obsession that would soon also be shared by Unity. Her passion for Blake and Milton both reflected and influenced her preoccupation with mystical, spiritual fantasy. In Janos she found both a kindred spirit and a sexual alchemist, who succeeded in fusing together her fantasies and her erotic realities, thereby awakening in Unity a passion akin to religious ecstasy.

She later told Gaby that one morning, after a rich, late-night supper and more champagne and sweet wine than she was used to, Unity followed Janos into his dark satanic library where they indulged in 'savage fornication'. Between explosive bouts of physical passion, they lay by the fire while Janos expounded the principles of necromancy, the summoning of spirits and manipulation of mortals. 'To drive them mad. To enflame to love or hatred. To gain their favour or to constrain them to do or not to do some deed.' He also spoke of the manipulation of death and Unity's role as a Valkyrie or 'chooser of the slain' and how obvious it was that their coming together had been preordained by the Norse gods, for whom pain and death was the ultimate sacrificial rebirth.

As Unity once again rose to ecstasy in the firelight, Janos revealed these to be the same gods that had chosen Hitler to lead the reborn Germanic master race and Unity to be the Führer's personal Valkyrie, while in a trance-like state she whispered Blake's immortal words, 'Fiery the angels rose, and as they rose deep thunder roll'd. Around their shores: indignant burning with the fires of Orc.' And dreamt of Hitler.

The following day, Unity awoke determined to gain more knowledge of Norse mythology. With Janos' guidance and the contents of his library she soon learnt that it comprised 'the myths of North Germanic pre-Christian religion or German paganism, rooted in mediaeval Iceland, Iron Age Scandinavian and Romanticist Viking revival.' She also discovered the importance of Snorri Sturluson's thirteenth-century epic *Prose Edda* and the gods Odin and Thor, and that Norse mythology was perfectly suited to her fantasies, being full of death and war, human sacrifice and slaves. Janos also explained to her the importance of Norse mythology and necromancy to both Wagner and her beloved Führer.

Until Unity chose to die, Janos fulfilled his role as her high priest and lover. But he was also married, though his wife Marie, who was confined to a wheelchair, was said to have accepted his other relationships. She got on well with Unity, who stayed for long periods of time at Bernstein, while Janos frequently went with her to Munich. They also spent time together in Venice.

His reputation as an astrologer was greatly enhanced by the fact that in 1939 he cast Hitler's horoscope, in which he warned of 'portended catastrophes, collapse and death by his own hand.' Hitler took his own life on *Walpurgisnacht*, 30 April/1 May, the night when witches meet on the Brocken mountain, or Blocksberg, in central Germany, and party with the gods.

★   ★   ★

While Madame Laroche's other girls studied the piano, singing, painting and other subjects considered suitable for well-bred young women, Unity rarely attended formal lessons apart from German language. She had her own agenda and adopted a considerably more 'à la carte' approach to Laroche's 'academy' than the rest of the girls, especially after dark.

Unity also developed a particularly close friendship with her language teacher, Fräulein Baum, known to everyone as 'Bäumchen', principally because she was extremely pro-Hitler and the Nazis. 'One was told by the Baroness that if one saw anything like a scrimmage, one was to hurry by and not stand and stare.'[2] Unity's anti-Semitism was even more extreme than Baum's; on being told of Jews being beaten she used to say, 'Jolly good, serves them right, we should go and cheer', having no regard that the victims often included women and children.

Armida Macindoe, a contemporary of Unity's and a pupil at the school, remembered:

During the autumn term Diana came out and took a flat off the Ludwigstrasse, she came again early in November. I also met Putzi Hanfstaengl with Unity, he was more of a means than an end, he introduced her to Nazis. I think I got on well with her. She used to go to the Osteria Bavaria restaurant and sit waiting for Hitler. She'd sit there all day long with her book and read. She'd say, I don't want to make a fool of myself being alone there, and so she'd ask me to go along to keep her company, to have lunch or a coffee.

Often Hitler was there. People came and went. She would place herself so that he invariably had to walk by her, she was drawing attention to herself, not obnoxiously but enough to make one slightly embarrassed. But the whole point was to attract his attention. She'd talk more loudly or drop a book. And it eventually paid off.

That summer and autumn term, we sat there in the Osteria Bavaria. At last one of the henchmen was sent over. It was what she had been waiting and praying for. It was after lunch, we'd had a cup of coffee. I must go, I said, and hurried off. She was thrilled when she came home that the object of the exercise had been achieved, and she'd been noticed.

Rosemary Macindoe, Armida's younger sister, said:

In October 1934 I went to Baroness Laroche's ... Unity had not yet met Hitler; every Friday he lunched at the Osteria Bavaria, and she used to go in blind adoration. He came in with a rain-coat, an Alsatian, and a whip in his hand, and Unity said, 'Don't you think his eyes are marvellous?' She had a phobia about Jews, she used to make us write on letters 'Juden sind hier nicht erwünscht'. This was a Stürmer slogan which translated as 'Jews are not welcome here', and was often to be found posted up by Nazi mayors of villages and by shopkeepers.

Diana used to have dinner parties in her flat and I went there quite a lot ... there were three SS men in particular, Max was the first name of another of them, a curly-blond SS man whom we saw in the Brown House. As well as Max, Unity regularly recruited the services of two other 'Storms', Erich Widmann and Julius Stadelmann.

They had records of the 'Horst Wessel Lied', Unity was always singing that, as well as the 'Wacht am Rhein' and 'Unsere Fahne'. She was always on about the Hanfstaengls too. The only other thing we did, Diana, Unity and I, was when we went out to Schleissheim [where the famous Schloss was at Hitler's disposal] to see army manoeuvres, or perhaps a flying show, and found we were somewhere near Dachau. There were endless jokes about it.

So, even as early as 1934 they were under no illusion as to the pur-pose of the camp as an incarceration and extermination centre for members of the human race, that for racial, physical, mental, political or religious reasons, the Nazis considered unacceptable as members of German society; and if they knew what was going on there, then so did everyone else.

Mary Gerard Leigh, who was later to become Countess Kapnist, was only 15 when she arrived at Laroche's in September 1932, staying until the autumn of 1934 when the Mitfords started to descend on Munich. She had few illusions of what was going on, even though her memories remained somewhat coy:

> When Lady Redesdale came round with Diana, and with Jessica who was out there in September, they could hardly cram into the Baroness's little salon. I have a firm memory of the Oktoberfest, with the daughters all losing their mothers in the public gardens on purpose … Unity used to bring SA or SS men back and ask them to spend the night, but probably there was no sex in it.

But as Klaus Theweleit, quoting Hans Blüher, pointed out, 'What was most immediately striking about Hitler's bodyguards was their handsomeness. Hitler surrounded himself with young men of extraordinary beauty. Men worthy to become the pride of our line, with the delicate features we know as "Nordic".' Many of them were from upper-class families, raised from birth to adopt a military bearing and attitude; as such they would have been extremely attractive to Unity and Diana, both physically and socially.

Of course there was sex in it. That was certainly Nancy's opinion. According to Gaby Bentinck and Milly Howard-Brown, it was Diana's opinion too, but it was only when the latter returned unexpectedly one evening that she realised the full extent of her sister's bizarre sexual ritual. On entering her apartment, lit only by the reflections from the street lights, she was immediately aware of the sound of carnal activity and through Unity's partly open door, in the candlelight, could just make out three or four partly clothed, uniformed SS officers, one of whom was aggressively 'taking' her sister, who was splayed across the bed. Blindfolded and dressed in her black and grey BUF uniform, complete with leather gauntlets, her skirt removed, Unity appeared to be tied to the bed. A record of *Horst-Wessel-Lied* played quite loudly, while the waiting men looked on in silence.

Later, with considerable pride and no hint of shame, Unity apparently admitted that sex with the SS officers was her Eucharist. Her bed, draped with swastika flags, surrounded by candles and surmounted by iconic images of the Führer, was an altar devoted to her messiah on which she gave her body to those closest to him; his personal warriors or disciples. She explained that remaining blindfolded minimised her personal involvement.

Diana confessed to finding her role as a voyeur exciting and by mutual consent would often repeat the process. From time to time she apparently also took SS lovers, but only one at a time.

Sex with the Storms (as they were known) from the Brown House was also one of the ways in which Unity managed to get inside information concerning Hitler's whereabouts. Julius Stadelmann was particularly valued, as despite the fact that he wore spectacles, he was one of Hitler's junior adjutants and would have been a mine of information.

*   *   *

If one reads between the lines, some of Unity's young English friends were obviously quite appalled by her behaviour and the openness with which she spoke about it, though such views were rarely expressed in print and never in intimate detail. The rather 'fey' Tim Martin's comments concerning Diana and Unity were typical of the humorous anecdotes that have been encouraged by subsequent accounts:

Late in 1934, my mother came out to visit me, and shared a sleeper with Diana. Early in 1935 we were invited to lunch with her, on a hideous day of pouring rain. At the top of the lift stood these two great blondes, obviously stunning, who took our

mackintoshes. One of them [Unity] said, 'I've met the most mar-
velous storm'. 'Really, what was that?' 'My dear, a storm trooper'.

Another contemporary, Derek Hill, who was to become one of
Ireland's greatest society portrait and landscape painters but at the
time was studying theatre design in Munich, insisted:

Unity wasn't sexy [or not to Derek who knew very little about
girls' sexuality and had little desire to find out] and I should be
surprised if she got up to anything. References to Max or others in
her letters are probably a tease. Although she talked a lot about it.

One often gets the impression that witnesses had been heavily cen-
sored, not least, perhaps, by their own sense of loyalty to people
they considered to be of a similar class or out of respect for those
higher up the social scale. Particularly 'Hons'. This would have been
especially relevant after the war, when a number of reputations, but
those of the Mosleys and Mitfords in particular, were in desperate
need of censorial cleansing.

* * *

Back in London, the BUF was reaching what was considered the
peak of its success when on 7 June 1934, 'the biggest and most
important meeting to date took place in the huge Exhibition Hall
at Olympia'[3]. But just as Mosley rose to speak, a heckler shouted,
'Hitler and Mosley, what are they for? Thuggery, buggery, hunger
and war.' It was also around this time that Lord Rothermere, under
pressure from his newspapers' advertisers, withdrew his support. His
apparent change of heart, regardless of its hypocrisy, was a devastating blow to the party. If not the coup de grâce, it was certainly the
turning point in the fortunes of the BUF.

Despite the fact that Unity still awarded The Leader a considerable degree of hero worship, in Germany she was in the presence

of the real thing and could hardly contain her excitement. Particularly when, only three weeks after she had first laid eyes on Hitler, he would be personally involved in the first major act of violence since he had assumed absolute power.

Unity was excited by the ruthless brutality of the Night of the Long Knives, but publicly disguised her excitement with a face of girlish sympathy:

> The excitement here over the Röhm affair is terrific, everyone is horrified ... I am so terribly sorry for the Führer – you know Röhm was his oldest comrade and friend, the only one that called him 'Du' in public ... it must have been so dreadful for Hitler when he arrested Röhm himself and tore off his decorations. Then he went to arrest Heines and found him in bed with a boy.

It was somewhat paradoxical that this reputedly psychopathic leader, who would be responsible for the death of millions and whose ritualised violence Unity found so exciting, never actually killed anyone with his own hands. In the purest form of necromantic tradition, Hitler persuaded or inspired others to commit acts of atrocity on his behalf. He was a man who had an obsession with death rather than killing.

Of course there were those, and still are those, who firmly believe that despite his indisputable brilliance as an orator and socio-political strategist, Adolf Hitler was in fact suffering from schizophrenia, dissociative identity disorder, or some other form of psychotic condition. Perhaps he was just driven mad by the remorselessness of his own logic, but after four years in the First World War trenches Hitler would have almost certainly have been seriously unhinged. So, the question of whether he was mad was somewhat redundant. The only relevant question was, 'How mad?'

It was actually Heinrich Himmler who appeared to be the dottiest of all the Nazi leaders, claiming to believe that the inhabitants of Atlantis had been a super-race who had come straight from God, and that when Atlantis disappeared beneath the waves some of the priests had escaped by boat. For some inexplicable reason they had ended up in Tibet, or maybe Nepal. It was certainly the country furthest from the sea, both in distance and height. These same people had then apparently recreated their Nordic master race in their Himalayan retreat. Unfortunately, this race of 'God men' became polluted by the Jews and other lesser mortals. But Himmler was convinced that by means of a policy of racial purity and selective breeding, the race could be recreated.

Hitler also believed in the creation of a master race, as long as he was its leader and messiah. Fortunately for the success of his political ambitions, he sensibly chose to play down the Atlantis story; though he did support Himmler's decision, in 1939, to send an SS research team to Tibet to look for their Atlantean ancestors. In case they subsequently decided Nepal was a more likely location, Hitler gave the king a Mercedes.

The King of Nepal died in 1955, but his (by 2010) 90-year-old mistress was allowed to continue living in the palace by the recently empowered Maoist government, who had finally decided to sell the 70-year-old Mercedes. The Mitford girls would have considered it 'killing'.

It seems doubtful that the research team actually believed Himmler's ridiculous theory and far more likely that they chose to go along with it in order to facilitate their trip. By this time it was also becoming obvious that telling Himmler that he was barking mad would have been a potentially hazardous undertaking, regardless of the indisputable evidence.

When Hitler was out of town and she needed to relax from the intensity 'of it all', Unity used to go sightseeing and walking in the mountains with Derek Hill. Perhaps they amused themselves by speculating which of their other friends might have been in the habit of sharing Nazi beds, since many young English girls like Unity escaped from their parents' control and went to Munich to enjoy an active sex life with the Storms; as did a good number of their brothers and Derek's chums.

'It was Derek Hill who gave Unity her first glimpse of Hitler'[4] at close quarters. For a fascist dictator intent on world domination he was surprisingly casual in his habits, far more so than even the most liberal of today's democratic heads of governments.[5] He would have lunch at the Osteria Bavaria in Schellingstrasse, Munich–Schwabing, and sit for an hour or two chatting with friends, apparently without a care in the world. When the weather was fine, he sat out at a table in the garden. Another haunt was a café, the Carlton Teeraum, in Briennerstrasse. 'He would simply go to these places like anyone else',[6] accompanied by minimal security, an adjutant or two and various favourites, who were more often than not without any particular social or political qualification.

At around 6 p.m. on 11 June 1934, only eighteen days prior to the Night of the Long Knives, Derek Hill was taking tea with his mother and an aunt at the Carlton Teeraum when Hitler arrived. All too aware of how excited Unity would be, given the chance of being in the same room as her beloved Führer, he telephoned her with the news.

'Of course', she told Diana in a letter written the next day,[7] 'I jumped straight into a taxi, in which in my excitement I left my camera which I was going to take to the shop. I went and sat down with them, and there was the Führer opposite. Derek's aunt said "You're trembling with excitement", and sure enough I was, so much so that Derek had to drink my chocolate for me because I couldn't hold the cup.'

What was surprising was that Unity would have developed such a close relationship with a conscientious objector such as Hill while also retaining a relationship with Brian Howard, whose attitude towards the Nazis was so diametrically opposed to hers. He considered what the Nazis were doing to Jews, liberals, leftists and artists in the thirties, and what they were obviously going to do when they finally went to war, to be an indictment against not just the Germans, but the whole human race. He also failed to comprehend the wisdom of going to war to get rid of Hitler. 'In order to get rid of an unpleasant lodger, it is not only foolish, but criminal to set fire to the boarding house. Other people live there.'

But both Hill and Howard were highly intelligent and extremely entertaining which doubtless says a great deal about Unity; for neither man would have wished to have spent time in the company of the character subsequently portrayed by the Mitford family.

*   *   *

It was also somewhat surprising that, in 1934, so soon after Unity had taken up residence in Munich and been settled in by her mother, Sydney should have revisited Unity. What was even more surprising was that she should subsequently have chosen to make such politically charged statements; particularly concerning a regime that she had formerly claimed to have found appallingly disdainful, in a country against which her father, Thomas Bowles (so Jonathan Guinness claimed), had 'indoctrinated' her to believe everything was tasteless and without merit.

For someone whom her daughters had claimed was dizzy beyond belief, Sydney's statement was surprisingly erudite. Either her writing had been skilfully edited or, as seems far more likely, she was not as green as she was cabbage looking, particularly concerning politics:

From the time that the first German war ended, I believed that the victors had behaved badly and madly to the defeated ... the Germans had tried to get the Versailles treaty altered by peaceful means; now at last they turned to a man who might get something done by a show of strength.

And so when I went to Germany in 1934 [probably in late July] to visit Unity, I was hoping to see Hitler. Anyhow, what was this insignificant-looking man with a funny moustache and an untidy lock of hair, dressed in an old mackintosh? ... I found very great beauty and charm in Germany. Nothing I thought could be lovelier than the little baroque theatre in Bayreuth [a town that an English woman would only have been likely to visit to pay homage to Wagner]. The lovely white, gold, pale blue and pink churches seem to me to be admirably fitted to the worship of God in happiness.

There was certainly still no shortage of English support for Hitler and the Nazi Party, particularly by conservative anti-Communists. Such a man was Colonel (later Sir Thomas) Moore MP, whose attitudes were shared by more people than those who cared to admit it. In the *Daily Mail* on 25 April 1934, he had tentatively tested the public's fascist sympathies: 'Surely there cannot be any fundamental differences of outlook between Blackshirts and their parents, the Conservatives.'

By 15 August, in *The Times*, he was gaining confidence:

Rarely do we read ... anything of the social, educational or even moral achievements of the Hitler administration. Housing, maternity clinics, the purging of dens of vice, were a generation ahead of the rest of the world. Hitler may have been guilty, either personally or through his followers, of what may seem to us, without lack of knowledge, crimes against his own people, but they are his own people, and he is responsible to them, not to us.

The only member of the Mitford family to vehemently disagree was Jessica. By now she would have been under no illusions concerning the political and social developments in Germany, particularly regarding Hitler's banning of the Communist party.

By the late summer of 1933 she would certainly have known a great deal more about the past, present and future of the Nazis in general, after a group of exiled communist writers escaped to Paris where they published *The Brown Book of the Reichstag Fire and Hitler Terror*, which was almost immediately translated into English and published by Knopf.

The *Brown Book* had a major impact on the 18-year-old Jessica. 'It explained the new anti-Semitic laws in Germany and how they were being implemented, while pictures showed the effects of treatment meted out to Jews by storm troopers. At that stage it was beating and brutal handling, but the book also prophesied what would happen if the regime continued unchecked.' Conservatives claimed, 'There was little demand for such works in England and they were largely distributed through left-wing bookshops and Communist channels.'[8] The less politically bigoted accepted the fact that it became a bestseller and was translated into twenty-four languages.

Jessica optimistically introduced her mother and father to the book but they reacted in the same way as most of the English middle and upper classes by insisting that the book was nothing more than communist-inspired propaganda and a gross exaggeration. This was at the same time that they would subsequently claim to have been so appalled by Unity's decision to stay in Germany.

Much later, Jessica stated in an interview, 'People say they didn't know what was happening to the Jews until after the war, but they did know because it was all there.'

Unity and Diana certainly knew. According to Graham Stevenson, in 1935 Diana, Unity and her journalist friend Mick Burn were taken on a tour of Dachau concentration camp, which was quite close to Munich. Many of those who had known, but were loath to admit it, were only too pleased to accept the ever popular defence: 'But by this yardstick, those who supported Communism should have known about the millions of people being murdered by Stalin in the thirties. Vague reports of those atrocities also filtered into England only to be regarded by supporters of the regime as anti-Communist propaganda.'[9] But as Kathleen Atkins was so fond of saying, 'Two wrongs don't make a right,' and no amount of Communist guilt acquitted the Mitfords' support of Hitler and the Nazis.

An English translation of *Mein Kampf* had also been available since October 1933, the same year that Dachau concentration camp was opened, with the camps at Buchenwald, Sachsenhausen and Mauthausen in place by 1938. Although the book was dramatically unsuccessful initially, by the end of the war it had sold 10 million copies. But what is perhaps far more interesting is that it has continued to sell an average of 3,000 copies a year in the UK and 15,000 in the US, ever since.

★   ★   ★

'It was a subtly changed Unity who returned to Swinbrook for the summer. Photographs show that she had a poise and a singular beauty, where since the age of 13 she had merely looked fair and awkward.'[10] Of course this was hardly surprising as not only was she seven years older, but she had also just spent three months fulfilling her sexual fantasies, and no doubt those of a number of Storms.

Unity's stay in Swinbrook could, in fact, hardly be described as 'the summer' as by August 1934 she had returned to Munich. There, 'she was content to eat a light lunch, alone at the Osteria and read a book to pass the long hours of waiting for her Führer'[11]. It was to be a long wait, and one had to admire her determination, if not the object of her ambition.

That same year Mosley adopted anti-Semitism as part of the BUF agenda, though many, including the Mitfords, would hasten to reassure critics that his British version was more concerned with the Jews' financial power than their undermining of the country's racial purity.

Meanwhile, in a vain effort to moderate the committed anti-Semitism of the Mitfords and Unity in particular, Pryce-Jones suggested, 'Unity was a German-inspired anti-Semite of this Mosley stamp.' However, he then contradicted himself, continuing, 'When anti-Semitism, among other Nazi flies, was cast over her, she swallowed it hook, line and sinker.' But, however it was couched, explained or excused, Unity and the Mitfords never voiced any concern for Hitler's policy of extermination; in fact, quite the opposite. They and many of their ilk believed racial hygiene to be a reassuring basis for politics. Predictably, most Jews were more concerned with the effects of violent anti-Semitism, than the cause. The Torah True Jews (a division of Orthodox Judaism) would even blame Zionism and go as far as claiming the Holocaust was God's punishment for the Jewish return to Israel, prior to redemption, with a new messiah and before the predestined time.

To the Torah True Jews, Adolf Hitler was an envoy of God sent to punish Jews for their sins, claiming, 'It is common knowledge that all the sages and saints in Europe at the time of Hitler's rise declared that he was a messenger of devine wrath, sent to chasten the Jews because of the bitter apostacy of Zionism against the belief in the eventual messianic redemption.'

Hitler's appalling racial policies and the fact that his political, social and militaristic ideals were almost entirely male orientated also did nothing to reduce his quite astonishing attraction to millions of other adoring women.

In his book *Pathology of Evil*, George Victor maintained:

Women by the thousand abased themselves at Hitler's feet, they tried to kiss his boots, and some of them succeeded, even to the point of swallowing the gravel on which he had trod … As a figurehead, as a male in absolute power, Hitler's aphrodisiac effect was scarcely even sublimated in the more impressionable women who constituted his beloved mass audience. They moaned, they were hysterical, they fainted, for an introspective bachelor deficient in sexuality.

But of course it was not Hitler who they found sexy; it was the power that he represented.

John Heygate noted:

People in Germany are throwing off the Christian religion and openly worshipping Hitler. Hitler's portrait hangs above their bed. The day for a German boy and girl begins with the praise of Hitler. Hitler is a German's prayer and a German's answer. He is the Messiah who has come down from his mountain to earth, and has not contented himself with preaching and publishing a gospel; he has brought it to pass!'

Every one of the words he has preached and written, almost every word, he has accomplished. Is it a wonder the man has become a God in Germany?

But it was not only the men and women of Germany who worshipped Hitler as God, or simply Unity who believed him to be her messiah. So, indeed, did Hitler himself!

He first started to believe that he enjoyed some form of divine protection during his military service in the First World War. He spoke of a mysterious voice that had advised him to move away from a crowded dugout moments before an incoming shell scored a direct hit. There was also a confirmed story of a British soldier, who, given a clear shot, had lowered his gun and chosen to allow him to escape. Hitler spoke of being chosen by the gods to lead his people. Even Pope Pius seemed to be of the opinion that God might have been keeping a special eye on him.

*   *   *

Unity had returned to Munich early with the idea of going to the *Parteitag* again. A week or two later, Diana joined her there, but to their annoyance, Putzi Hanfstaengl was said to have declined their request for VIP tickets, offering them press-passes instead. He later admitted to have been criticised the year before for being accompanied by women in such heavy make-up.

It was not the first time that the Mitford girls had come under attack for wearing too much make-up. At this time only theatricals and prostitutes wore make-up in Germany, while in England the middle and upper classes plastered themselves in mascara, rouge, lipstick, 'foundation' and powder, which they constantly reapplied. It gave rise to the whole culture of the powder compact. Not only would such women carry them at all times, but they would use the excuse of powdering their noses to leave the table, either to give the men freedom to discuss male things or to swap girls' gossip. The thickness and brittleness of such make-up also resulted in women speaking without moving their lips and avoiding any facial expressions likely to cause cracks in their 'war-paint'.

Confident that they could talk their way into the VIP enclosure, Unity and Diana went to Nuremberg anyway. There they were said to have 'got talking with an elderly man in a beer garden who was wearing the gold party badge, which testified that he was one of the first hundred thousand members. He turned out in fact to have party card number 100: "Parteigenosse Nummer Hundert", they called him.'[12] Diana rose to the challenge (in other words, she turned on her most seductive charm) and in next to no time they had persuaded him to fix them up with tickets for everything and beds in a small inn.

Once again they were seduced by the theatrical extravagance of the *Parteitag* and the sight and sound of Europe's most powerful and, doubtless, charismatic man, whipping the crowd up into a state of mass hysteria with the promise of a thousand years of power and glory.

> The flash of his steel-blue eyes ... and now the screams of 'Heil!' erupt, becoming overwhelming, like some all-fulfilling wave that rips everything along with it. Fifty thousand voices merge into a single cry of 'Heil Hitler!' Fifty thousand arms shoot out in salutes. Fifty thousand hearts beat for this man who is now striding, bare-headed, through the narrow passage formed by all those thousands.[13]

Klaus Theweleit, author of *Male Fantasies*, a study of fascist consciousness, continued to describe and explain 'the enormous attraction of fascist celebrations and their overwhelming impact on participants', and the importance of the Führer and the Reich's celebrations, in a manner that quite galvanised academic historians. 'Hitler enabled fascists to have an erection,' he wrote. It was a particularly interesting analogy, as Hitler had already admitted that for him the act of public speaking was like sex, the crowd playing the part of a woman who he stimulated and excited to the point of simultaneous, orgasmic climax.

Needless to say, the rally intensified the Girls' enthusiasm and afterwards Diana, on the advice of Professor Lindemann, decided to remain in Munich with Unity and learn to speak German. This was the same Professor Lindemann, known to the Mitford girls (and later Churchill) as 'the Prof', who, armed with some rather fanciful statistics, would encourage the British to become involved in a terrifying and ill-advised campaign of bombing German civilian targets during the war.

Unity, having left Madame Laroche's restrictive 'finishing school', moved into a flat with Diana and the pair enrolled on a special foreign-language course at the university. Apparently Diana loved Munich, which, as Jonathan Guinness described, had 'its faint smell of brewing and cheap cigars, its heavily subsidized opera which cost nearly nothing to attend and its cheerful population made healthy by the proximity of the mountains for cheap Sunday skiing'. What Guinness avoided mentioning was that for those who failed to qualify as racially, sexually, politically, mentally or physically compatible with the Nazis' requirements, life in Munich was far from cheerful or healthy. But the Mitford girls were far more interested in the seemingly limitless supply of sexually available, physically attractive young SS officers who had recently taken a sacred oath of unconditional obedience, not to Germany but to their Führer; something that Unity found particularly appealing. One has to assume that Diana was also finding Germany and its 'diversions' more compelling than caring for her children or sharing Mosley with his numerous mistresses. Meanwhile, Unity's obsessive stalking of the Führer continued.

According to Diana, when Unity thought Hitler would be at the Osteria Bavaria, she used to insist on going to lunch there. She 'seemed to know by instinct' when Hitler was likely to be there. Her family and friends concluded that she must have had some contact in his entourage. What they seemed quite unprepared to consider was that her contacts were of course her appreciative Storms.

Diana's explanation would be particularly protective. 'She followed his doings in the newspapers, chatted to the doorman at the Brown House, looked to see if there was a policeman in the Prinzregentenplatz where he had his flat.' Diana's son Jonathan added:

> When they did see him in the Osteria it was (as far as Diana was concerned) liable to mean a lost afternoon, because of what Diana called his Spanish hours. He never arrived before two o'clock at the very earliest, and often not before three, driving up with an adjutant and a few friends or assistants in two black Mercedes cars. Unity then insisted on staying in the restaurant until he left, perhaps an hour and a half later, so as to see him go by her table. Needless to say, eventually Hitler noticed her and one of the waitresses told her that he had asked who she was.

Unity was beside herself with excitement. 'Did he really? ... I hope you told him I was an English Fascist and not just an English student.'

He would certainly not have been surprised to discover that she was English; as a result of Adolf Hitler and the Nazis' presence, Munich's popularity as a Grand Tour destination for the privileged classes of England increased. The exchange rate also continued to attract, as did the presence of the ci-devant aristocracy, especially in Bavaria and nearby Austria.

Even Pryce-Jones was minded to impart the time and the city with an atmosphere more redolent of Waugh's Oxford than the location for the dawn of an unimaginable horror:

Many of them were independently rich, on allowances, owners of cars, carefree and heart-free, which obliged the countesses to rein in their charges, and the tennis parties, the expeditions, the picnics with the girls in local costume and the men in lederhosen were innocently decorous. The Nazis welcomed them all with open arms in appreciation of the value of such influential potential converts to their fascist values.

If first impressions of Germany were favourable, and stuck, then their return home was likely to filter youthful Nazism through the English upper classes. Suitably formal occasions, such as the laying of the foundation stone of the Haus der deutschen Kunst in 1937 by Hitler (who broke the silver hammer as he did so, his superstitions erupting at once) were attended by massed rows of chic English girls. Unity was even present when the silver hammer snapped; she cast herself into whatever Nazi reception or ceremony there was, the captive slave perpetually bound to the wheel.

This last phrase gives what appears to be a clear indication that Pryce-Jones may have even begun to realise that Unity's relationship with Adolf Hitler and the Storms was not as naively romantic as the surviving Mitford girls would later have had their public believe.

★   ★   ★

While Diana was settling into Munich life, the BUF was holding a Blackshirt rally in Hyde Park in an attempt to inject fresh impetus into the campaign. For the next large meeting on 28 October 1934 at the Royal Albert Hall, tickets had been sold promising that visitors might witness 'yet another stage in the advance of fascism. 'This would turn out to be Mosley's declaration that anti-Semitism was henceforth to be one of the main planks of the movement.' It was not long before the Blackshirts were marching through the East End, chanting 'The Yids! The Yids! We've got to get rid of the

Yids!' But despite Unity's enthusiasm for the mantra, compared with Germany there just were not enough 'Yids' in England to generate the level of racist hysteria needed to revitalise the failing BUF. Fortunately, many potential BUF members were also discouraged by extreme anti-Semitism.

As Susan McPherson, the granddaughter of Norah Dacre Fox, one of Mosley's most ardent and committed disciples, recently stated, 'In the twenties fascism was viewed as a great new idea and a creative and positive movement; before it was taken to extremes by the Nazis.'

However, Jessica Mitford was more concerned by the 'extremes' than the 'great new idea':

> *The Brown Book* [*of the Hitler Terror*, written by exiled journalist, Otto Dix and published in 1933] had detailed and documented as much as was then known of the revolting cruelties to which the Jews were being subjected in Germany. It contained actual photographs of the bruised and bleeding victims of Nazi sadism, and related in horrifying detail how the new anti-Semitic laws were working out in practice. My parents maintained that the book was Communist-inspired, and that anyway the Jews had brought all this trouble on themselves, apparently by the mere fact of their existence. Unity and Diana, on their rare visits to Swinbrook, justified the atrocities as necessary for the survival of the Nazi regime.

For many of the English, all too aware that their country's fortune had been based on slavery and the subjugation of a large percentage of the world's population, this would probably not have been considered a particularly unreasonable policy. But things were undoubtedly changing; the subjugated were beginning to rise up against their foreign oppressors, slavery had been abolished for some time and while the English, particularly the middle and upper classes, were generally anti-Semitic, it was not manifest in physical violence and wouldn't become so without the persuasion of a considerably more charismatic and committed political leader than Oswald Mosley. There were also an increasing number of educated people who were devoting their energies to improving the lot of the oppressed rather than subjugating them. Unfortunately, they possessed insufficient sympathy with the plight of such people in Germany.

★   ★   ★

In the Mitfords' social circles, the concept of chance encounters between men and young girls was still considered quite unacceptable. All social intercourse was formalised by introduction, which made Unity's behaviour so extreme. The very idea of a young girl hanging around in a public place, alone, with the intention of being picked up would have been considered quite outrageous behaviour, redolent of a tart. But while Diana and Unity had yet to actually meet Hitler, let alone be formally introduced, 'they already knew one of the most intimate secrets of Hitler's life: that he had a mistress'[14]. They had even met Eva Braun, twenty-three years the Führer's junior, whose existence was then virtually unknown to members of the general public.

Eva modelled for Hitler's 'court' photographer and constant companion, Heinrich Hoffmann, and worked in his shop. It was there, one evening in 1929, that Hitler had first seen her. She was only 17; slim, pretty and athletic; a great deal more extrovert and uninhibited than has been generally accepted and remarkably similar in many respects to Unity, whose habits of wearing make-up and sunbathing naked she shared. It was not until 1932 that Eva and Hitler became lovers, though the exact details of their sexual habits, or whether they ever even had sex in any conventional form, are still the subject of conjecture. This is doubtless due to Allied propaganda that cast Hitler as a sexual pervert with scatological tendencies.

As early as 1 November 1932, Braun was said to have attempted to commit suicide with her father's pistol. There would be more attempts, largely as a result of Hitler's necromantic influences, but partly as a means of coercion. As far as Eva was concerned, if she was to remain at his beck and call, she wanted some tangible commitment on Hitler's behalf. The following summer he set her up in an apartment in Munich, close to his own at 16 Prinzregentenplatz, a square in one of the most expensive neighbourhoods in the Bavarian capital. His flat, in a corner house, was on the second floor, from where he would send for her whenever he came to the city.

It was inevitable that before long Unity would become aware of Eva Braun's existence and her relationship with the Führer. As a keen photographer, Unity often visited Hoffmann's shop to both buy and develop film. It was during one of these visits that she became aware of an extremely attractive girl working at the rear of the shop. In a letter to Diana, she deemed her worthy of comment. Some time later she saw the same girl, expensively dressed in the back of a chauffeur-driven white Mercedes and assumed she must have been the mistress of a high ranking party member. At the 1935 *Parteitag* she realised just how high the party member was; though she never revealed exactly how she discovered this information.

According to Diana, 'At the Parteitag we were given seats next to Fräulein Braun, and thought her pretty and charming.' There was apparently some jealousy on the part of Eva, who was later believed to have referred to Unity as 'the Valkyrie'. Unity, on the other hand, while appreciating Eva's physical attraction, regarded her as a mere shop girl and as such far too 'common' and of insufficient social standing to have even warranted any consideration, let alone communication.

While Hitler continued to prefer living in Munich, due to his status he was obliged to spend more time in Germany's capital city and, at the end of 1934, officially at least, took up residence at the Chancellery in Berlin, giving his first dinner party there on 19 December. 'Lord Rothermere and his son Esmond Harmsworth were among the guests in the 100-foot dining room with its red marble pillars, blue and gold mosaic ceiling and Gobelin tapestry from the museum in Munich.'[15] Theoretically, this move should have diminished Unity's chances of meeting Hitler. But due to his preference for Munich, where Eva continued to live and to which he returned regularly, in reality it made little difference. The German public remained quite unaware of the existence of either Eva or Unity.

Unity continued to frequent both the Carlton Teeraum and, especially, the Osteria Bavaria where 'she often saw Hitler, who would sometimes give her a friendly nod, an event always noted with delight in her diary'. The long period of waiting to meet Hitler should have diminished her enthusiasm but on the contrary; by her own family's admission, 'Hitler had become Unity's God and National Socialism ... "my religion, not merely my political party".'[16]

★   ★   ★

It was on 9 February 1935 that their relationship made the great leap of faith for which Unity had been waiting so long, finally moving from conceptual to realised fantasy. According to Jonathan Guinness, 'The night before she had been to a fancy dress dance for the foreign students. She spent much of the time with Brian (Howard)', but although Unity had not left until three o'clock in the morning 'she would not have been hung-over, as she never drank much'. Finally, after sleeping until noon, she wandered along to the Osteria for a late lunch at 2.30 p.m. and her patience was rewarded. Afterwards she was in heaven and in love and could not wait to tell her father:

> Forgy darling. Yesterday was the most wonderful and beautiful day of my life. I will try and describe it to you, though I can as yet hardly write. I went alone to lunch at the Osteria and sat at the little table by the stove where we sat ... last time you were there.[17]

In January Lord Redesdale, who had returned to Munich with Unity, had apparently accompanied her on her vigil at the Osteria, where Unity would later insist he came under Hitler's spell, despite the fact that he did not actually meet the Führer but only lunched in his presence:

> At about 3, when I had finished my lunch, the Führer came and sat down at his usual table with two other men … about 10 minutes after he arrived, he spoke to the manager, and the manager came over to me and said: 'The Führer would like to speak to you'. I got up and went over to him and he stood up and saluted and shook hands and introduced me to the others and asked me to sit down next to him.
>
> I sat and talked to him for about half an hour … Rosa (the fat waitress) came and whispered to me: 'Shall I bring you a post-card?' So I said yes, really to please her … I was rather embarrassed to ask him to sign it … and I said I hoped he wouldn't think it very American of me. He made me write my name (which I did as you may believe very shakily) and then he wrote on the card: 'Frl. Unity Mitford, zur freundlichen Erinnerung an Deutschland und Adolf Hitler' (For Miss Unity Mitford as a friendly memento of Germany and Adolf Hitler) … I can't tell you all the things we talked about.

Unity loved her father and the fact that he had introduced her to Blake, fascism and doubtless anti-Semitism and racism; but she also knew that any metaphysical references could all too easily result in his famous response to 'all that nonsense'. For while her sisters' belittling may have been limited to mere teasing, Farve could react with immediate, hysterical fury and 'one just never knew'.

But Unity did eventually tell Janos Almasy the story, who then told Gaby Bentinck. Adolf Hitler did not speak English and apparently asked Unity to pronounce her name as well as write it. But as the Germans share the English habit of adopting more than one Christian name, he also asked her for her full name.

Up until this point, Hitler's attraction for the young English girl had probably been based on her Rhine Maiden appearance. But when she gave her full name as Unity Valkyrie Freeman Mitford, he was both surprised and delighted, '… you are a Valkyrie. You choose who shall die in battle and bring these bravest of the warriors to Valhalla, the afterlife hall of the slain, ruled over by the God Odin. You serve them mead and take them as lovers …?'

Her name and its connotations immediately established a bond between them through the Teutonic mythologies that so inspired Hitler and his idolised Wagner. Pride surged through Unity and her confidence soared as the ecstatic fantasist delightedly agreed that she did indeed fulfil the full responsibilities of her role. Meanwhile, the equally euphoric Hitler was convinced Unity had been assigned to him by the gods as his own personal Valkyrie.

Unity also brought more to their relationship than her name and appearance, in the shape of her own cultural and mythological influences. She took copies of the works of both Blake and Milton wherever she went, particularly during the long hours of waiting at the Osteria. According to Gaby, Hitler questioned her as to the subject of her reading and was delighted by a phrase from Blake that Unity considered particularly appropriate. 'I must create a system or be enslaved by another man's.'

He was incredibly impressed by the fact that Unity could recite from memory whole passages, some of which, particularly Blake's 'A War Song of Englishmen', it was difficult to believe had not been written especially for them.

Hitler was even more impressed when Unity explained that Blake was an artist as well as a poet. She soon came to realise that his respect for artists, particularly visual artists (or at least those whose work he considered acceptable), was greater than for almost any other category of creativity; though he may have been less impressed if Unity had mentioned the fact that Blake abhorred any form of racism, believing in both racial and sexual equality. She was far more interested in underlining his interest in Wagner.

He asked me if I had ever been to Bayreuth and I said no but I should like to, and he said to one of the other men that they must remember that the next time there was a festival there.

He said he felt he knew London well from his architectural studies and ... believed it to be the best town, as a town, in the world. He thinks *Cavalcade* (a movie based on the show by Noel Coward) is the best film he ever saw. Isn't it just killing that John Betjeman and Adolf Hitler share the same taste in movies!

He talked about the war, he said ... that international Jews must never again be allowed to make two Nordic races fight against one another. I said no, next time we must fight together. He talked of the roads, the new buildings that were being put up in Nuremberg for the Parteitag, and other things.

In the end, he had to go. He kept the bit of paper with my name on. Rosa told me it was the first time he had ever invited someone he didn't know to sit at his table like that. He had also apparently said that my lunch was to go on his bill.

So, Forgy, after all that you can imagine what I feel like. I am so happy that I wouldn't mind a bit dying. I suppose I am the luckiest girl in the world. I certainly never did anything to deserve such an honor.

A very nice thing was that two very poor girls, who really work themselves to the bone for him – the 'Hungry Girl' and the girl you met in Café Hag – were sitting at another table. After he had gone, they waited outside for me and shook my hand for ages and congratulated me ... If I had been them, I would have been furious that a foreigner who had never done a hand's turn for him had such wonderful luck ...

You may think that this is hysterical. I'm sure Muv will, but when you remember that at any rate for me, he is the greatest man of all time, you must admit that I am lucky even to have set eyes on him, let alone to have sat and talked to him.

Unity's diary revealed that from then on, between February 1935 and September 1939, she met with Hitler on at least 140 occasions, approximately once every twelve days, which was quite remarkable when one considers what Hitler's schedule must have been like in the four years leading up to the outbreak of war.

Far from being brief, snatched moments they were, more often than not, lengthy, relaxed encounters, illustrating not only the importance of Unity in Hitler's life, but also, in his role as supreme dictator, how little time he devoted to the mechanics of actually running the country.

So quickly did the relationship between Unity and Hitler develop, that within a matter of months she had also introduced him to her entire family, with the exception of Nancy. Something which, with Sydney's success in achieving a considerable degree of press coverage, gave her tremendous kudos and added immeasurably to the Mitfords' notoriety.

This has not prevented various authors, with her family's subsequent encouragement, from attempting to play down Unity's relationship with Hitler. In her role as editor of the Mitford letters, Charlotte Mosley claimed, 'She was rarely alone with him and, in spite of what has often been speculated, there was no love affair.' But there was certainly a degree of unintentional accuracy in her pronouncement concerning 'love', for what Unity felt for Hitler far surpassed mere love. Both Gaby Bentinck and Milly Howard-Brown agreed that Unity 'worshipped him'.

They were in fact alone together on a number of occasions, but as far as Unity was concerned, even when accompanied, the intensity of their relationship transcended all others. Unity could often not even remember what her Führer had said, only the feeling of all that power focussed on her alone; concentrating her senses into a cerebral vortex of ecstasy. The same power that took the howling masses of half a million people to the point of hysteria; the same power that drilled into the very core of her soul. According to Gaby she said it could only be compared to the feeling she experienced when she was being 'taken' by his SS disciples; roped to her deity's altar, where her senses were concentrated to the point of orgasm. It appeared to be remarkably similar to the sensation that Hitler claimed to experience when bringing his adoring crowds to their climax at one of his numerous rallies.

★   ★   ★

In the spring of 1935 Diana also met Hitler, but despite the fact that she would remain loyal to his ideals for the rest of her life, by comparison with her sister her friendship with the Führer remained largely superficial.

That Unity and Diana were 'young, upper class and socially at ease' was obvious, but whether 'Hitler was always impressed by women who had the sophistication, assurance and polish which he knew he himself lacked'[18,] was open to conjecture. That was certainly not what he saw in Unity and if he had been so impressed by social sophistication he could certainly have chosen a considerably more sophisticated and aristocratic girlfriend than Eva Braun. However, in the surviving documentary footage, Eva comes across as a very different and far more attractive woman than the weak, pitiful character so often portrayed.

Hitler may have 'enjoyed their unafraid manner'. Diana and Unity may even have appealed to his 'penchant for the English aristocracy', if indeed he really had such a thing. Doubtless they were 'pretty, stylish, frank and amusing' and chatted away with all the 'Mitford inconsequence and insouciance' that 'made him roar with laughter'. But it is extremely doubtful that there was the merest crumb of truth in the claim that 'Hitler was very attracted to Diana' and that 'their relationship was further strengthened by this subterranean sexual link'[19]. While there is no reason to doubt that, like most men, Hitler found Diana aesthetically, though not necessarily sexually, attractive, she never became as close to him as her sister did. In fact, there is evidence to suggest that, motivated by unconscious jealousy, Diana may well have overestimated her own personal magnetism somewhat; certainly as far as Hitler was concerned.

He was also more than capable of seeing through Diana's rather superficial charm. His ability to judge people's true motives was illustrated by a George Washington-style anecdote.

Apparently Hitler called in to a small Bavarian inn on his way to Berlin. The Bürgermeister and the other leading men of the village all sat down at a long table with Hitler at its head. Hitler said he would take his customary Fachinger, a mineral water. The great big, beer-blown-up Bürgermeister said he would also take a Fachinger. 'One by one all down the table, the beer drinkers of Bavaria proclaimed themselves converts to the cold, clear water – All, that is except an inconspicuous citizen at the far end, who apparently had not been listening and who said he would have his usual – a large Stein of Dunkles.' His neighbours nudged each other and look scandalised. But Hitler called to him down the table, 'It seems you and I are the only two honest men in this village.'[20]

Hitler, who would eventually illustrate his contradictory values by marrying Eva Braun shortly before he persuaded her to commit suicide with him, would have been unlikely to have appreciated Diana's betrayal of her husband and position as Mosley's mistress, let alone her abandonment of her children.

Unfortunately, it was Diana whom Winston Churchill, having recently written that Hitler had 'succeeded in restoring Germany to the most powerful position in Europe', invited to lunch to question her about Germany's leader. The fact that the most profound opinion considered worthy of recording was her observation that Hitler found negotiating with democracies disconcerting – 'One day you are speaking to one man, the next day to his successor' – only illustrates her superficial understanding of what drove Adolf Hitler.

However, Diana was said to have 'found Hitler's aura of power profoundly exciting or, as she put it, "He was the person in control – the person that everyone was interested in"'[21]. Compared with Unity's belief that he was a deity and the incarnation of her deepest beliefs it was, while doubtless an accurate statement, once again a fine example of her somewhat facile understanding of the man.

Hitler may not have liked Churchill, but he was knowledgeable of England and fascinated by the ability of such a small island nation to control and subjugate such a vast empire and its millions of native inhabitants.

Most people of Churchill's social class and those in his own party, in the government and in the establishment in general, still regarded him as a bit of an adventurer and a warmonger, with the monstrous failure of his First World War Gallipoli campaign, and its huge loss of life, still casting a shadow over his future. But, like Hitler, Winston was a master political tactician, and in 1937 appeased the privileged classes while confusing the working class with the rather weasel-worded statement, 'I will not pretend that if I had to choose between Nazism and Communism, I would choose Communism.'

A few years later, during a conversation with Tom Mitford at a ball in Blenheim Palace, Churchill remarked, with a sweeping gesture of his hand to indicate the magnificent house and treasures earned through war by his ancestor, the Duke of Marlborough, 'Chamberlain says war produces nothing. But look at all this!'

Unity also 'introduced her brother Tom to Hitler on 8 June 1935, despite having wanted to avoid doing so'; apparently because she feared he may have displayed insufficient reverence:

> She took Tom to the Osteria Bavaria, obviously at his request, but did so at a time earlier than Hitler's usual one, her intention being to get Tom out of the restaurant before Hitler arrived, if he did. But for once in his life Hitler came at 1:45, and asked them over.
>
> In a letter to Diana Unity wrote: 'Although I didn't want him to meet him (Tom) I am quite pleased now. He adored the Führer. He almost got into frenzy like us sometimes, though I expect he will have cooled down by the time he gets home and I am sure the Führer liked him and found him intelligent to talk to. So I really think no harm is done.'[22]

In September 1936, 'when Diana was in Berlin making preparations for her forthcoming wedding to Mosley', Hitler invited her to dinner 'on the spur of the moment'[23]. Or that was how she claimed it had come about. She subsequently wrote to Unity:

He was so wonderful and really seemed pleased we had gone to the Party Conference every day ... He asked after Tom and I said 'Der Judenknecht ist fast Nationalsozialist geworden' [The lackey of the Jews has almost become a National Socialist] and he roared with laughter and said, 'Ihr Bruder ist ein fabelhafter Junge' [Your brother is a splendid boy] twice over. Isn't Tom lucky.

*   *   *

While the recounting of Unity's transcendental experience could all too easily be seen as something profound and magnificent, as with Hitler's relationship with the occult it was leading down a dangerous path, a path that would lead to the 'heart of darkness'.

For Unity, her meeting with the 'deity' was the equivalent of a confirmation, and the profound effect it had on her was manifest in her intensified hatred of Jews and her enthusiasm for the Nazis' increasingly aggressive laws threatening their very existence. Like millions of Germans, her revulsion was inflamed by Nazi propagandist Julius Streicher and his publication, *Der Stürmer*. Pryce-Jones wrote:

Streicher's own speeches were invariably on the same single note, but on 19 April 1935, for instance, at an Easter meeting in Nuremberg of Nazi teachers, of which he had been one himself, he said, 'The number of Jew bastards in Germany is terribly large. We must not believe that we have yet obtained the victory. A hard path lies before us'.

On 9 May, in another speech at Nuremberg, Streicher gave what must have sounded like encouragement from the home front to Unity. He had had occasion, he said, to congratulate the leader of the British fascists upon one of his speeches. The very next day the Nazi press published the text of the telegram in reply from Mosley to Streicher: 'Please accept my very best thanks for your kind telegram which greeted my speech in Leicester … the power of Jewish corruption must be destroyed in all countries before peace and justice can be successfully achieved in Europe'.

Meanwhile, Streicher's publication continued to advertise the Nazis' increasingly aggressive policy towards Jews:

> The *Stürmer* had been a provincial sheet with a circulation of 28,000 when Streicher bought it for 40,000 Reichsmark from the previous owner's widow and transformed it into a blend of anti-Jewish raving and incitement to violence. The *Stürmer* had to be bought by some institutions and distributors under compulsion, so its circulation figures, and even its influence, are uncertain.[24]

It had been in the very first issue of *Der Stürmer* in 1934 that the British fascists were attacked for their lack of aggression towards the Jews: 'Mosley is the tool of the Jews. Mosley has admitted that he had Jewish blood in his veins.' It was doubtless this criticism that encouraged Diana to make her 'little jest' to Hitler, when referring to her brother Tom as a 'lackey of the Jews'.

> But by the forty-eighth issue, in 1935, it would be the same paper that would announce, presumably in response to Unity's influence: 'Mosley is a great speaker, a fearless fighter but above all things a subtle diplomat. With his nationalist policies, he has for a considerable time been annoying and challenging the Jews'.[25]

*   *   *

After Unity's invitation to Hitler's table, she suffered considerable insecurity, wondering if it had been a unique coming together or the start of a relationship that she had previously only dreamt of in her most auspicious fantasies. But on 18 February 1935 her dreams once again became reality.

'Having tea at Carlton Tearooms, Hitler came and sent Brückner over to ask us to join them, Werlin, the Mercedes man and pressman Dietrich. Nobody else.' (The person with Unity during this episode seems to have been Mary St Clair-Erskine. It is difficult to establish Unity's company for certain events because she had five different friends all going by the name 'Mary', who were with her at one time or other, namely Mary Ormsby-Gore, Mary St Clair-Erskine, Mary Gerard Leigh, Mary Crum and Mary Woodise.)

Wilhelm Brückner, a dedicated Nazi, was 'more of a bodyguard than an adjutant'[26]; Jakob Werlin, director-general of Mercedes-Benz, was a political opportunist, while Dr Otto Dietrich was in control of press and publicity for the NSDAP. Following Hanfstaengl's fall from grace he would also assume responsibility for foreign correspondents.

Unity believed their encounter was to be more diversionary than transcendental. Bored by Werlin, Dietrich and Brückner, Hitler invited Unity to their table to enliven the meeting with light, sparkling conversation. Her intuition was sufficiently well attuned not to require telling that mystic conversations should only take place when they were alone or amongst very close members of Hitler's inner circle, who either shared his occult convictions or were sufficiently loyal to appreciate the extreme discretion with which such conversations must be treated.

Some friends had been grudgingly prepared to admit, 'Unity and Hitler were alone together rather rarely.'[27] But it is highly likely that, considering the lengths he went to in hiding his relationship with Eva from the public, by the time Unity had reached the stage of being invited to stay with Hitler, she would also have fully appreciated the importance of her discretion. It was said she 'stayed with him once or twice, if one can call it that, in a sleeper on his special train; his habit of taking her on train journeys accounts for her nickname among his entourage of "*Mitfahrt*" (travelling companion)'.[28]

Unity told Gaby Bentinck that she didn't always record her time spent with Hitler and there was certainly no evidence to suggest that Unity stayed with Hitler in Berlin. But on the weekend of 14 February 1935, incredibly just five days after allegedly meeting Hitler in person for the very first time, she apparently began to make regular visits to the city as a houseguest of the Goebbels family.

These visits gave Unity ample opportunity to spend time in the company of the Führer as her stays were often quite lengthy, lasting for weeks rather than days, during which time Hitler would often arrive, apparently unannounced.

> Like all well-placed Nazis, Goebbels acquired property, whether through fees or sinecures due to him as a propagandist and editor, as a Minister, and Gauleiter of Berlin. Schwanenwerder, where Unity stayed, on an island in the Wannsee just outside Berlin, was the home which he bought after the Röhm purge ...
>
> Although not a lecher like Streicher, Goebbels was a womaniser, and one wonders what impact Unity made on him. Mosley's autobiography states: 'Diana was very fond of Frau Goebbels, who, with her husband, was often at dinner with Hitler. Goebbels, distinguished in public by his qualities as an orator and master of mass propaganda, had in private life an almost exaggerated sense of humour which, surprisingly, Hitler shared; it was one of the bonds between them'[29].

But Unity's close friendship with the top echelons of the Nazi Party had a side effect that could prove dangerous for the unwary. In English society it would have come under the category of 'telling tales'; something which Nanny would have discouraged at the nursery stage and which also, for those with sufficient determination to develop the habit, would have been cruelly punished by fellow schoolchildren. Under the English rules of 'fair play', it was not something 'one did'. Yet in Germany it became the very bedrock of fascism; even amongst the privileged. Like all things Nazi, Unity adopted the habit with consider-able enthusiasm.

Pryce-Jones wrote of one such case:

> Paul Wallraf ... Dined ... with Lali and Freddy Horstmann, Ber-lin's most fashionable couple, in their house on the Tiergarten ... at this dinner party one Prince Lippe-Bisterfeld had openly railed against the Nazis to Unity Mitford, the young lady seated next to him, only to be arrested with his wife forty-eight hours later. 'Everybody knew that if you ran into Unity you had to be care-ful,' Paul Wallraf said, 'she was a very dangerous woman, I saw her afterwards at parties and kept well away.'

*　　*　　*

Unity's friend, and fellow English student in Munich, Mary St Clair-Erskine, was regularly recruited by Unity as a companion 'in waiting' in the early days of her pursuit of the Führer. Shy and retir-ing, she could be relied upon not to 'get in the way', as it were. She was with Unity at the Carlton Tea Rooms on 18 February when Brückner approached them, and later recalled the events:

> [Brückner said] 'The Führer invites you to his table', and over we went. We'd seen Hitler almost every day ... I went over to their table too, and had tea with them, about six of us in all.
>
> After that, a phone call would come to the pension from Brückner to say, 'Will you have tea with the Führer' and in case it rang, Bobo would sit by the telephone until about two o'clock, that became the pattern of her day, first the tension, then the anti-climax or the frenzy of getting ready. A car came for us.

Mary St Clair-Erskine was also somewhat more truthful than the various friends of the Mitford girls, who were so insistent that Unity rarely visited Hitler at his home:

> We went a lot to his flat in the Prinzregentenstrasse, it was round the corner. The curtains would be drawn and it was always dark. Lovely flowers everywhere. He ordered lots of cream cakes which he'd be disappointed if we left, but he'd eat a bit of *Knäckebrot* [crisp bread]. He had a great big globe on a stand; and liked to show us any new pictures he had. He was extremely nice and kind to us. A pleasant host.

Mary was extremely discreet, insisting that their conversation was limited to entirely innocent subjects, mainly concerning the state of the British nation. She made no mention of Unity's more personal conversation, partly because her German was not sufficiently advanced to understand what they were talking about, and if it had been, she would have been deeply embarrassed by such 'nonsense'. However, Mary was also bright enough to be aware that Unity and Hitler obviously had a very special and deeply personal relationship which, if she wished to continue her studies in Munich and remain on amiable terms with Unity and the Führer, made her discretion imperative; particularly in view of the fact that Unity would often insist in regaling Mary with the most intimate details.

Fortunately for Mary's somewhat sensitive, nervous disposition, she was not always required to act as Unity's companion, particularly when Hitler wanted to spend time alone with Unity or with his special inner circle of friends, who were sufficiently sympathetic to his needs to know when to involve themselves in conversation, leaving their Führer free to devote his attentions to his Valkyrie.

Hitler and Unity had actually met on several occasions on a rather superficial and, for Unity, somewhat frustrating level before she was summoned for afternoon tea, on the strict understanding that she should come alone. A car was to be sent for her. The fact that Hitler sent a car to collect Unity and that she spent the afternoon and early evening alone with him was confirmed by her friend, Mary. Gaby Bentinck's friend, Marie France Railey, recounted the rest of the story.

More by force of habit than for any specific reason, Unity probably gathered up her book of Blake as well as her notebook, which also served as a sketchpad. As the bell rang, she ran down the stairs and climbed into the black Mercedes. But it was only as they pulled up on Prinzregentenstrasse that she realised she had been summoned to Hitler's private apartment.

Unity was greeted with warm but formal affection by the Führer, while a maid took her coat, before pouring their coffee or tea and serving them with rich cream cakes. She then left them alone.

Once again Hitler took an interest in the books Unity had with her. He even opened her notebook before she had a chance to reply to his query of whether it was private. He was amused by her obvious embarrassment at the erotic content of her drawings and waived aside her apologies for what she thought might have caused him offence. He then complimented Unity on her skill as an artist and assured her that he was no prude, while gesturing towards the Ziegler nudes hanging above his fireplace. He also reassured her that, as well as being, like him, an artist, she was a Valkyrie and as such, beyond moral judgement.

Not for the first time Unity was excited by her conviction that he was referring to her adventures with his Storms. It also seemed likely that he enjoyed a degree of vicarious sexual excitement in his knowledge, for he would certainly have been kept aware of such things and should he have disapproved, could have put a stop to it immediately. But he did not.

*   *   *

Accounts of Unity's movements during the spring of 1935 appear somewhat variable. Lord and Lady Redesdale had accompanied

Unity when she travelled back to Munich after one of her brief visits to the family in England. 'Having outgrown even [Madame Laroche's] minimal supervision'[30], she had, supposedly against her parents' wishes, insisted on remaining in Germany. If in fact they had seriously objected they could easily have discouraged her by the simple expedient of 'tightening the purse strings' but there was no evidence of any such thing.

Pryce-Jones seemed quite prepared to believe that Unity 'put her foot down to her parents and they gave in, as ever'. Before returning to England, her parents also travelled to Berlin to introduce themselves to the British ambassador, something a family of their elevated status would have done as a matter of form.

Sir Eric Phipps, a small man whose forbears had fought both at the battles of Trafalgar and Waterloo, had taken up his post in Berlin rather inconsequentially in September 1933. Phipps was somewhat undecided about Hitler, vacillating between believing that 'he may perhaps be more moderate than his followers' and that he was 'possibly quite mad'. Perhaps there was also something to be read into the fact that he chose 1 April to warn Foreign Secretary, Sir John Simon:

> Let us hope our pacifists at home may at length realise that the rapidly-growing monster of German militarism will not be placated by mere cooings, but will only be restrained from recourse to its *ultima ratio* by the knowledge that the Powers who desire peace are also strong enough to enforce it.

The somewhat theatrical Lady Phipps, while appearing infinitely more dynamic, seemed quite prepared to accept the Redesdales' story. 'The Redesdales were distraught parents who came out in the winter of 1934–35. They'd been in Munich, they couldn't bear the idea of Unity having bolted.' It was difficult to know exactly who was responsible for this exaggeration.

Unity was only able to survive in Germany, or anywhere else for that matter, due to Lord Redesdale providing her, as he did all his daughters, with an allowance of about £125 a year. This was hardly a fortune, but due to the advantageous rate of exchange and her father also paying for her rent and travel expenses, which included her own car, it was more than sufficient for her to enjoy an extremely comfortable and highly independent standard of living.

Perhaps the Redesdales exaggerated their concern in order to gain ambassadorial protection for their daughter. But while Lady Phipps seemed quite prepared to accept the reason for their 'distress', she was less taken in by Unity or her parents' social status:

> They stayed at the Adlon, which was next to the embassy in the Wilhelmstrasse. I don't remember whether we'd already had Unity to lunch or not. These sloppy English girls were always having affairs with dreadful SS types, and Eric had the trouble of clearing it up. If you were at all snobbish you asked the ambassador for help. Anyhow Unity came as a *Deutsches Mädchen* battleship of a woman, walking upstairs into the drawing room, and giving a Nazi salute … I remember her telling me that her favourite among Nazis was Streicher (known as 'the Jew Baiter'). She brushed aside my protests, and said Jews were traitors … with Hitler I got on rather easily. I sat next to him at a New Year banquet with the whole diplomatic corps. He was affably trying a few words of English saying 'Young lady, young English lady, Freeman, honourable lady, charming lady'. Then I realised it was Unity Freeman-Mitford he was talking about.

Lady Phipps would have perhaps been less 'easy' towards Hitler if she had been aware that he referred to her as 'that sanctimonious cow'.

She was not the only person to notice that Unity's attitude towards Jews was becoming increasingly extreme. The writer and journalist Paul Willart's wife, Brenda, had invited Unity to visit them on Hayling Island in the summer of 1935:

When Unity arrived we were all out sailing. Father [Sir William Willart, one of the old-school correspondents of *The Times* and a great Liberal] received her and went off to do some work. Then he heard the sound of shooting and found Unity firing at targets with her pistol. He asked her why. 'I'm practicing to kill Jews', she said.

★   ★   ★

By now Unity's friendship with Hitler and her sympathies with the Nazi Party had become newsworthy. Predictably, Sefton Delmer, the Anglo-German Berlin correspondent for the *Sunday Express*, who was no stranger to Hitler's press office and had been accused of pro-Nazi sentiments, was one of the first to run her story:

Twenty years old, pretty with shining blue eyes and flaxen hair, she seemed when I met her in Munich, to embody the ideal of a Nordic woman. Her eyes lit up with enthusiasm as she spoke to me of Hitler. 'The entire German nation is lucky to have such a great personality at its head. I should like to remain in Germany, because I like the Germans very much.'

Unity was also getting to know other leading members of the Nazi Party. That April, after she had met Hitler on a number of occasions, he invited her to a luncheon party. Guests included Goebbels and his wife; Ribbentrop, whom Goebbels was to accuse of having paid for his title; the Duchess of Brunswick, only daughter of the Kaiser and a great-granddaughter of Queen Victoria; plus Winifred Wagner, the composer's English-born, widowed daughter-in-law who ran the Bayreuth Festival and was to become a close friend of the Mitfords.

Unity was said to have been surprised when, upon her arrival, she discovered that the lunch was in honour of Mosley, who was paying a private visit to Hitler. It was to be the first of only two meetings between the two men. Apparently, Mosley 'hoped to obtain financial support from Hitler'[31]; although Special Branch discovered that from 1933 to 1935 the BUF was, in fact, largely funded by the Italian fascists. Even while it was subsequently 'claimed that Hitler and Sir Oswald had "outlined an agreement" for the peaceful cohabitation between Germany and Britain'[32], there was no evidence that any funds had changed hands. However, Mosley remained optimistic.

He was also extremely impressed by how close the relationship had already become between Unity and Hitler, and not a little jealous. Hitler, on the other hand, was claimed by Jonathan Guinness to still be unaware of the relationship between Diana and Mosley, and thus surprised by Unity's familiarity with the British fascist leader.

The lunch was also a somewhat grander affair than Unity had become accustomed to at the Osteria Bavaria, Hitler's favourite restaurant, which her friend, Mary, had also grown particularly fond of:

> We always went there for lunch, it was cheap. Herr Deutelmoser, the owner, we called Domodossola, a sweet gentle old bachelor. Bobo, like everybody, loved him. The two waitresses, Fräulein Rosa and Fräulein Ella, had been there for years and years. My husband's parents belonged to a club of painters and artists, the 'Klub der Lebenskünstler', whose headquarters were there, so they had their *Stammtisch* and came every day.

Exactly why Hitler, a man of seemingly limitless desire for power and operatic fascist grandeur, should have chosen to spend so much time in such a small, undistinguished restaurant, in a city with no shortage of impressive restaurants and beer cellars, remained a mystery. But the fact that Schwabing was a district popular with students and artists may have appealed to Hitler's frustrated artistic ambitions.

Unity also lunched at Hitler's flat with Diana and Mary Woodisse. She wrote to Sydney, 'We had a most lovely lunch, none of which of course the Führer ate.' She does not say why. It was certainly not because Hitler was a vegetarian or a teetotaler, as claimed. Although he rarely ate meat or drank alcohol, contrary to popular belief, Adolf Hitler was in fact particularly fond of sausages, stuffed pigeon, beer and watered wine. It was more likely that he was suffering from an upset stomach, apparently a regular occurrence. However, for his guests he would always order food to be sent round from the restaurant.

★   ★   ★

In June 1935, Unity initiated another story in the *Sunday Express*, despite Sydney claiming that a full-blown 'press persecution' had already commenced with their 'She Adores Hitler' story. There was certainly a marked lack of sympathy for Unity's aggressive anti-Semitism – a reaction that many found somewhat reassuring. It was also difficult to believe that the letter that Unity, with the encouragement of her friend Streicher, penned to *Der Stürmer*, had not been written with the sole intention of publicising the Mitford name and their political sympathies in the British press:

Dear Stürmer

… the English have no notion of the Jewish danger. English Jews are always described as 'decent'. Perhaps the Jews in England are more clever with their propaganda than in other countries. I cannot tell, but it is a certain fact that our struggle is extremely hard. Our worst Jews work only behind the scenes. They never come into the open, and therefore we cannot show them to the British public in their true dreadfulness. We hope, however, that you will see that we will soon win against the world enemy, in spite of all his cunning. We think with joy of the day when we shall be able to say with might and authority: England for the English! Out with the Jews! With German greeting, Heil Hitler! Unity Mitford.

P.S. If you find room in your newspaper for this letter, please publish my whole name. I want everyone to know that 'I am a Jew hater'.

Diana was said to have regarded Unity's outburst 'with the eye of one accustomed from the nursery onwards to Unity's headstrong convictions and her desire to shock. Diana was neither alarmed, nor outraged, nor even mildly disgusted; it was, she thought, "a piece of silliness. A wild thing to say"[33].' Like Mosley, Diana was far more concerned with her social life than any real commitment to political beliefs, and while she no doubt agreed with everything Unity had to say, she also had many, socially important Jewish friends whom she had no wish to provoke. But she certainly didn't see fit to contradict or excuse her sister's opinions.

The comings and goings of the Mitfords and their friends continued unaffected. But while the opportunity of being introduced to the Führer gave Unity a considerable cachet and added immeasurably to Munich's attraction, it presumably only did so for those who were sympathetic to Hitler's policies and methods.

> Sister Pam's arrival on 14 June was jotted down in Mary's diary. Pam was with the Heskeths and Billa Cresswell, now married to the economist Sir Roy Harrod. Lady Harrod said: 'We had driven along the Rhine, through Wiesbaden to Munich, in three cars, Roger Hesketh's, his sister Joan's, and Pam's. Cuthbert Hesketh and a footman called John were also with us'.[34]

They also brought with them flashes of humour, a somewhat rare commodity at the time; even amongst the Mitfords, who had perhaps never been quite as amusing as they thought they were, and were now anything but. Certainly, there was little to match Lady Harrod's brilliant flash of self-promoted wit:

> For two days we stayed at the Vierjahreszeiten. Pam rang Unity up and she came round to see us. We were all five sitting in the foyer of the hotel, and Unity was looking at her watch all the time as she was going to meet Hitler. She was on tenterhooks, she didn't seem too sure of him. It was the year of the Jubilee and I had on a

check cotton dress, red and white with a round collar. I'd got buttons covered with Union Jacks from Woolworths. The conversation turned to patriotism and Bobo said to me, 'Would you think of joining the National Socialist Movement?' I answered, 'I would if I could get the buttons'.

Another rare moment of humour concerned Unity's reported conversation with Hitler when he asked, 'What is your father's name?' Lacking the knowledge required to understand how Unity Mitford could have been legitimately sired by Lord Redesdale, he patted her hand and commiserated, '*Mein armes Kind*' (My poor child).

But as their relationship developed, the humour diminished while their mutual fantasy intensified, particularly in the case of Unity's realised erotic fantasy. This was exemplified in a statement contained in one of her letters. 'Hitler is so kind and so divine I suddenly thought I would not only like to kill all who say things against him but also torture them.' As a sadomasochist, Unity derived sexual pleasure from pain, both from giving and receiving it. This was confirmed by Gaby Bentinck and her friend, Marie France-Reilly. In Hitler's case there was no evidence of such tendencies. His necromantic pleasure, of the most extreme and appalling degree, appeared to have been facilitated by his indulgence in persuading others to slaughter and torture on his behalf.

* * *

While the development of Unity's relationship with Hitler was a deeply personal matter that few if any people, possibly not even her own family, fully understood, it appears Mosley may have started to take advantage of the situation in order to promote himself and his cause. Certainly, the interviews Unity gave were beginning to display a suspiciously sophisticated style and content that suggested she may have been briefed, or that the BUF press office may even have written them for her. One obvious example was published in the weekend *Münchener Zeitung* for 22/23 June 1935, under the title 'Eine Britische Faschistin erzählt' (Confessions of an English Fascist girl):

> ... our anti-Semitism has called Jewry in England to account ... Oswald Mosley has a military disposition, he was educated at a military college, was a combat airman in the World War, he certainly did not find his homeland brought low and conquered, as Adolf Hitler did, but for all that the country was bitterly divided ... anyone who has ever heard Mosley speak knows that he is a man imbued with his sense of mission and an unshakeable belief in the victory of his cause. Oswald Mosley is our Leader, and we English fascists are behind him with the same enthusiasm as today the whole German people are behind their wonderful (herrlich) Führer. We British fascists have a lot to learn from Germany.

The British Embassy was certainly beginning to suspect that the motif for Unity's presence in Munich may have been more political than had previously been suggested by her friends and family, and forwarded the interview to the Foreign Office:

> You may like to know that the *Münchener Zeitung* of the 22 June contains an interview with the Hon Unity Mitford on the subject of Fascism in England. Miss Mitford, although only 20 years of age, appears to represent Sir Oswald Mosley in Munich, and has been living there since September ... the Embassy do not seem to know about Miss Mitford's acquaintance with the Chancellor which is very curious indeed. She is a student in Munich and it is true that her family are friends of Sir Oswald Mosley but I can't believe she 'represents' him. I understand that she sees Herr Hitler very often in Munich.

They appeared totally ignorant of Diana's relationship with Mosley, despite the fact that there was little secret of it amongst many of the more fashionable members of London society.

The *Münchener Zeitung* interview was published to coincide with a celebration on the Hesselberg, a hill outside Nuremberg and the historic site for a midsummer night (*Sonnenwende*) pagan celebration involving bonfires, dancing and ritual offerings of bread and ham. The Nordic god Baldur (god of peace), numerous spirits and fire were all a traditional part of the solstice celebrations. The Nazi Party exploited the festivities in which the people wearing traditional costume were also obliged to wear swastika armbands and celebrate the symbolism of people (i.e. the German people, the *Volk*), blood (and specifically its purity) and fire (the great cleanser).

Afterwards, Unity proudly wrote to her mother:

> At 9.30 pm we started for the high hill … we drove in a column, seven giant black Mercedes rushing through the night, all full of men in uniform, all open, I was the only woman. When we reached the top of the hill, we marched through the crowd, band playing, between cordons of SA men with torches, to the speakers' stand.

This particular night had been stage-managed as a tribute to Streicher and his journal. At ten o'clock he started his rant of revenge against the Jews.

Accompanied on the platform by his adjutant, König, Göring was also due to address the crowd but on the spur of the moment, Streicher first introduced Unity. The *Fränkische Tageszeitung* reported:

> We have one thing to say to those witnesses among us from England. You have no idea as yet that it is the Jew who first split our people into political parties. You still do not realise that the Jew brought political parties and strife to you too. The English people are ready for an honourable peace, but it is the Jew who does not want peace.

The 'Frankenführer' then called Unity to the microphone, where she affirmed her solidarity with the German people and the struggle of Julius Streicher:

Göring then turned to the question of Anglo-German relations and expressed Germany's pleasure [specifically Adolf Hitler's] at the recent declaration of His Royal Highness the Prince of Wales [the future King of England]. The German ex-servicemen and the German nation cheerfully grasped the hand which had been stretched out at them [contained in an unfortunate speech he had given to members of The British Legion on the theme of old soldiers' comradeship and alluding to his possible support of the BUF].

The Fränkische Tageszeitung on Monday 24 June published another interview under the title 'Miss Mitford Replies' in which she further established her support for the BUF ... 'plenty of Englishmen, and certainly those of better stock (Rasse) can be found to subordinate themselves to one man's leadership ... at present the Mosley movement is ignored in the main papers, as once happened in Germany to the national socialists ... the Jews in England were not so visibly a danger as in Germany. But Mosley very soon recognised that the Jewish danger may well work its evil way from country to country, but fundamentally it poses a danger to all the peoples of the world ... for years I have been a personal friend of Mosley and so committed myself early to his political way of thinking'.

They were hardly the words of a naïve romantic, despite Nancy's attempts to establish her as such in the role of the somewhat vacuous Eugenia Malmains in her latest book, the satirical *Wigs on the Green*, and in a letter to Unity dated 29 June 1935: 'Darling Stoneyheart, We were all very interested to see that you were the Queen of the May this year at Hesselberg [in parody of Tennyson's, 'The May Queen']. Call me early, Göring dear, For I'm to be Queen of the May! Good gracious, that interview you sent us, fantasia, fantasia.' At least Nancy recognised her sister's propensity for fantasy.

In the same letter Nancy also teased Unity by claiming:

We were asked to stay with somebody called Himmler or some-thing, tickets and everything paid for, but we can't go as we are going to Venice and the Adriatic for our hols. I suppose he read my book and longed for a good giggle with the witty authoress. Actually he wanted to show us over a concentration camp, now why? So that I could write a funny book about them. We went to Lord Beaverbrook's party last night, it was lovely and I told him about how Göring called you early and he roared. I must say you are a wonderful noble girl, and everyone who has read my book longs to meet you.

Wigs on the Green was so obviously autobiographical and so aggres-sively critical of her family, including the thinly disguised figure of Diana, whom she described as 'intellectually pretentious' and 'ambi-tious', and their support of fascism, that it was said to have caused lifelong family rifts. But it was also somewhat hypocritical, as Nancy had already joined the British Union of Fascists in 1933. It also seems more than likely that while she could appreciate the humorous silli-ness of Mosley and her family, it didn't affect her fascist sympathies.

Even prior to the book's publication, Nancy was obviously fully aware of the impact it would have within the family, par-ticularly regarding her relationship with Diana. Though in this letter to Unity she also appeared to be amused by the challenge of faking concern:

Darling Head of Bone and Heart of Stone,

Oh dear oh dear the book comes out on Tuesday.

Oh dear, I won't let Rodd give a party for it, or John Sutro either, who wants to.

Oh dear I wish I had never been born into such a family of fanatics.

Oh dear.

Please don't read the book if it's going to stone you up against me ...

Oh dear do write me a kind and non-stony-heart letter to say you don't mind it nearly as much as you expected, in fact you like it, in fact after I Face the Stars it is your favourite book even more favourite than mine comf [*sic*].

Oh dear I am going to Oxford with Nardie [Diana] tomorrow, our last day together I suppose before the clouds of her displeasure burst over me. She doesn't know yet it's coming out on Tuesday.

Oh dear, I have spent days trying to write her diplomatic letters about it.

Oh dear, I wish I had called it mine uncomf now because uncomf is what I feel every time I think about it. So now don't get together with Nardie and ban me forever or I shall die ... I did take out some absolutely wonderful jokes you know and all the bits about the Captain [Mosley].

OH! DEAR!

In fact, Diana had already seen the book in manuscript form because the publisher, understandably fearful of a costly legal action, had persuaded Nancy to allow her to read it. Diana then suggested a 'rash of edits', many of which Nancy subsequently claimed to have accepted, after Diana and Unity had told Nancy they would never speak to her again if she published the book in its original form. Nancy appealed to her sisters, 'I really can't afford to scrap the book', accepting that following its publication communication between the sisters remained somewhere between tense and non-existent.

How much of the outrage was genuine and how much it was designed to help promote the book is difficult to tell. The publication was certainly timed to take maximum advantage of Unity's various anti-Semitic, pro-Nazi and pro-BUF letters and speeches and the resulting coverage in British newspapers.

The *Stürmer* letter was reported in the *Evening Standard* on 26 July 1935 and in three morning papers the next day. The *Daily Mirror* ran the story with the headline 'Peer's Daughter as Jew-Hater'.

The Jewish Chronicle had a leader pointing out the obvious. 'Here was a scribbler so obscure that she begged Herr Streicher to "publish her whole name". She realised that without her title, which was, of course, a mere accident of birth, her vaporing's could have been of no more concern to the public than those of any other irresponsible young hussy out to get her name in the papers.'[35]

Exactly who had alerted the media, reminding them that Nancy's books were such thinly disguised accounts of this aristocratic, 'eccentrically' fascist family is not known, but it must have helped the sales of Nancy's books no end.

Once the newspapers had got the bit between their teeth and realised what a good and potentially long-running story they had, the Mitford girls in their various guises made regular appearances. If they had managed to gain knowledge of Unity's sexual 'Sturm und Drang' nights, the practice of which had increased dramatically since Hitler had given the impression of accepting, if not actually *blessing* her erotic 'Eucharists', one can only imagine how much coverage she would have been awarded. As it was, Unity and Diana's various Nazi-related appearances and utterances remained a particularly rich source of material.

On Monday 11 September 1935, the *Daily Mirror* ran yet another news feature about Unity being a guest of honour at the Congress of Nazi Groups Abroad, held at Erlangen, Bavaria. 'She and her sister, said the British United Press, were given seats at the speaker's table, where Julius Streicher, Germany's Jew-baiter Number one was addressing the congress.'

Streicher had apparently interrupted his speech to introduce those present to his guests of honour, the ladies Leni Riefenstahl; Frau Troost, wife of Paul Ludwig Troost, Hitler's foremost architect; and Unity and Diana Mitford.

*   *   *

Diana and Mosley had been together, on and off, for more than three years but while they were said to have, 'remained very much in love', he was still sexually involved with Baba Metcalfe and numerous other women. Diana was encouraged to 'treat Mosley's philandering as he had once advised Cimmie to do', as a 'tiresome silliness' that was beyond his control. But, despite the fact that she also took lovers, Diana claimed to have suffered 'agonies of jealousy'[36]. The only contradiction to this opinion was the amount of time she spent in Germany, with no record of being distraught by their separation.

Diana's celebrated beauty assured her of a constant stream of admirers, which, while reassuring for her, proved less pleasing for Mosley, who like most philanderers was 'apt to be jealous'[37]. Such mutual jealousy inevitably resulted in major rows, particularly concerning Baba Metcalfe.

Despite Mosley's extracurricular activities, the active membership of the BUF had reached 10,000, plus a claimed 30,000 non-active members and supporters, while Mosley insisted that fascism in Britain had grown faster than anywhere else in the world. In an early Gallup poll, 70 per cent of people under 30 apparently chose fascism rather than communism because they were all so terrified of the threat of communism. Though many of the privileged classes might indeed have been in favour of a fascist style of government to protect them from the lower orders at least and the Communists at most, what these English fascist sympathisers had in mind was a long way from Germany's violent, extreme right-wing dictatorship.

While Hitler had undoubtedly displayed flashes of genius in his ability to sell his message to both the masses and the social and industrial elite, his financial and industrial achievements (underwritten by direct and indirect loans from American banks) would be overshadowed by his appalling social and racial policies.

On 14 September 1935, Unity and Diana heard Hitler read out the Nuremberg Laws, which deprived German Jews of their citizenship and most of their legal and humanitarian rights, thus recalling the 'eugenic' principles of Houston Stewart Chamberlain and initiating policies that would lead to the extermination camps of Treblinka, Majdanek, Sobibor and Auschwitz.

News of the Nazis' treatment of Jews and other social and political victims was beginning to filter through to Britain, not only through political publications but also through national newspapers which were running stories about those people, particularly Jews, who were being humiliated and stripped of possessions, and whose shops and businesses were being looted and closed. There were also reports of German towns erecting signs boasting that they were 'Jew free'. Park benches were marked 'Aryan' and 'Jew', while shops proclaimed that Jews would not be served.

When questioned about the Nazi regime's attitude to Germany's Jewish population, Mosley replied, 'Whatever happens in Germany is Germany's affair, and we are not going to lose British lives in a Jewish quarrel.'

Despite her commitment to fascism both in Germany and England, Unity, like Mosley, displayed no inclination to curtail her social life. She spent most of October on an excursion to the mountains with her sisters Pam and Jessica, and Erich, one of the few SS officers with whom she enjoyed a relatively conventional, one-to-one relationship.

*   *   *

It was hardly surprising that Hitler still preferred Munich to Berlin, where he was constantly under the inevitable pressure that went with the role of Reich Chancellor, pestered by statesmen, diplomats and journalists. In Germany, Berlin was, and still is, famous for the ill humour of its people and, being at the political centre of the Reich, when he was there Hitler was left with little time to enjoy long lunches or tea with young women. However, when Hitler returned to Munich, his senior staff and ministers had little choice but to follow him to the city and even establish secondary homes and offices there. Goebbels, for one, hated it, but was all too aware that to remain in power one needed to be in constant attendance, as Hitler tended to view absence as a form of betrayal. So, it was through her regular attendance that Unity would soon meet 'everyone who was anyone' in the upper echelons of power.

Her presence was not appreciated by everyone; many failed to see why they often had to share Hitler's attention with an English girl and sometimes her friends and family, who were quite reasonably considered as being of little consequence or importance. There was a great deal of gossip, particularly amongst the wives, concerning the reason why Hitler chose to spend so much time with Unity, as he had a perfectly good mistress who appeared quite prepared to share his bed without the need to share his table and the company of his various friends and ministers.

Back in Munich, Diana having returned to England on 21 October, Unity and Mary Woodisse moved to Pension Doering, 17B Ludwigstrasse, and Unity returned to her constant vigil. Success apparently warranted a red-ink announcement in her diary and over-excited letters to either Sydney or Diana, usually the latter:

I didn't expect to see the Führer, as he apparently hasn't been to the Osteria for weeks. However today at last he came, it was wonderful and he was tremendously surprised to see me. He immediately asked me, as he came in (himself, for the first time), to go and sit with him. A bit later Max Schmeling came with Hoffmann and sat on the Führer's other side. He remembered you and me from the Parteitag. The Führer was heavenly, in his best mood and very gay. There was a choice of two soups and he tossed a coin to see which one he would have and he was so sweet doing it. He asked after you and I told him you were coming soon. He talked a lot about Jews, which was lovely …

The most amazing piece of news of all is Baum [Unity's language teacher] is out of the Partei! She was in the Osteria yesterday and Rosa told me. According to Stadelmann she was discovered to be a half-Jüdin (Jewess). Isn't it amazing. She also hasn't any work poor thing, as there was a big row in her Mütterheim at Starnberg and she was kicked out. I am really sorry for her, as the Partei and her hate for the Jews were really all she had.

This seemed particularly hypocritical, as the increasingly jealous Ms Baum had previously attempted to denounce Unity for having an affair with a Jew. The Jew in question was Brian Howard, both homosexual and Christian by birth. The fact that Baum's information was so inaccurate had not diminished Unity's fierce retaliation. She actually gained considerable satisfaction from Baum's fate, introducing her Führer to the English expression, 'People in glass houses shouldn't throw stones', which apparently made him 'roar'.

*   *   *

In the autumn of 1935, when Duff Cooper was made British Secretary for War, Chips Channon, the wealthy American political socialite now at home among Britain's aristocracy, observed that 'everyone (was) enchanted', which seemed a rather strange choice of words. But when the pro-Nazi Emerald Cunard, an enthusiastic member of the Anglo-German fellowship, telegraphed him 'Hail Mighty Mars', it is not unreasonable to assume that, like many politicians, Duff may not have been quite as anti-fascist, anti-appeasement as he claimed. Having been awarded an ambassadorial posting to Paris, he could make no greater contribution to international intelligence than seeing fit to warn the British government that they should be wary of a Russian-German alliance! Like Mosley, Duff spent too much time jumping in and out of bed with other peoples' wives to be capable of contributing anything very useful in his role as a diplomat. Unfortunately, the British Empire had been remarkably effective at breeding such men.

Of course, what so many people, including Hitler, failed to appreciate was that the British Empire had been both created and held together by 'boxwallahs' (those involved in commercial activities), not the aristocracy or the military, who still considered trade in any form as frightfully common and something one paid others to do. Unfortunately, the upper classes had a dreadful habit of offloading their surplus sons or 'remittance boys' into the diplomatic or foreign service, where they developed a remarkably inflated opinion of their own importance and often did untold damage.

Back in Germany, Hitler and Göring continued to recruit their own redundant aristocracy, while they also courted the British royalty. Sometimes they used one to achieve the other, as in the case of Duke Carl Eduard von Sachsen-Coburg and Gotha, whom in 1936 they persuaded to approach his 'cousin, the new British monarch Edward VIII, in order to explore the possibilities of a meeting (with an eye on a rapprochement between the two countries)'[38]. But, unfortunately, at this time the British Crown was heading towards the buffers, while the social elite was frantically taking sides, both pro- and anti-American, in the matter of Wallis Simpson. In Chips' case, his sympathy lay more with Wallis than King Edward VIII. Or that was what the snob in him claimed after the king was inaccurately said to have sympathised with the striking miners, describing him as 'Over democratic, casual and a little common'. A view he shared with many of his English chums.

*   *   *

By 1936, the Anglo-German Fellowship boasted forty-one corporate members including Thomas Cook, Dunlop, Price Waterhouse, Unilever, Midland Bank, Lazards, Vickers Steel and British Steel:

> Among the many members were The Marquis of Clydesdale, Sir Thomas Moore, A.T. Bower, Loel Guinness, Sir Ernest Bennett, Sir Asshelon Pownall, Sir Robert Bird, JRJ Macnamara, Duncan Sandys … plus Ministers such as Lord Londonderry, known derisively as 'The Londonderry Herr', plus peers Lord Brocket, Lords David and Malcolm Douglas Hamilton, Lord

Redesdale, Lord Galloway, the Duke of Wellington, Lady Downe and Lord Nuffield.[39]

Apparently, Guy Burgess and Kim Philby infiltrated the organisation on behalf of the Foreign Office; or so it was said. 'Burgess even managed to mix business with pleasure when he and Macnamara went on a "fact-finding" mission to Germany, which became "homosexual escapades with sympathetic members of the Hitler Youth".' According to Martin Pugh, the Anglo-German Fellowship's forte was:

> The monthly 'At Homes' and the lavish dinners graced by Joachim von Ribbentrop, the Duke of Saxe-Coburg-Gotha, Rudolf Hess (Hitler's deputy), Field Marshal von Blomberg (German War Minister) and the Duke and Duchess of Brunswick. Members also organised country-house parties where they shot game, with delighted visiting Nazis, discretely raised the swastika among the rhododendrons, dressed up in jack boots and drank toasts to the Führer.
>
> Such activities appealed to a clutch of society hostesses, including Lady Emerald Cunard, Lady Sibyl Colefax, Lady Londonderry and Nancy Astor (whose marital family had German roots), who happily entertained von Ribbentrop and helped to make Nazism fashionable in smart circles. Many of these hostesses along with the Redesdales, Lady Ravensdale ... Lady Diana Cooper ... eagerly awaited invitations to Nuremberg rallies and Nazi dinners in Berlin; it was there that Ernest Tennant (in a brief moment of inspired observation) spotted 'the young and beautiful Miss Unity Mitford who really believes that Hitler is divine in the Biblical sense'.

Chips was, of course, frantically impressed by high society's adoption of the Fellowship and, to a lesser degree, by von Ribbentrop; if not by his wife:

> Frau von Ribbentrop is distinguished in the Berlin manner, that
> is she has intelligent eyes, appalling khaki coloured clothes and an
> un-powdered, un-painted face. How can the Germans be so silly
> about things that don't matter, or is it because their women are
> so unattractive that the race is largely homosexual? ... The Rib-
> bentrops are intimate with the Londonderrys and he is known as
> the Londonderry Herr.

Many of the Fellowship were frantically impressed when they
were invited to attend the 1936 Berlin Olympic Games as Hitler's
VIP guests.

★   ★   ★

From an international public relations point of view, the 1936
Berlin Olympics were the Nazi Party's finest hour.

Lavishly entertained, every opportunity was used to impress the
English contingent. They appeared to remain totally unaware that all
the gypsies, or anyone who looked like one, had been arrested and
placed in camps, and that all anti-Semitic signs had been removed and
the police instructed not to enforce the law against homosexuality.

Aides-de-camp in Mercedes cars chauffeured by storm troopers
'whizzed' the guests to and from the Olympic Stadium. After an hour
or so of watching the hurdling and running, the crowd suddenly bel-
lowed 'Heil!'; there was a sudden movement and a surge forward
towards the large, rotund figure of Göring in his white uniform,
followed by the brown-uniformed figure of Hitler with his Charlie
Chaplin moustache. The frequent German victories were rewarded
with the playing of *Deutschland über Alles* and the *Horst-Wessel-Lied*.

Later that evening, there was a state banquet at the Opera House
and a lavish party, hosted by Göring who was reported to have
been 'flirtatious, gay and insinuating'. No one could have failed
to have been impressed by the 'surfeit of hospitality', particularly
Chips Channon:

The end of the garden was in darkness, and suddenly, with no warning, it was flood-lit and a procession of white horses, donkeys and peasants, appeared from nowhere, and we were led into an especially built Luna Park. It was fantastic, round-abouts, cafes with beer and champagne, peasants 'dancing' and 'schuh-plattling', vast women carrying pretzels and beer, a ship, a beer-house, crowds of gay, laughing people, animals, a mixture of Luna Park and White Horse Inn. Old Heidelberg and the Trianon ... Reinhardt could not have done it better. The music roared, the astonished guest wandered about. 'There has never been anything like this since the days of Louis Quatorze', someone remarked, 'Not since the days of Nero', I retorted, but actually it was more like the Fêtes of Claudius, but with the cruelty left out ... Frau Goering asked if we would like to see the house, and eagerly we followed her indoors into the vast Ministerium where the Goer-ings live in theatrical magnificence.[40]

*   *   *

While many amongst the privileged classes remained superficially impressed by little more than the lavish excess of the Nazis, others displayed a great deal more, albeit displaced, commitment. With increasing enthusiasm for the Nazi cause and impatience at media criticism, Lord Redesdale pointed out in the *Anglo-German Review* of November 1936, 'Has any one of (Hitler's) critics stopped to consider ... what Europe would be like today if Germany had gone Red? By holding Bolshevism on the flanks of Western civilisation, a tragedy was averted.' Even Churchill found himself on the same side as Mosley, in the sense that he regarded fascism as a necessary bulwark against communism.

Martin Pugh would later claim, 'The main obstacle to improved relations between the two countries remained the Nazi persecution of the Jews and the gypsies, political opponents, homosexuals and cripples.' But this was somewhat contradicted by the apparent lack of effort by the British government, or anyone else for that matter, to persuade the Nazis to stop. In 1936 the BUF were still exploiting the value of anti-Semitism for the rejuvenation of their party. Fortunately, a far smaller percentage of the 'lower orders' (than the aristocracy) were impressed by the fascist regime.

October heralded the BUF's march through London's East End, which many considered to be the beginning of the end of the party. Even the police were taken by surprise by the size of the 100,000-strong force of aggressive anti-fascists who beat back the BUF in what became known as 'The Battle of Cable Street'. In fact, most of the fighting had been between the anti-fascists and the police. But as a result, the Public Order Bill was introduced on 16 November 1936, giving the police greater powers to prohibit such political marches and ban the wearing of political uniforms. It could also be used to punish incidents of violent language and actions against Jews.

The British public also had more pressing matters on their mind, as it became increasingly obvious that the new King of England was obsessively in love with the American Wallis Simpson, particularly after he had opened parliament with a decidedly American accent. They were perhaps less concerned about the persecution of Jews and gypsies in Germany than with rumours that Wallis was about to divorce her second husband.

★   ★   ★

By 1936 it had also become increasingly obvious that the king was intending to become directly involved in negotiating with Hitler. This may have contributed to the determination of the prime minister to force the abdication of the new king in December 1936. It was an extraordinary episode, which has never been credibly explained.

In a conversation with the pro-Nazi Duke of Saxe-Coburg, Edward described an Anglo-German alliance as an 'urgent necessity'. When the Duke enquired about arranging for Baldwin and Hitler to talk it over, he heatedly responded: 'Who is the King here? Baldwin or I? I myself will talk to Hitler, and I will do so here or in Germany. Tell him that please!'[41]

Leading opponents of Edward's abdication included Winston Churchill, Lord Beaverbrook, Lord Rothermere, Lord Lloyd, Walter Monkton, Oswald Mosley, Lady Houston, Duff Cooper and Sir Archibald Sinclair, the Liberal leader. They wanted to force Baldwin to resign and for the Prince of Wales to form a 'King's Party'. A number of junior ministers even thought a coup d'état was possible.

Popular opinion was unmistakable as people took to the streets with banners that read 'Hands Off Our King' and 'Abdication means Revolution'. The BUF even adopted the slogan 'Stand By The King'. But the prince caved in to Baldwin's demand, probably because he was made aware that while he might indeed be king, Wallis Simpson was never going to be accepted as his queen. As Beaverbrook said, 'Our cock won't fight.'

6

THE GREAT AFFAIR

1936–38

Not God but a swastika
So black no sky could squeak through.
Every woman adores a Fascist
The boot in the face, the brute
Brute heart of a brute like you.

Sylvia Plath

There were certainly many in Germany, and not a few in Britain and America, who considered Edward VIII's abdication in 1936 as a thinly disguised political conspiracy to remove a Nazi-friendly king.

After the Windsors visit to Germany and well-publicised, 'cordial' meeting with Hitler in 1937, even *The New York Times* included the observation that the duke 'demonstrated adequately that the abdication did rob Germany of a firm friend, if not indeed a devoted admirer, on the British throne'. A further demonstration of the Duke of Windsor's enthusiasm for fascism took place after the war, when the Mosleys left England to live in France and became close, personal friends with the duke and duchess.

There was also the question of Edward's German roots. Jonathan Petropoulos claimed:

> The Duke spoke fluent German and continued to correspond with family members 'auf deutsch' throughout the 1930s. Privately, he considered German to be his *Muttersprache* (mother tongue) and, according to Diana Mosley, 'remembered as a child [how] the older members of the royal family waited until the English courtiers were no longer in the room, and then comfortably lapsed into German'.

Chips Channon believed that the German and Italian dictators should, if not encouraged, at least be left alone. Harold Nicolson recorded a conversation in September 1936, in which Chips told him, 'We should let gallant little Germany glut her fill of the reds in the East and keep decadent France quiet while she does so.' While his statement was breathtakingly hypocritical, one could certainly not question Chips' qualifications for being able to recognise decadence when he saw it, nor the threat that communism presented to his own particular brand of indulgence.

The events of 1936 forecast the shape of things for the next decade. In the spring, Ethiopia (then known as Abyssinia) fell to the Italians and Hitler marched his troops into the demilitarised Rhineland (an area in which no military activity was permitted) without any opposition from Britain or France. Some even publicly voiced the opinion that it might be possible to encourage Hitler to head towards Russia before further embarrassing onslaughts were made in the direction of Western Europe. Lloyd George went as far as warning that the overthrow of Nazism might result in the far greater threat to Britain; that of a communist Germany.

According to the *Daily Mail*, 'The sturdy young Nazis of Germany are Europe's guardians against the Communist danger. Once

Germany has acquired the additional territory she needs in western Russia, the problem of the Polish Corridor could be settled without difficulty.'

Sydney, who *had been* frightfully proud of her family's relationship with Churchill and dropped his name at every opportunity, reluctantly admitted that 'cousin Winston', who was obviously beginning to sense the opportunity for another scrap with the Germans, was 'a dangerous man'. 'Good thing he had so little following among the Conservatives,' she added. Milly Howard-Brown said he was a warmonger, which meant the same thing. She also spent time in Munich, learning to speak German in optimistic anticipation of Hitler reaching her new husband's estates in Hungary before the Communists. As it turned out, the rigors of indolence and the roulette tables of Monte Carlo would prove a far greater threat to their fortune.

In July 1936, General Franco had launched his attack on the Spanish Popular Front government, with the considerable help of Mussolini and Hitler and their troops and planes. British and American 'pinkos', 'lefties', 'commies' and other anti-fascists joined the International Brigade and fought with the Republicans against Franco. Shortly after the outbreak of the Spanish Civil War, the newspapers reported that 'Winston Churchill's nephew and Jessica's boyfriend, Esmond Romilly, had been "invalided out" of the Spanish war [where he had served with the International Brigade] and was back in England recovering in hospital'.[1] Much to his embarrassment, he was recovering not from a bomb, bullet or bayonet wound, but from 'a bad case of dysentery'.[2]

Churchill, who at that time was writing regularly for the *Evening Standard*, continued to warn of the aggressive rise of Nazi power and the dangers of appeasement, yet his articles on Spain were strongly pro-Franco. This may have had something to do with the fact that the Duke of Alba, Franco's envoy in England, was also an old family friend of Churchill's and a constant visitor to his home, Chartwell.

Back in Munich, Unity, having taken up residence in 1934 and first met her Führer in 1935, was still devoting her life to Hitler and writing to Diana complaining of others she considered quite unworthy of sharing his presence; including Lord and Lady Londonderry and their youngest daughter, who had apparently visited the Führer in the Reichskanzlei (Reich Chancellery). Hitler also admitted to having met Lord Beaverbrook, otherwise known as Max Aitken, which horrified Unity even more, though whether this was for social reasons, as she would doubtless have considered him both a 'nouveau-rich colonial' and 'frightfully COM', or because he appeared to be campaigning for both appeasement and confrontation at the same time, is not known. But then he was also considered by many, including Martin Pugh, to be 'an unscrupulous opportunist'. There is certainly documentary evidence to suggest that in 1933 Lord Beaverbrook may have invested in the German military aircraft industry, specifically the Messerschmitt-Aitken-Gesellschaft, prior to accepting the post of Minister of Aircraft Production under Churchill. So, perhaps Unity recognised this rather unfortunate side to his character.

What Hitler did say that filled Unity with both excitement and hope that some form of appeasement was possible was that 'with the German army and the English navy we could rule the world'. Perhaps, as many suggested, Hitler did in fact use Unity as an information conduit through which he could float concepts which he knew she would leak to the 'right people' in London, though whether he ever seriously considered sharing global power with Britain is questionable. As Unity would doubtless have agreed, deities are not prone to sharing their power.

Another visitor to Hitler was Lloyd George, who, to many people's shock and amazement, greatly admired the German chancellor. They got on extremely well, unlike Hitler and Mosley, and this led to theories that the Führer, having invaded Britain, may have intended to appoint Lloyd George, rather than Mosley, as a fascist overlord. Certainly, Lloyd George's admiration for Hitler is a historical fact, and as late as 1936 he still regarded him as 'the greatest leader in the world'. He even told him so during a visit to Germany.

Amongst the Mitfords only Jessica was sympathetic to the communist cause and horrified by the fact that so much of the British press echoed 'her parents' opinions that "Hitler and his Nazi troops were a bulwark for the rest of Europe against the threat of Communism"'. Even Beverley Nichols, the author and playwright, seemed to have changed his tune, asserting, 'There is so much in the new Germany that is beautiful, so much that is fine and great.' Particularly the young SS officers who, presumably, like Unity and Diana, Beverley would have found particularly appealing.

*   *   *

In the spring of 1936, somewhat surprisingly, Sydney managed to persuade Unity to accompany her, Jessica and Deborah on a Mediterranean cruise. One has to assume Hitler must have been out of town or otherwise engaged in affairs of state during this period, otherwise Sydney would never have managed to drag Unity away from Munich.

The *Laetitia* was a Lunn Hellenic Travellers cruise ship that included evening lectures as part of its program. When the socialist Duchess of Atholl gave a lecture critical of modern despots, Unity insisted on being allowed equal time the following day to preach her fascist gospel.

But more surprising than Unity having presumably been encouraged to do such a thing was that her mother saw fit to alert *The Daily Telegraph* in a letter 'taking the Duchess of Atholl to task ... and telling her that "Nazism is from every point of view preferable to communism"'.[3] This once again illustrated Lady Redesdale's quite sophisticated use of the media to promote her offspring, though of course it is possible that it was as much her intention to promote fascism. Whatever her intention, her skill at gaining such press coverage remained at odds with the image that has been promoted of her as a delightfully eccentric, if capable, woman more interested in the advantages of wholemeal bread than actively promoting her daughters and the family's commitment to fascism.

Unity's absence from Munich and her Führer, combined with her exposure to sea air, appeared to intensify rather than diminish what had by now developed into a full-scale religious conviction.

Peter Lunn, grandson of the travel company founder Sir Henry Lunn, was employed on board the *Laetitia* and later wrote to David Pryce-Jones:

It was Jessica whom I knew best, and what I learnt about Unity really came from her. She shared a cabin with her sister, who would lie on her bunk while she said her night prayers to Hitler, whose large signed photo would be propped up before her; at the end of her prayers, she would, still lying on her back, raise her arm in solemn Nazi salute. Unity was unabashed when I tackled her as to the truth of this story. I asked if she believed Hitler knew somehow she was praying to him and that he then interceded for her with God. Unity said she did not know how it worked; she simply knew that it worked.

In Paris, prior to boarding the ship they had spent a week in the company of Dolly Wilde, daughter of Oscar Wilde's brother and a noted lesbian. Attractive and witty, she was a prominent member of the city's racy artistic milieu. Nancy had apparently provided the introduction but while it was later claimed by Jessica that she and Unity 'deliberately irritated Sydney by pretending to be "in love" with Dolly, fighting to sit next to her in a taxi, stroking her fur collar and accepting gifts of frilly night-gowns from her',[4] Baroness Bentinck's French companion, Marie-France Railey, seemed to think the girls' sexual advances, particularly in the case of Unity, were somewhat more genuine than the subsequently claimed 'pretence'.

However, the Mitfords preferred to give the impression that their escapades were little more than schoolgirl pranks, full of sun-filled fun and jolly japes, while friends spoke of them 'following Unity's lead as they set out to shock while appearing models of innocence'.[5]

★   ★   ★

By now Unity's relationship with Hitler was causing his inner circle to ingratiate themselves with her. Diana Quilter, whose marriage into the Tennant family had offered her similar social advantages among the English aristocracy, was someone else introduced to Unity by a local aristocrat, Countess Anna Montgelas. She reported that 'Unity had been staying with [the Countess] at Oberau during the Winter Olympics in February 1936 … when Unity burst in to return a book, saying, "I'm in a hurry because I have the entire government waiting outside". I didn't believe her and went to the door to see her get into the back of the leading car with the Goebbels.'

It was the type of remark that not only illustrated Unity's privileged position within the Nazi hierarchy but also the type of profound social arrogance that was so much a part of both the English and German aristocracy; a quality that Hitler particularly admired.

Unity's friendship with Goebbels was particularly relevant; for while he appreciated the wisdom in total discretion concerning her transcendental relationship with the Führer, as the minister of propaganda he, more than anyone else, would have appreciated the potential value of her public relationship with Hitler and the party.

Quilter continued:

> Every year I went back to Anna Montgelas, and she arranged for me once to share Bobo's [Unity's] flat. We had a thundering party, with bodyguards in uniform, they got drunk, their ties came adrift early. I think we started at the opera; in any case we ended in an all-night café with Bobo dancing on a trestle table in that camelhair coat with a belt at the back, which she wore …

Her confusion concerning the order of the night's events had apparently been the result of the evening ending for her when Unity started lighting candles in her bedroom and the obviously, sexually aroused Storms removed more than their ties. Lacking Diana's sexual appreciation of voyeurism, Quilter remained locked in the kitchen until the early hours of the morning, her ears blocked to the sound of Unity's erotic sacrament. She was apparently mortified when, the following day, Unity appeared totally unconcerned or embarrassed.

But the more extreme details of Unity and Diana's sex life came not from Quilter but from Unity's friend Gaby Bentinck, whose equally exotic sexual reputation had predominantly been gained in Cairo, during the war, where she forged a close and personal relationship with King Farouk and enjoyed the attentions of a rather large number of British and allied officers. Some of her information on Unity and Diana was gained directly, some through her intimate liaison with the 'raffish' Janos Almasy, and the rest through the indiscreet wives of her husband's ambassadorial colleagues.

Robin Campbell was a Reuters correspondent in Berlin from February 1937 until early in 1939, and he became Unity's close friend and occasional lover. He and his wife, Mary Ormsby-Gore, had a flat in Charlottenburg, in the Flensburgerstrasse. He rather inadequately and inaccurately described Unity as 'a solitary figure in a mackintosh who everyone had tried to keep away from Hitler'. But on a more accurate level he did admit that Unity had once said to him that she had to sleep with the Führer's aide-de-camp in order to gain an audience.

It may have seemed a dramatically dangerous statement to make, especially to a journalist, but presumably she felt safe in the knowledge that no newspaper would be prepared to print such a story for fear that they would immediately be sued by Lady Redesdale. But her admission certainly answered the question that had puzzled so many people for so long, as to how she managed to gain so much information concerning her Führer's schedule. Even though it would be forty years before her admission appeared in print, it didn't take long for the revelation to become common knowledge amongst Munich's English set.

Despite her passion for the Führer and his Storms, Unity continued her complex, occult, sexual relationship with Janos Almasy, her necromantic high priest, paying regular visits to his and his wife Marie Esterhazy's Austrian schloss. It was there that she would meet Milly Howard-Brown, through her second husband, a Hungarian formerly known as Count Joseph von Schossberger, a close friend of Janos'.

The village of Bernstein is situated in Burgenland, one of the most remote, agricultural corners of Austria; an area that remained unspoiled, if cruelly feudal, long after much of the rest of the country had modernised. Many members of the Austro-Hungarian aristocracy owned estates in the area, only appearing to hunt or enjoy brief periods of pastoral indulgence. The village consisted of some fifty or sixty peasant houses or smallholdings; single story buildings, painted in pale Habsburgian yellow, green and pinkish washes, with decorated plasterwork and casements. The few larger farmhouses featured doorways high enough to allow horse-drawn hay-carts into the enclosed farmyards. At the village centre was a pond, with ducks and geese and chestnut trees while nearby stood the imposing eighteenth-century baroque Hotel Post.

Unity was enchanted and apparently considered it 'the most beautiful and thrilling place I have ever seen'. While Janos and his guests sat up till dawn discussing the advantages of National Socialism, an endless supply of colourful servants tended to their every need with stoic resignation.

But staying with Janos was not limited to the rural charms of Bernstein, which for his cosmopolitan guests could pale after a while. When they required more sophisticated entertainment they all traipsed off to stay at the Almasy apartment at 29 Horthy Miklos Körut (now Bela Bartok út) in Budapest, close to the famous Gellert Hotel by the side of the Danube.

In the city, Unity forfeited her intimate physical and cerebral relationship with Janos for relaxation with friends and the more transient attractions of hairdressers and dress-shops. Budapest was also attractive to them in part due to the fact that it was a city in the last days of lavish decadence where the aristocracy could still live in a style and behave in a manner that was quite impossible in the rest of Europe.

*   *   *

Diana and Unity had also been part of the enormous British contingent invited to attend the Berlin Olympics. They could not help but be impressed by the Games, but the social competition to meet 'the most powerful man in the world' was so intense that the frustrated Unity had to make do with an occasional nod, smile or wave through the fawning crowd. It proved quite impossible for her to spend any time alone with her Führer until the following, infinitely more precious event, the Wagner Festival at Bayreuth, to which the sisters were transported by chauffeur-driven Mercedes, personally provided by Hitler. He also arranged the best seats for them for both *The Ring Cycle* and *Parsifal*; tickets that money could not buy, for twenty hours of magnificent, if challenging, opera that imbued Unity with the same ecstasy with which she reacted to her Führer's impassioned, evangelical performances. It was a reaction that was further enhanced by her appreciation of the operas' (or musical dramas') mythological content and monumental style. Diana, on the other hand, was bored to distraction and only got through it by drinking a great deal of champagne both beforehand and during the breaks, while also resorting to a considerable amount of snoozing.

Unity made no mention of meeting Winifred Wagner, the English-born widow of Siegfried Wagner, who ran the Bayreuth Festival with considerable skill from 1930 to 1945 and would almost certainly have been present. But by now it was becoming evident that while Winifred remained a loyal friend of the Mitford family, and was still extremely close to Hitler and sympathetic to his Nordic fantasies and racist principles, she was very jealous of Unity and vice versa, so little mention was made of the other by either protagonist.

Winifred's humour would not have been improved by Hitler's end of festival invitation to the Mitford girls. According to Unity:

> In Bayreuth a message came that the Führer wanted us to return with him on his private train, so they came rushing along to pack for us, and get us on board. Thousands of people were shouting 'Heil! Heil!' all alongside the track and we didn't sleep a wink in the excitement.

*   *   *

In September 1936 the Mitfords were once again represented at the Nazi Party Rally. Not merely as friends or sympathisers, but in conspicuous celebration of their elevated position as full blown VIP guests of the Führer himself. Initially they had been seated in the third row, but Hitler soon had them moved. By the following afternoon, Tom, Diana and Unity, her friend Mary, and even Janos, had been re-seated in the front row of the Congress Hall to listen to Hans Frank, the Nazi lawyer who was to become governor of Poland; Otto Dietrich; and Max Amann, the publisher of *Mein Kampf* and the *Völkischer Beobachter*.

The celebrations continued each night as they were invited to a different function, including a bivouac dinner given by and for the SS, who dined at long tables in a huge tent, while their band played and the men sang. Unity was in her element; dashing between the official host, Himmler, to Streicher, Graf Helldorf, the chief of the Berlin police (a dangerously powerful man), to Gauleiter Wagner (mayor of Munich) and many others.

It was hardly surprising that such super-heated socialising would result in some 'frayed nerves', which in turn led to Unity having a flaming row with Mary. The altercation was caused by jealousy concerning her friend's closeness to Janos who, if truth be known, would probably have been just as happy being 'closer' to Unity's brother, Tom, with whom he had long enjoyed a close physical relationship; something Unity must have been aware of!

On the last day, unconsciously or otherwise, Hitler contributed yet further to Unity's nervous tension by arranging to have her seated in his reserved stand to watch the march-past. Unfortunately, she once again found herself on the seat next to Eva Braun.

There was no record of their conversation and it is more than likely that they cut each other dead! It was said Eva believed the reason for Hitler's interest in Unity was the result of her similarity to his niece, Geli, who had committed suicide in 1931. By 1936 Eva had apparently been suffering from some degree of insecurity concerning their relationship, but this situation had improved considerably when Hitler installed her in the Berghof near Berchtesgaden in the Bavarian Alps.

In her diary, Eva, who possessed an extremely slim, athletic body, displayed an unusually spiteful side to her character by explaining, in words to the effect:

Herr Hoffmann lovingly and tactlessly informs me that he (Wolfie) has found a replacement for me. She is known as Walküre and looks the part. Including her legs. But these are the dimensions he prefers. If this is true, though, he will soon make her lose thirty pounds, through worry, unless she has a gift for growing fat in adversity.

*   *   *

For Diana's Berlin wedding on 6 October 1936, some three years after her divorce from Bryan Guinness and the transferral of her affections to Oswald Mosley, both she and Unity were the houseguests of the Goebbels family, while Mosley stayed with two of his friends in the Hotel Kaiserhof. A brief account of the wedding apparently survived in Unity's diary:

Frau Dr., Diana and I drive to Hermann Göringstrasse about 11.30, I in my car to Kaiserhof to pick up Leader ... to Hermann Göringstrasse. The Führer and Doktor [Goebbels] arrive at 02.30 ... the Standesbeamte [Registrar] performs the ceremony. Bill [Allen] and I are witnesses. All sit and talk afterwards, then Frau Dr. and I drive to Schwanenwerder [the Goebbels' home], the others follow, the Führer last. Lunch there ... then an interpreter arrives and the Führer and the Leader go off and talk alone ...

According to Oswald Mosley:

Frau Goebbels, who was a friend of Diana's, helped to arrange the marriage and after the ceremony she gave a luncheon for us at her villa near Wannsee. Hitler was a guest. From this incident arose the rumours that Hitler had been my best man, while in fact this duty was performed by an English ex-officer of the 10th Hussars who accompanied me.

Later that evening, Hitler celebrated the occasion by entertaining Diana and Mosley at dinner in the Reichskanzlei, with Joseph Goebbels and his wife and other members of the Nazi hierarchy among the guests. Following the dinner, Hitler set off back to Munich on his train, taking Unity with him. It would be the last time Mosley and Hitler were to meet.

It was said that his decision to marry Diana well beyond the gaze of his English supporters was the result of Mosley's fear that his remarrying after the death of such a hugely admired wife would compromise his popularity as a political leader. It seems more likely to have been the result of his fear that the change in his status from single to married may have had a detrimental effect on his philandering. The press remained silent and very few people knew of the marriage until it was publicly announced two years later when *The Daily Telegraph* and the *News Chronicle* both broke the story on 28 November 1938.

The marriage certainly had a positive effect on Lord and Lady Redesdale's relationship with Mosley. It was all too predictable that while his charm would result in Sydney becoming a close and personal friend, David, apparently, remained somewhat disapproving. However, Lord Redesdale would doubtless have gained some satisfaction from the fact that it was his Christian name that very nearly forestalled the whole ghastly business.

Apparently there had been a little contretemps beforehand. When Diana was in the registrar's office making the preliminary arrangements, she had been required to give all her personal family details, including the names of her parents. David's Christian name had made the official look up sharply, because in Germany David is regarded as an exclusively Jewish name, thus indicating that the union may be contravening the Nuremberg Laws against marriage between Jews and gentiles. The adjutant accompanying Diana assured him that there was no problem, explaining that in England the name David could, and was, often used by 'Aryans'.

*   *   *

Unity now lived in Munich almost permanently, only returning to England for brief periods of time. She still socialised with English acquaintances who were in residence or visiting Munich, but most of her waking hours were spent either in the company of Hitler, waiting for him to arrive, or submitting to his divine power through the loins of his Storms.

Diana also joined Unity and Hitler when she visited Munich, even taking lunch with them at his apartment. But her relationship with the Führer developed mainly in Berlin, where Unity seldom went. Whenever Diana arrived, increasingly by aeroplane, she would telephone the Chancellery to announce her arrival at the Kaiserhof Hotel.

Because Hitler was an insomniac who seldom went to bed before two or three o'clock in the morning, their meetings usually took place at somewhat unsocial hours. The rendezvous were said to have been regarded with deep suspicion by British intelligence, but in truth, while they kept a file on Diana there was little in it of any consequence, apart from gossip concerning her relationship with Mosley; there was certainly no evidence that she was ever approached for information or for any justification for her visits to Germany. But this was in the days when the understaffed, wildly inefficient MI5 had considerable difficulty describing itself as an *intelligence* agency. At that time it was also considered quite unthinkable that a member of the privileged classes could possibly be involved in anything that would be a threat to national security.

So, it is doubtful that, at the time, the authorities would have been aware of the British Union of Fascists' attempts to raise funds by starting a German-based radio station to be beamed at the United Kingdom. With her Nazi connections and seductive physical attraction, Diana was the obvious person to try and secure permission for the establishment of such a radio station. Despite having no knowledge or interest in radio, Diana appeared more than happy to spend extended periods of time in Germany. She would doubtless have preferred to remain in Munich with Unity and her chums, but Mosley wanted the Nazis to finance the project, and for that she needed to be in Berlin.

Despite enjoying the comfort of the Kaiserhof, arguably one of the most luxurious hotels in Europe, it is no surprise that initially Diana was both bored and lonely. Indeed, she wrote to Unity saying, 'I did not mean to write, but I am so bored and miserable that I feel I must. I have been here a week tomorrow and I have been alone the entire time.'

However, she soon started to enjoy regular meetings with Hitler, without Unity, and could not resist rubbing it in. 'I must tell you how sweet the Führer was. He came into the room and made his beloved surprised face, and then he patted my hand … he looks in blooming health and his skin is peeling from so much sun.'

In fact, there is no evidence that this resulted in any jealousy between the sisters, which supports my theory that their respective relationships with the Führer were entirely different. Although Diana was undoubtedly the most conventionally attractive of the sisters and, according to both Milly Howard-Brown and Gaby Bentinck, equally as promiscuous, she was, as far as Hitler was concerned, a married woman and a good deal less cerebrally attractive than Unity. Hitler's sexual needs and greeds were anything but conventional, so his relationship with Diana involved none of the erotic fantasy and spiritual alchemy that he shared with Unity, who, because of these tastes, held far greater sexual appeal for him. As a result, his conversations with Diana would have concentrated on fascism and the English and, eventually, the financing of Mosley's radio station.

Whether or not Oswald Mosley actually *wanted* a radio station subsequently became somewhat questionable. Particularly when the contents of Joseph Goebbels' diaries were revealed and it became rather more obvious that the BUF was frantically short of funds and that Hitler's contributions, when they finally arrived, were being used to prop up the party. To this end Mosley appeared quite prepared to use his wife's physical attraction in order to further his political ambitions, and she likewise. As can be seen from extracts from the Goebbels diaries they were, at least initially, rather successful:

24 April 1936: (Lady Mitford) wants Germany to give £50–100k credit to the Morgan Bank ... the Führer will investigate this.

5 December 1936: The Führer has now released the money arranged for Mrs Guinness. As a result there will be peace. [An undertaking not to oppose the Reich or some form of appeasement presumably having been the carrot.]

7 February 1937: Mrs Guinness wants more money. They use up a fortune and accomplish nothing.

Obviously the cracks in the arrangement were already becoming visible; while the change in address of both name and title was ominous. By the end of 1936 the BUF was nearly bankrupt and Mosley's own finances were far from healthy. This was largely due to his personal refusal to become involved in anything so vulgar as commerce, expecting others to do so on his behalf.

*   *   *

One of the friends that Unity made in Munich was Henriette 'Henny' Hoffmann, daughter of the photographer Heinrich Hoffmann, Hitler's friend and raconteur. After the premature death of Hoffmann's wife, Henny accompanied her father everywhere. Hitler called her 'mein kleiner Sonnenschein' (my little sunshine). A year younger than Unity, she was only 17 when, in 1932, she married Baldur von Schirach, leader of the Hitler Youth movement, with Hitler and Röhm as her witnesses. There were rumours that he was a homosexual paedophile but he still managed to father four children. Meanwhile, Henny remained part of Hitler's inner circle.

There were also rumours that Hoffmann gained his position by blackmailing Hitler after he had subjected Henny to masochistic-coprophiliacal abuse. As Hitler had friends and acquaintances assassinated for a great deal more innocent knowledge of his personal habits and background, it seems highly unlikely that anyone could have blackmailed him for very long before they met with an unfortunate end. It seems eminently more likely that the rumour was British propaganda.

Hoffmann would certainly have been in a good position to gain intimate knowledge of Hitler, having written a number of authorised books about him, including *Hitler Was My Friend*, in which he confirmed Hitler's opinion of Unity as that of 'the personification of German womanhood'. He also spoke of her desire to see 'Britain and Germany closely united. "She often said to me, she dreamed of an impregnable and invincible alliance between the

Ruler of The Seas and the Lord of The Earth; the land of her earth with the country of her hero could, she was convinced, achieve world domination".'

Henny also wrote a book, called *The Price of Glory*, which was mostly about her time in Vienna at the end of the war. In it she described the Mitford sisters as 'two pale blond English girls wearing sky-blue sweaters' and how Hitler had explained that their peach-like complexions were the result of so much walking in the English rain; choosing not to mention their reliance on heavy make-up of the type that, it was claimed, he so abhorred in German women.

She recounted their remarkably relaxed leisure activities together and Unity's independence:

> We all used to go on picnics, and she (Unity) was on one of the biggest of these. We'd set off towards Austria, we sat on the ground, 5 or 6 girls … my father and Hitler more to one side, reading the papers … she used to drive right across Germany in her own car. She seemed very rich and rather too much the lady for me. But the back of her car was a jumble of books and pullovers all any old how.

Henny Hoffmann also claimed that Hitler had once said, 'Unity talks so much that whenever I have anything to announce to the world, I have only to tell her.' Again, it seems rather unlikely, unless he said it in the form of a tease. Hitler's facilities for the dissemination of propaganda were highly sophisticated. Henny's account of how, rather than why, Unity came to possess a pistol seems a great deal more believable:

> The gun she had was a 6.35 Walther. We girls all learned to shoot, we had to swim, ski and ride too. To Hitler sport was all-important. I'd learnt to shoot a revolver of this calibre at the Foehring shooting range, where she [Unity] had also learnt. We were

taught to handle guns, to load and clean them, and to practice target shooting. Whether Hitler actually gave her the gun I don't know, and it would be dangerous to say so, in case it created the impression that he was trying to get her to do away with herself.

In fact, all five of the key women in Hitler's life would either attempt or succeed in committing suicide. It is a detail that gives very considerable credence to the belief in Unity's and Hitler's obsession with necromancy. Not in the original occult practice of raising the dead but in the more modern concept of the control over life and death, as in the Norse legends' glorification of death and the afterlife, and also in their beloved Wagner and, arguably, in Teutonic culture in general.

★   ★   ★

Another witness to the Mitford sisters' behaviour in Munich was Lady Donald St Clair Gainer, wife of the then consul and friend of Gaby and Adolphe Bentinck. She remembered the somewhat bizarre situation of her husband who, like Hitler, tried to avoid having anything to do with Oswald Mosley – though for somewhat different reasons. 'Diana was to have married Mosley in Munich. Witnesses were to have been Hitler, Goebbels and my husband. He had been dreading it, prevaricating as best he could and he was very pleased when they switched to Berlin.'

Her ladyship was also sufficiently well informed to appreciate that Unity's attraction to Munich, like many of her contemporaries, was likely to have been sexual:

Lots of English girls got tied up [!] with SS men, you know, the boots, the red leather in their cars. We had a lot of trouble. Unity was a dumb blonde. She came quite often to see us at home in the Mauerkirchestrasse, but was at the consulate more often still, turning up without an appointment.

Lady St Clair was not the first person to underestimate Unity's intelligence. Understandably, her opinion may have been coloured by Unity's Nazi-based attitude towards Jews. 'They had taken a lot of Jews to an island in the Danube and stranded them there to die, and she said, "That's the way to treat them. I wish we could do that in England to our Jews".'

The consul's wife apparently also underestimated both Unity's and the Mitford family's Nazi sympathies. Or perhaps she was too polite, or too much of a snob, to admit that such people could possibly be sympathetic with such a ghastly little man as Adolf Hitler. But both Unity and members of her extended family made the extent of their sympathy obvious by their conspicuously exulted position at the London banquet of the Anglo-German Fellowship on 15 December 1936.

In the main speech of the evening, Ribbentrop demanded the return of German colonies, lost after the First World War. This was also one of Lord Redesdale's favourite subjects, which he raised in several speeches in the House of Lords. He and Lady Redesdale were seated with Unity at the top table, as were Lord and Lady Rennell, Nancy's parents-in-law. There was no mention of Nancy having been present, though it seems highly likely as she had already been a member of the BUF for some three years; something that her public tends to overlook.

* * *

In 1936, while the rest of the family were becoming increasingly enthusiastic concerning Adolf Hitler and the Nazis, only Jessica continued to swim against the tide by eloping to Spain with her 'red cousin', Esmond Romilly; having finally met and fallen in love. In fact, their motivation for heading for Bilbao was more as a result of their commitment to socialism than marriage. But, wherever the Mitfords went, publicity was never far behind. This time Esmond even managed to report their own 'goings on' by persuading the

News Chronicle, presumably encouraged by the fact that he was Winston Churchill's nephew, to commission him as their Spanish correspondent.

Meanwhile, as a cover for her elopement, 19-year-old Jessica had pretended to be staying in Dieppe with her friends, the Paget twins. When they discovered the truth, the Redesdales reacted with customary predictability. Drawing upon their social contacts to do something, within a miraculously short space of time they had enlisted the aid of Anthony Eden, then foreign minister and, somewhat unsurprisingly, cousin Winston. This was claimed to have resulted in the unlikely despatch of a Royal Naval destroyer carrying Nancy, who had been instructed to retrieve the errant couple. The destroyer had, in truth, probably been sent to Spain to rescue British nationals marooned by the conflict, and, as a result of the family's political connections, Nancy was permitted on board as a passenger. She had no particular interest in their moral welfare but recognised the publicity value and doubtless enjoyed the adventure.

In the meantime, Sydney had also alerted the media with the story, 'Pretty teenage daughter of a peer of the realm, eloping with a younger cousin who also happened to be the notorious and rebellious "red" nephew of Winston Churchill.' The *News Chronicle* was beside itself with excitement. Young Romilly was already proving an extremely valuable investment and, with the assistance of the Mitford family, was dominating the newspaper headlines with their story. The story was further enhanced when Lord Redesdale had Jessica made a Ward of Court, which was frightfully fashionable at the time, but of course had no legal status south of Dover or north of Carlisle.

Some cynics even suggested that the couple had initially refused to board the naval destroyer in Spain in the knowledge that the press needed more notice if they were to organise appropriate coverage. Others claimed that a week later they all met up again in the south of France. It looked good in print, although Saint-Jean-de-Luz, where the Navy were dropping off some of their rescued charges, is actually in the Basque area of south-western France, just across the border from Bilbao and rather a long way from the Cote d'Azur. But the press felt safer in France than war-torn Spain, and Nancy was able to organise even more publicity.

Having arrived, the mothers of both Esmond and Jessica soon decided, to the obvious delight of the press, that their respective son and daughter would indeed make a 'good match', and the wedding was swiftly organised to take place on 18 May in Bayonne, the closest large town to Saint-Jean-de-Luz. It was, the newspapers said, 'the wedding that even a destroyer could not stop' (for by now Sydney's claim that the foreign secretary had sent a destroyer whose sole purpose was to find Decca, had been enthusiastically adopted by the press).

Esmond also continued to fuel the story by referring to the entire Mitford family as Nazis and Lord Redesdale as 'the Nazi Baron'. This did not prevent Sydney and Nellie Romilly from attending the wedding while Unity, in a letter to Decca, explained in what she no doubt considered her rather 'conciliatory' manner:

> My attitude to Esmond is as follows – and I rather expect his to me to be the same. I naturally wouldn't hesitate to shoot him if it was necessary for my cause, and I should expect him to do the same to me. But in the meanwhile, as that isn't necessary, I don't see why we shouldn't be quite good friends, do you? I wonder if he agrees.

Meanwhile, Nancy doubtless sold more books and the press more newspapers, while the Mitford girls further enhanced their celebrity status. Even Esmond appeared to be learning a thing or two from the Mitfords as, in order to take advantage of the substantial press coverage, he spent his honeymoon writing an account of his Spanish experience, which was subsequently published under the title *Boadilla*. Later, Jessica managed to get even further mileage from their story by suggesting that her husband was in fact the illegitimate son of Winston Churchill, obviously having scant regard for the fact that if this had indeed been true, it meant she had married the offspring of half siblings; a somewhat incestuous arrangement.

For a brief period of time, Unity's celebrity status was quite over-shadowed by the Esmond and Jessica story.

★   ★   ★

By now Unity's sister Pamela had also married well, though with a great deal less drama and publicity. Her new husband, Derek Jackson, enjoyed important financial and political qualifications for entry into the Mitford family. He was bisexual and very rich, having inherited a large fortune from his father. He also shared many of Mosley's and Adolf Hitler's fascist and racist opinions. Following their wedding at the end of 1936, Pamela and Derek set off to spend their honeymoon, somewhat predictably considering their political leanings, in Vienna.

Derek's father, Sir Charles Jackson, and his friend Lord Riddell had, at one time, invested in a number of newspapers together, including *The News of the World*. Riddell, an honouree member of the British Medical Association was, in Derek's case, more impor-tant than Jackson, due to the influence he appeared to have had on the boy (whose father died when he and his twin brother were only 14 years old). It was a relationship that developed into a shared enthusiasm for fascist and Nazi principles.

In 1932 Lord Riddell's socio-political beliefs became public knowledge when he wrote a small but worrying pamphlet entitled 'Sterilisation of the Unfit'.

A man of exceptional intelligence, Derek became a lead-ing atomic physicist with an international reputation and a chair at Oxford. He could variously be considered as mad as a March hare, extremely amusing, annoyingly arrogant, deranged, or, indeed, all four. He was certainly blessed with sufficient financial privilege to practice eccentricity on an advanced level.

There was also something of the notorious wit and friend of the Mitfords, Brian Howard, in Derek Jackson's humour. Able to speak both French and German, with as strong an English accent as he could muster, he was once overheard 'announcing to a group of bewildered Viennese: "Ich bin steinreich, bildschön und weltberühmt" (I am rich as Croesus, pretty as a picture and world-famous).'[6]

The RAF, in which he served with considerable distinction, provided him with a particularly satisfying, reactive audience, especially to his pronouncements concerning the attractions of homosexuality (also interesting in light of the fact that Pamela would eventually adopt that mode of sexual preference) and Nazi politics; quite openly voicing the opinion that all British Jews should be killed. But there was apparently little doubt, certainly amongst the Mitfords and their peers, that Derek, as well as being a committed fascist, an extreme anti-Semite and a screaming snob, was also considered an all-round 'good egg'!

*   *   *

While Unity's relationship with Hitler appeared rather benign to many observers, there was increasing evidence of collateral danger for those who got too close. One of those who found himself in this position was Putzi Hanfstaengl, following a bizarre assassination plot in which Hitler was the instigator rather than the victim. Their friendship ended abruptly on 11 February 1937, Putzi's fiftieth birthday.

Hitler had arranged for him to be thrown out of a military aircraft over the Spanish Nationalist-held lines. With or without a parachute, his German uniform would have guaranteed his immediate demise. Fortunately, the pilot, a fellow Bavarian, saw fit to forewarn Putzi and let him off the plane after making an excuse for an emergency landing at Zurich (or Leipzig, depending on who you believe).

A loyal friend of both Unity and Diana, whom he had looked after at party rallies and Brown House functions right until his downfall, Putzi was convinced that a remark made by Unity, either intentionally or otherwise, had started the chain of events.

The story was that some time previously Putzi had said to Unity that he rather regretted the Nazi Party's achievement of its unassailable position of power, as he missed the years of struggle and conflict, and that the only place where such things continued was in Spain, and that, consequently, he now envied those who were fighting for Franco. Unity then repeated this story to Hitler, which seemed harmless enough until Hitler, who obviously had doubts concerning Putzi's loyalty, said, 'I'll tell you what we'll do, we'll let him fight for Franco if that is what he wants,' and issued orders for Putzi to be dropped into Spain.

Having fled from Switzerland to England, Hanfstaengl would eventually end up working for the Office of Strategic Services (OSS, forerunner of the CIA) in America, before returning to Germany after the war. His work for British and American intelligence could of course have been seen as validating Hitler's suspicions that he was being plotted against, as well as confirming what many considered to be Hitler's highly developed ability to sense disloyalty and treachery (even while Hitler also possessed an undoubted paranoia).

★   ★   ★

Unity may have returned to England in 1936 to celebrate the coronation of George VI, to which her parents had been invited, but it was far more likely that she only really went to take delivery of a brand new, shiny black, four-seater MG car that her father bought for her; yet further evidence of his appreciative encouragement of her relationship with Hitler and his 'warriors'.

Now she would be able to scream up and down the autobahn with … total freedom and so, with no further ado, she was soon heading back to Munich, for neither London nor Swinbrook held any further attraction for her.

By now, Unity's friendship with Hitler had reached new levels of intimacy, and in contradiction of various claims that she never spent time alone with her Führer, Unity's letters reveal that Hitler 'often' invited her back to his flat, where 'We sat for hours, chatting, quite alone'.

After Hitler had given one of his hysterically energetic performances at yet another party rally, he would return home quite exhausted. With insufficient energy to even talk, they listened to music together, particularly the 1927 live recordings of Wagner's *Ride of the Valkyries* from Bayreuth, which would have left them both in a trance-like state of ecstasy.

Sometimes they would also talk about politics. On more than one occasion Hitler commented on the mistakes he thought Mosley might be making concerning the BUF. Unity later told Diana:

> He said very emphatically that he thought it might have proved a fatal mistake in England to call them Fascists and Blackshirts instead of something typically English and suggested that if he had been starting a party in England he would have gone back to Cromwell and perhaps called his SA Ironsides.

One wonders if he had been aware that it was Cromwell who allowed the Jews to return to Britain after they were expelled by Edward I in 1290. Apparently, Hitler told Unity that he sometimes wondered if England was ready for fascism. He may also have reminded her how long the English had lived with democracy, particularly in comparison to Germany, and that the last absolute ruler in Britain had in his opinion been William of Orange in 1689.

But Unity and Hitler also shared a highly developed, if potentially life-threatening, sense of humour, and Gaby Bentinck, whose husband was a direct descendant of one of William's pages, heard tell that Unity reminded him, 'You know the first city William of

Orange took was not London but Exeter, which he rode into on a white horse, with two hundred black men forming a guard of honour, dressed in white with feathered turbans. Doesn't it sound just so much like Reichsmarschall Göring?'

Tears would have rolled down Hitler's face as, roaring with laughter, he may even have reminded Unity of the other reason why the English would probably never willingly adopt fascism. 'Your sense of humour, you find everything so funny! Even Reichsmarschall Göring and all those niggers!'

Many years later, during an interview with the *Sunday Express*, Nancy, still as bitchily jealous as ever, would support Hitler's opinion of Unity's humour with considerably less generosity, while belittling her intelligence and political knowledge: 'With [Unity] the whole Nazi thing seemed to be a joke. She was great fun. She used to drive round Central Europe in a uniform with a gun. Unity was absolutely unpolitical. No one knew less about politics than she did.'

This was also a perfect example of the Mitfords' subsequent trivialisation of the relationship between Adolf Hitler and Unity.

★   ★   ★

Hitler and Unity undoubtedly shared a reliance on the influence of fantasy. In the latter's case it was manifest in her love and belief of Milton, Blake and subsequently Wagner, her worship of Hitler and willing participation in physical devotion through sexual submission to his SS disciples. There was also, in Unity's case, an increasing erotic pleasure in necromancy, gained from submission to Janos Almasy's physical and spiritual influence.

Quite how Gaby Bentinck knew such intimate details was never revealed but she was certainly in no doubt that while Janos practiced the more traditional form of occult necromancy, his sexual manifestation of this black art was apparently the practice of asphyxiophilia, erotic oxygen depletion or what he and Unity referred to as 'gaspers'. It was apparently her willingness to take part in such dangerous practices, in order to heighten the pleasure of their 'comes', that endeared her to Janos, on a sexual level at least.

While Hitler may not have been as susceptible to the more extreme levels of the occult as Himmler, or have relied so heavily on the advice of his crazed spiritual adviser, Karl Maria Wiligut, he certainly accepted and encouraged its influence on the development of the Nazi Party, particularly via Dietrich Eckart, his mentor, a founder member of the NSDAP. Meanwhile, Hitler's susceptibility to the influence of fantasy during his rise to power would be well recorded, while his obsession with necromancy would become increasingly evident in his belief that he was Germany's new messiah and in his subsequent responsibility for the deaths of millions.

The fifteenth-century *Munich Manual* described the purpose of necromancy to be, amongst other things, 'To manipulate the mind and will of another person (or people). To drive them mad, to enflame them to love or hatred, to gain their favour or to constrain them to do or not to do some deed' (translated from Latin). But it cannot be overemphasised that there has never been any evidence that Adolf Hitler ever personally killed anyone, apart from himself.

It was entirely logical that Unity and her Führer, who had already admitted the sexual euphoria he experienced during his frenzied public speeches, should also achieve sexual fulfilment through shared erotic fantasy.

According to Gaby Bentinck, who Unity avidly confessed to, the first enactment of this fulfilment took place when Hitler was feeling sufficiently relaxed to take the development of his transcendental sexual relationship with Unity onto another level altogether. Although she knew that, contrary to popular belief, Hitler enjoyed the occasional glass of wine, she had apparently bragged to Gaby that during one of her visits she had been surprised to see a bottle of champagne in an ice bucket and lighted candles on the table in his apartment. Ecstatically apprehensive in the belief that her beloved Führer was intending to seduce her, Unity was somewhat surprised when, after pouring them both a glass, he sank back into the cushions and in the best bedside manner of a family doctor, quietly asked her for details of her erotic *devotions* with his elite disciples.

Initially shocked and embarrassed, she found it extremely difficult to answer such direct questions, particularly from someone whom she worshipped. But when it became obvious he had no intention of assigning guilt or being judgemental, she began to relax and as his questions became increasingly more intimate and detailed so did the erotic explicitness of her replies. Also, as Unity became increasingly aware that Hitler's arousal was heightened by her personal revelations – in the same way that Diana had, in their early days together in Munich, been excited by watching her have sex with her Führer's Storms – so she in turn was aroused by his mounting excitement.

Thus, she realised her fantasy of him not only being her deity, but also a participant in her sexual Eucharist. To his obvious pleasure, this became apparent to him, when, in answer to his whispered question of what she thought about when she was being taken by his warrior disciples, she assured him that she only ever thought of him and that they were purely a symbol of her submissive devotion and total commitment to his control of her destiny.

And so it was that for the first time, they not only shared a sexual experience but Unity acknowledged her unconditional acceptance of Hitler's necromantic power.

⋆   ⋆   ⋆

While the intimate details of Unity's relationship with Hitler have never previously been publicly revealed, there have been a number of rather vague but pointed references made, particularly by Nancy, that lead one to believe that within the Mitford family they were an open secret; but something, they decided, that was best kept to themselves. Many years later, Nancy could not resist claiming that Unity and Hitler's relationship had developed to the point where marriage had been considered. While Sydney may indeed have harboured such ambitions, Unity believed their relationship transcended such a dreary, temporal union. There was also no evidence, despite Nancy's claims, that Hitler had told Unity that he 'could not think of marrying someone who had been behind the hedge with half his army'. It was much more likely that Nancy was hinting at Unity's group sex activities in an effort to intimidate the family. There was no doubt a degree of resentment in the publicity that her sister was attracting and the fact that Unity was now a frequent guest at gatherings of Hitler's inner circle.

While Hitler's clique seemed to have accepted the fact that she regularly saw their Führer alone in his apartment, there is no evidence that the details of her physical and transcendental relationship with him were of any concern to them. This group of privileged associates were all too aware that discretion was the safest option. Of far greater concern would have been the security risk she posed.

Major Gerhard Engel, Hitler's adjutant representing the Wehrmacht, always claimed to be ignorant of Unity's relationship with the Führer; this was of course highly unlikely, but perhaps advisable. 'The great enigma,' said Engel, 'was what did Unity Mitford *want*?'

There was also an ever-increasing degree of jealousy involved. They could not help but notice that Hitler addressed her as 'Walküre' or that she now signed her name 'Unity Walküre' in the German manner, adding a small swastika underneath.

No one else in his life, apart from Eva Braun, who was rarely present in either Munich or Berlin, dared to treat him in the casual manner that Unity adopted. Even during the time that Diana spent alone with Hitler, which was far more than most people realise, she was always respectful of his position and her radio station agenda and addressed him accordingly with the formal 'Sie'. Only Unity had been invited to address him with the familiar 'Du', in the same way that the equally ill-fated Ernst Röhm had before her.

*   *   *

By the end of May 1937 Unity had returned to Munich, accompanied – or joined soon after – by Sydney. Unity then drove her mother to stay with the Heskeths, who had rented the frightfully grand Princess Starhemberg's villa at Ischl, once the summer residence of Emperor Franz Joseph.

According to Peter Hesketh:

> When they arrived at Ischl, Unity's car had swastika flags on it and one long banner given to her by Hitler. We had English servants and the loyal Starhemberg servants who were strongly opposed to Hitler. Muv and Unity spent a few days there. My mother took them over to Engleiten, a charming little castle not far away belonging to Lucy Goldschmidt-Rothschild, married to Baron Spiegel. When Unity was asked to sign the visitor's book, with a flourish she put a huge swastika opposite her name, Lucy picked the book up, hugged it and said something to the effect that it was her first swastika.

The Mitford family, like Baroness Bentinck and Milly Howard-Brown, seemed quite impervious to the rising tension in Austria and continued dashing about as if they owned the place. Their constant stream of letters gave little indication of the socio-political eruption that was about to take place. Even Deborah's letters to Jessica, the supposedly committed socialist, reflected little in the way of social or political conflict:

> Yesterday [2 June 1937] we went to stay with Janos [von Almasy] and Baby [Countess Palffy-Erdödy] took us in her car. We found Mrs Janos in a great state because Janos had been taken off by the gendarmes because he was thought to be plotting for the Nazis and the soldiers had been through all his papers and writing desk and they had found the picture of Bobo [Unity] and H [Hitler] and were in a state about it.

The Mitford party did not seem particularly concerned by the incarceration of their host; no mention was ever made concerning the outcome of this charade, or of why the police or the army should suddenly become suspicious of a man who had already been flying a swastika flag over his house for some time. One can only assume that the Mitfords knew that poor Countess Almasy's husband was being somewhat less than truthful with his wife concerning his relationship with Unity and decided the best course of action was to politely change the subject.

On 13 June Deborah wrote Jessica another letter with no mention of Janos or what may or may not have happened to him:

> There is a wonderful band led by the most wonderful and sweet man called Barnabas von Geczy and they play at a delicious café called the Luitpold. Dear, there is a man in that band who simply makes your hair stand on end to look at him. We don't know his name but he plays the violin the second from the right so that is what we've called him. He is the personification of my type – awfully like Franchot Tone and he sometimes makes the most fascinating faces like Maurice Chevalier ... if it hadn't been for Geczy and the second from the right I should have longed to go ages ago. I think Munich is no end nice all the same. If I had to live anywhere abroad I should certainly live here.

What was so remarkable about these letters was that they were – and are – so unremarkable, yet the Mitford sisters considered them worthy of preservation. Indeed, countless writers have referred to them, and in some strange and bizarre manner the letters have contributed to the girls' elevation to iconic social and literary status. Sometimes their superficiality and humour appears to be a concerted effort to avoid their Nazi sympathies being taken seriously.

A typical case in point is a letter from Deborah to Jessica concerning their parents:

Everyone does the same old things here. Farve goes off to
The Lady and the House of Lords and Muv paints chairs and
reads books called things like 'Stalin: My Father' or 'Mussolini:
The Man' or 'Hitler: My Brother's Uncle' or 'I was in Spain' or
'The Jews – By One Who Knows Them' etc. etc. etc. I haven't
read a book for eight months now …

Other letters, while avoiding specific intimate details concerning
Unity's relationships and sexual adventures, certainly gave strong
hints. In the middle of July 1937, Jessica announced that she was 'in
pig' and Unity, who appeared genuinely pleased to hear her news,
announced her own breeding plan which was apparently to include
having 'eight darling little bastards, all with different fathers'. Lord
Redesdale, who had obviously read the letter, reacted to this information by drafting a new will disinheriting any illegitimate grand-
children he might be presented with.

Her statement and her father's reaction gave a rather clear indication of Unity's sexual habits and the fact that she made no attempt
to hide them, even from her own father. In fact, quite the opposite;
Unity appeared to be flaunting her unconventional behaviour, Mitford letters being anything but private.

Unity also gave a good indication of her provocative behaviour
and lack of inhibitions, casually informing Jessica, 'The other day
when it was boiling hot I found a secluded spot in the Englischer
Garten where I took off all my clothes and sunbathed, luckily no-one
came along.' While nudity had become a national pastime during
the Weimar days, such things were far less acceptable under the Nazi
regime, particularly in the middle of an urban park, thus leading one
to believe that Unity's behaviour was more of a celebration of the
protection afforded by her privileged position, than a desire for an
all-over tan. Doubtless she also enjoyed a degree of erotic excitement
from the possibility of being observed.

But, as with all family archives, as much was revealed by the Mitford girls' choice *not* to publish certain letters, as by the contents

of those that were made available for public reading. Many years later Deborah – by then Dowager Duchess of Devonshire – would shrewdly admit, 'There's bound to be some things which you don't want everyone to read … but I don't think that it affected the story at all.'

*　　*　　*

While she continued to roar round Europe in her new motorcar, staying in grand hotels and even grander houses, for Unity, as for Hitler, the preferred location for their meetings (apart from his apartment, which was relatively modest by fascist dictator standards) remained the Osteria Bavaria; even when she had to share his company with 'the Osteria circle'. This group included the photographer and author Heinrich Hoffmann; Adolf Wagner, the gauleiter of Munich; Martin Bormann, head of the party chancellery and Hitler's private secretary, chief aide and adjutant; Otto Dietrich, chief press officer and confidant; Julius Schaub, another chief aide and adjutant; Hitler's doctor Theodor Morell; Dr Karl Brandt, another of Hitler's physicians who headed the euthanasia program and was involved in criminal human experiments and abortions; and Wilhelm Brückner, another chief adjutant and bodyguard.

But none of these members of Hitler's dining club ever seemed particularly welcoming, as Unity recounted in yet another letter to Diana:

> I had lunch with the Führer in the Ost the day before the Duce came … the little Doktor [Goebbels] was there. We had rather a stormy scene as all of them, except the Führer, set on me because I said I didn't like Musso, and bullied me till I was almost in tears, it was dreadful. I thought I wouldn't be able to prevent myself crying. However, the Führer took my part (without of course saying anything against Musso) and he was perfectly sweet. Of course the one that led the attack was Dr Brandt.

But there were also contradictory reports concerning the reactions to Unity's presence. Bella Fromm, diplomatic columnist of the *Vossische Zeitung* before she fled to America, claimed, 'Unity is most unpopular with the Nazis. Ribbentrop dislikes her. Hess is jealous and suspicious.' But, apparently, when confronted with this statement Frau Hess could not recollect her husband having any such reaction of jealousy and suspicion and thought it most improbable.

Albert Speer, an occasional participant and observer remembered:

> For those close to Hitler [she] was a nuisance. Schaub was angry that she was coming again. It was amazing that someone not German was around Hitler and could listen to details of party politics and far-ranging policy ... Her German was good enough to make herself understood. She was never bored and never boring. Her features were those of a woman with some intelligence, thinking in her own way, not the type of Eva Braun who had no serious interests.

In fact, Hitler rarely encouraged Eva to accompany him personally to any public events, even lunch, at which any of his staff were present, except at the Berghof. Though it has to be said, there is no evidence that Eva was particularly interested in politics or the working of the party. Judging from the considerable amount of surviving home-movie footage she was extremely extrovert and spent her happiest times fooling around with 'Wolfie' and their dogs or her numerous girlfriends.

★   ★   ★

While Unity's obsession with Hitler continued to develop, her car had given her a great degree of independent mobility which she obviously enjoyed exploiting.

David Pryce-Jones claimed that in August 1937:

Unity had completed another of her mammoth drives, to Bernstein. The next ten days of summer slipped idly by. Tom was there as from Friday onwards. So were Marie-Eugenie Zichy, Kisebb, Baby and Jimmy Erdödy. Herr Pohl, the factor on the estate, was [according to her friend Mary] 'misguided enough' to take the Bernstein party to a service in the Szombathely synagogue.

What Mary does not point out is that Janos, despite being pro-Nazi and politically anti-Semitic, was quite prepared to employ Jews and fascinated by the more mystical, messianic and Kabbalistic branches of the faith. It also seems likely that Pohl, like many of the Austrian and Hungarian estate factors, was Jewish and that Janos had persuaded him to take them to the service, either to increase their understanding of the faith or in an attempt to manipulate Unity. If that had indeed been his intention, it backfired quite dramatically.

First Unity had refused to attend the service and then she was publicly abusive towards Pohl. The result was that she had an electrifying row with Janos and threatened to report his actions to her Führer. She rather accurately predicted that Hitler would be occupying Janos' miserable little country in the very near future, when he would doubtless have him and all his Jews slaughtered. Realising that he had overshot the mark, Janos arranged for Jimmy Erdödy to drive Unity into Vienna to cheer her up with some shopping and an appointment at the hairdresser's. But somehow Unity managed to make contact with a local SA Stormführer who, much to Janos' horror, turned up at the schloss the following day. Unity then insisted on spending the morning incarcerated with him in the library.

The good-looking, young SA Stormführer was called Lajos Mezriczky. It is unlikely that he had ever actually met Hitler personally, so he must have found it extremely exciting to be in the presence of someone who had spent so much time with the Führer. 'They were closeted together all morning.'[7]

After he had left, Unity explained in detail to the increasingly terrified Janos how much she had enjoyed Mezriczky's company and gave him a full account of the young Stormführer's planned *Fememord*. This was the term the SA used for the part of their initiation that consisted of the assassination of a Jew or a Communist or another political opponent. Janos could feel his necromantic power ebbing, but even worse was his realisation of its transference to Unity.

The Kohfidisch and Bernstein crowd of fellow houseguests, including Baroness Bentinck, despite having initially teased Unity about her worship of Hitler, had been desperate to know what he was *really* like. They now took to teasing the unhappy Janos concerning exactly what had taken place in the library that morning between Unity and her young Storm and what Janos' punishment might be. There was also endless speculation concerning Unity's relationship with Hitler and her various pet Storms, particularly the ones with whom she had been connected publicly; most of whom it seems likely she had also been involved with sexually.

A rather typical example was Stabschef Viktor Lutze, who had become the leader of the SA after Röhm had been murdered. Unity even joked about his glass eye, which she insisted he used to remove before they had sex.

There was evidence that she had also sought advice concerning contraception from Dr Beckett Overy, the family gynaecologist whose name, having been obviously personalised by the Mitford girls, made it somewhat difficult to take the evidence seriously. But there can be no doubt that Unity had an extremely active sex life. Regardless of claims to the contrary.

*　　*　　*

In September 1937 Diana and Unity again visited the Nuremberg Nazi Rally, once more accompanied by their brother. By now a sophisticated hospitality service had been developed to attract foreigners and their welcome currency. Anne de Courcy described it with somewhat disturbing enthusiasm. 'The cheerful, bustling friendliness, the optimism and enthusiasm of the people, and the ritualistic, compelling drama of the rally itself, affected Tom deeply.' Apparently, Tom Mitford was so impressed by the event that shortly after his return to England he felt obliged to join the BUF.

As with the rest of the Mitfords, there was no evidence of him finding fault with the Nazis' use of concentration camps or their policies on euthanasia, racial cleansing or selective breeding, or the use of extreme violence to achieve social and political ambitions.

The *Daily Express* and the *News Chronicle* reported the presence of Diana, Unity and Tom at the rally, while one of the paper's readers voiced a question that was becoming of increasing concern to many Britons. 'Once more members of the Mitford family are attending the Nazi Congress at Nuremberg. Why are Lord Redesdale and his children so interested? Why are they Britain's Fascist Family Number One?'

Doubtless Lord Redesdale, like many of his class, was motivated by the ever-present socialist threat that he would continue to blame for his declining fortune, a decline that was beginning to make it increasingly difficult for the Mitfords to maintain both their country estate and appropriate town house. While the gradually increasing independence of his offspring, which reduced the size of the resident family, could have been used as an excuse for his decision to sell Swinbrook and the estate in 1936, its loss would have been a huge blow to his ego as well as his family's social status. However, its replacement with a private fiefdom would have gone some way to repairing his loss.

In 1938 one of Lord Redesdale's chums at the Marlborough Club asked him if he was interested in buying an island on the west coast of Scotland, at the mouth of Loch Na Keal, next to Mull. It was called Inch Kenneth and David bought it almost immediately. One mile long and half a mile wide it is virtually treeless but wildly beautiful with magnificent views of its better-known sister. Sheltering amongst the low hills and distant hillocks, known locally as 'humpies', was a rather plain, pretentiously castellated and large four-storey mansion. There was also a small cottage and the ruins of a medieval chapel; something that proved extremely useful for Unity's subsequent, somewhat theatrical, religious exploration.

★   ★   ★

Despite Unity's fight with Janos, Milly Howard-Brown confirmed that their relationship continued, though not, it was said, without a good deal of ill humour on her part.

In October, after an exchange of angry letters and telegrams, Janos arrived in Munich, accompanied by Baby Erdödy and Kisebb. It appears his conciliatory initiative worked, as they were soon plunged into the familiar social round of the Luitpold, the Regina Bar, the Osteria, Walterspiel, Platzl's and Janos' favourite restaurant, the Franziskaner (still unchanged today).

Baroness Redwitz gave a cocktail party that was attended by Iris Mountbatten while Kisebb entertained them with his hilarious drunken behaviour. The following day he and Janos returned to Bernstein while Unity drove by herself to Stuttgart, where another of Janos' chums lived, a gifted amateur pianist called Hubertus Giesen, or Hubsie. He was a close and personal friend of Janos', and his particularly lewd sense of humour was said to have appealed to Unity.

There were unconfirmed though highly likely stories of Unity having enjoyed sex with Hubsie; in the full knowledge that Janos knew where she was and what she was doing. Her enjoyment would have been enhanced by his resulting jealousy. Her pleasure may also have been supplemented by Hubsie's skill as a pianist, for in the lulls between their carnal activities, he was apparently in the habit of drinking cocktails and playing the piano. Unity was particularly impressed by his interpretation of Wagner, and it would have taken very little pressure on his part for her to be persuaded to sing along to those movements whose librettos she had learnt by heart. Never having sung before, or not with any serious intent, Unity would have surprised them both with her considerable natural talent, and what she had initially entered into for fun soon became an extremely satisfying devotion. Hubsie even gave her some records, probably by Bruno Walter, the legendary German-born American conductor, so that she could practice when she got home. 'Perhaps you can sing for your Führer. I'm sure he would be enchanted.'

And sing for him she must have done, at some point; presumably when they were alone, because there was no record of her singing for him in public. But Hitler certainly developed a genuine appreciation of her talent and was indeed enchanted. He even insisted that she accepted his offer of singing lessons with Juan Raventos, the Spanish tenor who was adamant that Unity had the most beautiful voice and was quite capable of singing the part of Elsa in *Lohengrin*, 'till her heart's content.'

Now Adolf Hitler not only had his own personal Valkyrie, but a Valkyrie who could sing Wagner and also fulfil his sexual fantasies. All Unity had to do now was to fulfil his necromantic ambitions.

*　　*　　*

Meanwhile, both Bavaria and Austria remained as popular as ever for the English whose social equivalents continued to offer them the type of feudal hospitality that it had become increasingly difficult to find in Britain.

Of particular notoriety in the *right* social and political circles were the fun-loving Wrede twins, Princesses Carmen and Edda. The Wrede family's ancestral home, Schloss Fantaisie, was particularly popular amongst the English, not only because it was as fantastic as its name suggested, but also because it was situated only 5 kilometres from Bayreuth.

Unity's special relationship with Hitler continued to grant her a privileged position amongst many of the German and Austrian aristocracy. Princess Carmen remained particularly impressed:

> Unity's *Heil Hitler* was very graceful, she had aplomb and self-confidence, she knew her own worth. She was to be met in

Berlin at the Adlon or the Kaiserhof, or in Munich at the Vier-jahreszeiten [Four Seasons], or at any official reception. Once we had supper in the cellar of the Vierjahreszeiten and Hitler was giving a big speech in the Hofbräu, which was being relayed on the radio. We heard how the Führer had finished and the meeting was breaking up and he was leaving for Berlin. Unity said, 'Quick, come and stand in the street opposite, we can line up as he passes'. The huge Mercedes came, with Hitler standing up in it, and Unity shrieked, '*Mein Führer*'! He stopped for her, he took her two hands in his, and said, 'Unity what are you doing here?' She answered, 'Tonight I'm going to Berlin'. He said, '*Melden Sie sich gleich*, let me know as soon as you're there'. And she took the night train. It was 1937.

In Berlin, my sister and I lived in the Rauchstrasse, and Unity was there often ... Unity went with each big Nazi, c'était frère et cochon. Her snobbery was to know everyone.

This seemed rather hypocritical as, according to Gaby's French 'social-secretary', Marie-France Railey, Carmen's facility for snob-bism and enjoyment of a healthy sexual appetite certainly appeared to lack little in comparison with Unity's, while her bitchiness was not dissimilar to Nancy Mitford's. Unity, Diana, Sigi von Laffert, Hella Khevenhüller, were too fine, really too aristocratic for him (Hitler). Eva Braun was his social level.

The princess, who had become aware that Unity 'liked her lovers in jackboots', would also gain intimate knowledge of the previously Jewish-owned Munich apartment that Hitler would eventually *arrange* for Unity's use. Apparently it consisted of 'a drawing room, a bedroom and a little spare room':

> Her furniture was Deutsche Werkstätte style ... behind her bed two big flags with swastikas crossed over, and their ends folded down on the pillows like drapes ... on her bed-side table stood Hitler's photo, with the lips and eyes painted in. 'I did that',

she [Unity] said, 'because it looks so nice'. In the sitting room she had a writing table, and in one of its drawers a revolver, a little silvered revolver, and she took it out and waved it around, saying, 'When I'm obliged to quit Germany I will kill myself'.

Although it was undoubtedly the necromantic Janos who had originally introduced Unity to the mystical attractions of death as an altered state rather than a source of tragedy, it was Hitler himself who would eventually convince Unity of the part her death must play in their relationship; as it was only in death that she could fulfil her true role as his Valkyrie.

7

RIDE OF THE VALKYRIE

1938–39

> While I thought that I was learning how to live,
> I have in fact been learning how to die
>
> *Leonardo da Vinci*

With war looming on the horizon and increasing evidence of appalling human rights abuses emerging from Germany, pro-Nazi, pro-fascist and anti-Semitic organisations continued to flourish in Britain. They included the British Union of Fascists, the Nordic League (formerly the White Knights of Britain), the Anglo-German Fellowship, the Link, English Array, the Imperial Fascist League, the National Socialist League, the British Council Against European Commitments, the British People's Party, the Right Club and the National Association, amongst others.

The likes of Lord Redesdale, Lord Brocket, the Duke of Buccleuch, the Duke of Westminster, Sir Arnold Wilson MP, Ernest Tennant (of the AGF), Arthur Bryant, Henry Drummond Wolff and Lord Aberconway still wended their way to Munich and Berlin, like so many commercial travellers, selling appeasement.

But, according to Martin Pugh, the attractions of appeasement were not always entirely moral or political: 'Lord Brocket reminded Chamberlain that "middle and upper class people here see no hope for the future owing to the appalling taxation which a long war makes necessary".'

Rothermere continued to contradict himself: he maintained his personal enthusiasm for Hitler and yet claimed that he could no longer support the BUF due to their unacceptable anti-Semitism. This situation was doubtless affected by the withdrawal of advertising by Jewish companies following pro-BUF and Nazi articles in his newspapers.

Meanwhile, Oswald Mosley was reinvigorating his party's membership by pushing hard for appeasement. While suggesting a whole package of concessions to Germany, he seduced many English by reminding them of the losses they had endured in the Great War and the moral responsibility of sending the following generation to die in yet another war 'to come to the aid of small nations'.

But Mosley still insisted on keeping his party's anti-Semitism alive. At an indoor rally at Earls Court on 16 July 1939, attended by 20,000 people, he suggested that the Jews would be responsible for the impending conflict: 'We fight for Britain, yes, but a million Britons shall never die in your Jews' quarrel.'

By September 1939 the British government had admitted that some 70,000 Jewish refugees had arrived in the United Kingdom; Mosley tried to capitalise on this situation but it was too late. For the majority of English people, what was going on in Germany was unacceptable.

*   *   *

Five months before Britain declared war on Germany, Unity wrote to Diana:

> I had lunch with the Führer on Sunday and Monday, and he asked me to send you viele Grüsse [many greetings]. Both days

he was in his very sweetest mood, particularly on Monday, he held my hand most of the time and looked sweet and said 'Child!' in his sympathetic way because he was so sorry about England and Germany being such enemies. However he said nothing but wonderful things about England and he completely gave me faith again that it will all come right in the end.

Unfortunately, Hitler's march into Prague on 15 March was in fact an invasion of Czechoslovakia rather than the re-occupation of those areas of the country (the Sudetenland) he considered to be rightfully the property of Germany, and thus violated the Munich Agreement (drawn up in 1938 and signed in 1939), in effect bringing all efforts of appeasement to an end.

Considering how close Britain was to war with Germany and how much time Unity spent in the company of Hitler and the various heads of the Nazi Party, the subsequent lack of attention paid to her by the British authorities was puzzling. This was probably due to the fact that Britain did not really have a properly organised intelligence service, even at this late hour. For foreign intelligence they relied largely on their somewhat naïve diplomatic service under Foreign Office control.

According to Foreign Office documents, after Hitler's invasion of Austria, Donald Gainer was replaced as consul at the Munich consulate by J.E.M. Carvell, who on 27 March 1939 sent a despatch to Sir George Ogilvie-Forbes, first secretary in the Berlin Embassy, who forwarded it to the Foreign Office:

Unity Mitford called on me today with the object of informing me that she would be resident in Munich until the autumn of the year. As I thought it likely that she would have visited Herr Hitler while she was in Munich, I engaged her in conversation and learnt that she had taken luncheon with him on the day of his arrival in Munich and also on the following day. Miss Mitford told me that Herr Hitler had said that he was confident that

friendship between Germany and Great Britain was still possible
… (She) then volunteered the statement that Herr Hitler considered Italo-German friendship as unnatural and that he did not
expect the Berlin-Rome Axis to last.

Carvell remained mystified why Unity appeared so sanguine about
the forthcoming war, believing that she must have been aware of
how inevitable conflict now was. Of course, there was no way that
he could have known that for Unity, having decided on a course of
action for herself, a war was really of little importance.

Unity was also still enjoying her Eucharistic activities with her
enthusiastic group of young Storms, who were an additional incentive for remaining both mortal and in Germany, for she had yet to
be entirely convinced their services would be replaced in Valhalla.
Though, ever since her Venetian adventure, Janos and his skilful use
of the silk noose had become, at least as far as Unity was concerned,
an addictive alternative.

So, soon after her meeting with Consul Carvell, she set off for
Austria once again, this time via Budapest, where she paused briefly
for a frantic interlude in the company of her lover's entourage.

Apparently, she first 'stopped at Devecser in the hopes of leaving
Boy (her dog) in the care of Countess Tommy Esterhazy'[1]. But the
countess was unable or unwilling to keep the animal and admitted
to being far more interested in Unity's love life than her dog. 'The
"on dit" was still, did she or did she not sleep with Hitler? The fact
of gossiping about it gave her a cachet.'

David Pryce-Jones recounted the social extravagance of the society comprising Budapest's 'best and brightest' among which Unity
moved in a manner reminiscent of those halcyon days when Europe
still belonged to the aristocracy. Unity was immediately:

Whirled into the social round with Marie-Eugenie and Imre Zichy,
with Anty and Erzsi Szapary, Baroness 'Gaby' Bentinck, 'Millie'
Howard-Brown, Count Strachwitz, Count Csekonics, Baby

Erdödy in a new flat, Jimmy and Lady Patricia Russell together, lunch with the Malagollas at the Italian Legation, meals at the smartest restaurants like Krist and Ludlab, late-night drinks at the Ritz with the Duke and Duchess of Mecklenburg, a call on Countess Wenckheim, a garden party with Countess Nora Hadik and her sister, a Luise Rainer film, Dramatic School, in a cinema in Vaci utca, the whole spiced with the hairdresser, Countess Julia Apponyi's shop, new blouses, even a fur coat made to measure, and of course Boy to be exercised on St Margaret's Island on the Danube.

After indulging herself in the city's privileged extravagance, Unity retired to the Almasy castle where she was welcomed by Janos and Marie. She spent blissful days locked away from the spring storms before the library fire or with Janos in the intimacy of his study. 'On 20 April they walked down to the village for her to send a telegram to Hitler. It was his 50th birthday.'[2]

According to Gaby Bentinck, Janos had mixed emotions concerning Unity's departure. While he greatly enjoyed her company, both physically and emotionally, her addiction to 'gaspers', was extremely stressful, as Janos was fully aware of the lethal danger involved in such sexual practices; though he had to admit that he found the empowerment it conferred on him exceptionally arousing.

On the way back to Munich, Unity spent a night in Vienna at the Wintzinger Hotel. Then, after a brief stay, she set off to meet with Hitler in Berlin. Two weeks later, she was in a state of considerable excitement as for the first and, as it proved, only time she was invited by her beloved Führer to visit the Berghof, his mountain retreat.

It was everything that Unity could have hoped for. The afternoon was spent walking and taking tea in the Tea House. But while there was rather a lot of coming and going of visitors and messengers, she soon realised Eva Braun was nowhere to be seen and thus it was even possible for them to spend some time alone together.

Unity subsequently revealed to Gaby Bentinck that she was also astonished to discover that her Führer was not only fully aware of the fact that she had visited Venice with Janos Almasy but also that she had taken him as her lover. Even more surprising was his opinion of Janos as an intelligent man and a good Nazi but most of all his knowledge of Almasy's necromancy. Indeed, Unity's fear that Hitler may have been jealous had soon been dispelled by his desire, not for details of their sexual adventures, but for confirmation of Janos' encouragement of Unity to take her own life.

He had been particularly delighted by Janos' insistence that unless she did so, Unity could not hope to fulfil her true destiny as Hitler's Valkyrie. For it was only there, on the other side, that her fantasy could become reality; once again illustrating the fact that Hitler and Unity shared a propensity for fantasy that was way beyond most mortals' wildest imagination.

Not only was her Führer allowing her to worship him; now he was offering her the honour of dying for him. For Unity it was to be both the supreme sacrifice and the ultimate experience. For Hitler it was the quintessential fulfilment of his necromantic powers and a reminder that he gained his obscene gratification not from killing, but from having others kill on his behalf; particularly themselves.

*   *   *

On her return to Munich, Unity discovered that Hitler had instructed his office, under the direction of Rudolf Hess, to find an apartment for her. Many Jewish-owned properties had been requisitioned in the aftermath of Kristallnacht and to her delight she was invited to choose one for herself. On 5 June she made her decision, and shared her excitement in a letter to Diana. 'At last, we found the perfect flat in Schwabing, in a modern block … it belongs to a young Jewish couple who are going abroad.'

It was said that while Unity was making plans for redecoration and furnishing, the terrified Jewish owners had still been present prior to their forcible dispossession. Witnessing their fear and despair would presumably have entertained Unity and increased the flat's attraction for her no end.

Her new address was to be Agnesstrasse 26, Flat 4, with the telephone number 372-338. The flat, together with its decoration and furnishing, were all to be paid for by the Führer. As he had only ever provided his mistresses with such a facility, it was officially accepted that Unity had fulfilled that role.

The general consensus of opinion is that Hitler was for some reason deceiving Unity by lulling her into a false sense of security, as by 23 May he had already alerted the Wehrmacht to his plans for an invasion of Poland in September. 'I doubt the possibility of a peaceful settlement with England,' he told the chiefs of the armed services. 'We must prepare ourselves for the conflict.'

One of the contributory reasons for Hitler's insistence on relocating Unity at this time concerned his rift with Putzi Hanfstaengl, with whose sister, Erna, Unity had been staying while her new flat was being refurbished. Due to the fact that she was running short of money, Erna had persuaded Unity to deliver a letter to Hitler in which she asked for the return of money that her brother had lent to the party. Predictably, Hitler reacted to the letter with one of his incandescent 'piggy-fits' and insisted Unity left Erna's immediately and moved into her new apartment.

However, his intentions were often in conflict with his actions, as Hitler was a man of endless contradictions. While he lusted after the power and glory of controlling a war, he would doubtless have preferred to go to war with Britain as an ally rather than an adversary. In the case of Unity there was an added complication: he yearned for the puissance to cause her to take her own life in fulfilment of their fantasies so she could wait for him 'on the other side', yet was undecided as to exactly when this should take place as he was still enjoying her mortal company.

Britain, of course, would display similar indecisions and contradictions by claiming to have gone to war in protection of Poland, while not lifting a hand in her defence for some seven months; by which time, the Reich controlled the west of the country including the prized Danzig, while Soviet Russia had taken the east.

Despite the appalling conflict, Hitler managed to retain his sense of humour, which Unity still managed to appreciate. 'In a letter to Diana of 15 May she says he told her that he had made a new speed limit for the protection of German agriculture, because of a time when she and Diana had crashed into a manure cart.'[3]

Regardless of his humour, however, Unity admitted to Gaby Bentinck that the Führer's apparent aversion to killing and thus qualifying as a warrior, continued to prey on her mind. Try as she might to remain steadfast, she was regularly, if briefly, suffering from moments of self-doubt concerning Hitler's immortality and the whole basis of their transcendental relationship. If, as she still believed, Hitler *was* Odin the deity, what would be her relationship with him as a Valkyrie? How many other Valkyries would she have to share him with? Furthermore, as Odin was the god of gods, overseeing wisdom, war, battle and death as well as magic, poetry, prophesy and victory, or even if he was a marginally lesser deity such as Thor, surely he should be capable of killing her, rather than her having to do it.

Unity was all too obviously becoming less assured of her future. Even Jonathan Guinness recognised the change manifesting itself during that period, when she wrote to Diana:

> (Adolf) Wagner said to me, 'You are so silent', and Wolf took my hand and said in his wonderful voice (you know what I mean) 'The poor child is unhappy', and then turned to me, with the sweetest look in his eyes, and said: 'Child, you needn't take it so tragically'. So then, as you can imagine, I felt that none of it mattered any more, just for the moment, but I felt I could kill the Umbrella (Chamberlain).

To reassure herself, Unity increasingly relied on the services of Max, Julius, Erich and other anonymous Storms, for fierce nights of 'Sturm und Drang'.

*   *   *

Between 12 June and 7 July 1939, or thereabouts, Unity returned to England to see her parents and various other friends and relatives. With an introduction from Mosley, she also visited the gifted strategist and military historian, Major-General J.F.C. Fuller CB, CBE and DSO.

His theories and practice in the use and strategy of mechanised armour were to have a profound influence on the British Army, though it was the Wehrmacht, where his tactics became known as 'Blitzkrieg', who would prove to be his greatest proponents. Fuller was also the inventor of 'artificial moonlight', a means by which searchlights were used to facilitate night attacks. But it was his role as a fascist, mystic, occultist, disciple of Aleister Crowley, guest of Adolf Hitler and one of Mosley's closest allies that attracted Unity, for she desperately needed divine reassurance from a man whose intelligence and metaphysical beliefs she respected and with whom she had no sexual agenda.

Major-General Fuller was the perfect choice, for according to Kathleen Atkins he was under no doubt that Hitler was indeed an earthly manifestation of Odin and that the same higher forces that had elevated him to that position had chosen Unity as Hitler's own personal Valkyrie.

Shortly before she had arrived back in England, Lady Redesdale had also been busy reassuring Unity, while illustrating her political commitment and determination to keep 'The Mitford Girls' in the public spotlight and canvas support for the Nazis by writing an article 'published on 10 June, for the *Daily Sketch*, arguing that National Socialism eliminated class warfare, raised living standards and strengthened religion, unlike its deadly opponent, Bolshevism'.[4]

As Unity was about to return to Germany, Mabel, the Redesdales' parlour maid made an astonishingly profound statement. It was also one of the only instances where any of the Mitford biographers have seen fit to give any of the staff an independent voice while failing to award her the respect of a surname:

> Unity had pictures of Hitler; she used to boast about meeting him and all of them. She was dead against the Jews. I said goodbye to her outside Rutland Gate, she was just going away the summer the war started, and she went and put her arms round me, Goodbye, she said, and don't hate Hitler so much, you'll come in with Germany, you'll see.

It was not the rarity of such comment, or the equally rare identification of any of their many servants (apart from nannies and governesses) by name, that justified its inclusion, but her subsequent statement. 'Then I prayed, kneeling upstairs in my little kitchen, "Please God will you let Russia help us" and it came out that way.' So saying, Mabel displayed a remarkable political awareness and wisdom.

*   *   *

Diana, who was still spending a considerable amount of time in Germany, had returned home in time for Mosley's 'last hurrah': the 'demonstration for peace' in the Earls Court Exhibition Hall on 16 July. Anne de Courcy recorded:

> The backcloth to the platform was, as usual, a huge Union Jack; as Mosley marched up to the platform many of the 20,000-strong crowd gave the fascist salute … speaking for 2 hours, as usual without notes, Mosley gave a 'virtuoso' performance that played on what he held to be his despairing longing for 'peace'. His peroration roused the crowd to a delirium of hope as he [who had obviously heeded Mabel's advice] urged that Hitler should be allowed unrestrainedly to go east, 'and then he would not want to fight Britain'.

According to Mary Lovell:

> Tom [Mitford also] attended Mosley's huge 'peace rally' at Earl's Court. Here, Tom, by now an officer in the Territorials, greeted his brother-in-law with the Fascist salute as he walked past them. The newspapers took it amiss that a serving officer in His Majesty's Forces should behave like this. Tom's commanding officer was interviewed by reporters, who [according to Mary Lovell] were clearly hoping to 'stir up trouble', but the colonel merely told them he wasn't going to be deprived of one of his best officers over the matter of a salute.

After Hitler had invited Unity and Diana to Bayreuth again, for the last time, Diana was soon on her way back to Germany, leaving her with little time to support her husband or his political ambitions, let alone her children. It was also at Bayreuth that Gerhard Engel (Hitler's adjutant) reported a statement by Hitler that displayed a far greater appreciation of the English character than the English could display themselves, or certainly those for whom fascism held any attraction. He pointed out the main and rather simplistic reason why Mosley's seduction of the English would never be successfully requited:

> At Wahnfried [Wagner's house in Bayreuth] we would sit down 10 or 12 at table, with Frau Winifred and her daughters. In 1938 and 1939 Unity was there with her sister Diana, and very interesting conversations developed about England and the English fascist movement. At one lunch in particular Lady Mosley launched out into optimism about the movement's future. She believed that anti-Semitism had at last taken firm hold. Not for the first time, Hitler answered that fascism did not lie in the English character and that although Mosley might be a fine person and had grasped the weakness of English politics, he could not seduce a whole nation.

This statement appeared to consist of two opinions, the latter concerning Mosley's lack of political commitment in his refusal to curtail his womanising and other recreational activities. One suspected that it was only out of respect for Diana that Hitler made any attempt to disguise his impatience and lack of respect for Mosley. The former opinion concerned the reason *why* the English did not adopt fascism. This could have been to do with the fact that they would have had to abolish the monarchy together with the entire courtly process of privilege, power and snobbery and the aforementioned 600-year history of democracy. The threat of a communist revolution was not sufficiently immediate to justify such sacrifice. Finally, there was the English sense of humour, which Hitler had also admitted would have made the seizure of power by the likes of Göring in his music-hall uniform extremely difficult.

Unfortunately, for the future of both the Mitfords' and the Mosleys' political ambitions, embracing anti-Semitism would do little to increase the attraction of fascism in England. Lady Diana Mosley was also almost certainly making an assessment based on the fervour of her and, particularly, her sister's extreme anti-Semitism. There can have been no doubt that Unity considered:

> Streicher's act in making Jews crop grass with their teeth amusing and that she approved when a group of Jews were taken to an island in the Danube and left there to starve. She told a friend, Mary Ormsby Gore, how an old Jewess, heavily laden, had approached her in the street and asked the way to the railway station. She deliberately sent her in the opposite direction and thought it an amusing thing to have done[5].

But although many English people did not like Jews, or 'wogs', 'wops' and 'diddicoys' (pejoratives still in common usage at the time) for that matter, the Reich's exterminatory policies were, for most English, more than a step too far; even when given the quasi-scientific title of 'racial hygiene'. Furthermore, the adoption of forced sterilisation for alcoholics would have been unacceptable for the simple reason that it would have decimated the English upper classes.

A day before they were due to leave Bayreuth the sisters lunched with Hitler, and Diana remembered that he told them he believed England was determined to go to war. When they were alone together after luncheon, Unity again told Diana that if war were to be declared between England and Germany, she would shoot herself. Diana refused to take her threat seriously, considering it quite pointless as she was quite convinced that Britain would eventually be forced into some kind of capitulation and Mosley would assume the role of chancellor. While it was said that the Redesdales were growing more and more concerned about what would happen to Unity if and when war was declared, they did not seem sufficiently concerned to try and *force* her to return home. Presumably they were also still convinced of the victorious inevitability of fascism.

★   ★   ★

On 2 August, Hitler spoke to the sisters once again of the war that he claimed to be so determined to avoid and the British so determined to enter into. Unity's diary quoted him as telling them, 'If there is no miracle I see the outlook as very black. And I do not believe in miracles.' Yet again Unity told Diana that she would kill herself if there was war; yet again Diana told her not to be so ridiculous. If she had known more about her sister's mystical beliefs she may have tried harder to talk her out of it, which was probably what Unity was hoping for, but Unity remained inhibited by the risk of exposing herself to Diana's ridicule.

According to Jonathan Guinness and Unity's diaries, 'she saw Hitler on 4 and 5 August, both times at the Osteria; on the fourth, he was "fascinating about his new buildings", on the 5th he was "sweet"'. What she would later admit to Kathleen Atkins was that while they were having lunch and Hitler's *stammtisch* (reserved table) friends were talking amongst themselves, the Führer's sweetness consisted of him quietly announcing to her that their mortal relationship was coming to an end.

He would almost certainly have warned her of the inevitability of the impending war, how he would now need to spend more time in Berlin and the impossibility of spending time with her. When she asked how long he thought the war would last, he reminded her of her pledge to terminate her mortal existence and wait for him on the other side, where time did not exist. And while Unity's eyes silently filled with tears, she whispered the words from her beloved Milton: 'Death is the golden key that opens the palace of eternity.' Hitler took her hands in his and gave her one of his 'loveable smiles' before rising to his feet and announcing loudly, 'Now I have work to do. Tyrants' work', and while everyone roared with laughter, he strode out of the restaurant with his entourage.

It was some time before it sunk in that this was probably also to be the last time they would meet as mortals. Unity remained seated at the table for some time, staring down at the small silver automatic pistol she had removed from her handbag and now held in her lap. She reminded herself how fitting it was for a Valkyrie to use the declaration of war as a signal for her move to the afterlife. She said later that decision had a surprisingly calming effect.

*   *   *

In order to fill the time, Unity set about decorating and furnishing her new apartment. She had even arranged the transport of various furnishings and books from Rutland Gate to Munich.

Her flat, comprising three rooms and a kitchen, was on the third and fourth floors of a three-storey block some ten years old. Its solid build prevented the transmission of any sound from other residents. Apart from the chatter of her cleaning lady who came every morning, the flat was silent, which could have contributed to Unity's feelings of isolation and abandonment, as most of Munich's foreign residents had already left or were in the process of doing so. But by 8 August Janos had arrived to help celebrate her twenty-fifth birthday by once again fulfilling her paraphilial demands while reinforcing his necromantic powers.

The following day, after lunching outside at the Osteria, Unity and Janos made contact with Max, Unity's favourite Storm, and Hubsie, her other lover who joined them for dinner in the Vier-jahreszeiten cellar. Afterwards, all four of them returned to Unity's apartment to assist her in celebrating her forthcoming adventure.

While Max returned to work, Unity's friend Rudolfine 'Rudi' Simolin came round to the flat the following morning, and after lunching at the Regina Hotel they spent the afternoon searching for furniture amongst Munich's antique shops. According to David Pryce-Jones:

> Hitler had offered her drawing-room furniture, Janos matched him by buying her a dining-room table and a set of chairs to go with it … Hubsie [then] returned home to Stuttgart, but the others dined out at Lombardi, an Italian restaurant and later occupied the box at the opera which that night Gauleiter Wagner had put at Unity's disposal … 'All the singers knew [Adolf] Wagner's box', Rudi remembers, 'so we received special bows from them'.

Surprisingly, there even appeared to be a few English left in Munich whose company Unity could enjoy. 'Debo's friend Mr Douglas Home [William – the playwright] and a … clergyman friend of his have been here for two days. I showed them round a bit and I dined with them at Walterspiel … Last night we all went, with the English Vice-Consul and his wife, to Platzl.'[6]

By now the imminence of war was becoming manifest in petrol and food shortages, obliging Unity's friends from the country to arrive bearing gifts of butter and eggs. According to Jonathan Guinness, Unity wrote to Diana:

I wish I could make out … whether there is going to be a war or not. When I heard about the (non-aggression) pact with Russia, [which briefly gave the impression that Mabel's prayers were to remain unanswered] I thought not. However, now it looks worse than ever. It's nearly three weeks since I saw W.

The frustration of not knowing how long she had on this earth was compounded by the fact that, apart from Janos (and subsequently Gaby Bentinck and Milly Howard-Brown), there was no one else to whom she was prepared to disclose her reasons for being so insistent on remaining in Munich. Even when Wolston Weld-Forester, the British consul, 'summoned' Unity and 'ordered' her to return to England, she refused, only to be informed that she would forfeit British protection if she did not leave with the few remaining British subjects. Unfortunately, the Mitfords were not good at being either 'summoned' or 'ordered', particularly by members of the diplomatic service. The consul's wife made this evident after she ran into Sydney on their return to London. 'Lady Redesdale turned up on the very first morning "demanding" to see him (Weld-Forester). She wanted to know things my husband didn't know.' And doubtless things he was not prepared to tell her, particularly in view of her ladyship's habit of treating members of the diplomatic service as extended members of her staff.

Unity's general well-being improved immensely when Janos and Rudi returned once again. Apart from the not knowing, her life remained remarkably carefree. After nights of passion, she would spend the morning at the hairdressers before meeting with Janos for lunch at the Osteria. The afternoon would be spent swimming in the lake at Seeseiten. Despite a brief moment of ill humour between Janos and Unity, Unity was feeling sufficiently mollified in the evening to cook them all a supper of scrambled eggs; a feat of domesticity that was, for a Mitford girl, quite remarkable.

Rudi and Janos apparently left the following morning to visit Hubsie in Stuttgart without Unity, who now avoided lengthy travel in case there was a declaration of war while she was driving. Instead she organised the collection of Rudi's Salzburg Festival tickets from the American Express office, leaving them for Rudi's collection at the Regina Hotel before lunching alone at the Osteria.

Not knowing if she would ever see Janos again as a mortal, she spent 20 minutes with him in the Munich Bahnhof café while he waited for a connecting train to Vienna. The fact that she did not accompany him back to Bernstein illustrated her determination to fulfil her promise.

★   ★   ★

On 23 August Hitler received word from Moscow that the non-aggression pact with Stalin had been signed during the preceding night, thus leaving him free to declare war by marching into Poland.

On 24 August, Unity happened to run into her friends the Wrede twins, who she took with her that afternoon:

… to Tutzing, a village on the Starnbergersee, to have tea with Anna Montgelas in her house, Frauenberg. Leaving at about half past six, Unity and the twins went on to Schloss Buch on the Ammersee, an estate belonging to Count Hubert Deym, who [according to Pryce-Jones] said: 'That night we had a large dinner party perhaps thirty or forty people. I'd seen Unity twice before with friends, she was an acquaintance. I was always being told about her, so I asked her out to Buch …

After dinner, Unity begged to be allowed to switch on the radio, she ran to it, there was something very important which she had to listen to, a speech by Halifax.' [The foreign secretary that night broadcast on the crisis, reiterating the government's resolve to stand by Poland in accordance with the repeated pledge to do so … Unity came back distraught.]

On 27 August Unity wrote to Diana displaying some degree of indecision:

I feel awfully cut off, since all the foreigners and even journalists left; not that I knew any of them, but the feeling of security
is gone. Tomorrow, I shall go round and see if the Consul is still
there … on thinking things over, I have done nothing else the
last few days. I thought I might disappear into the mountains in
the Tyrol perhaps, if war is declared. Of course, the other thing
seems the easiest way out, but it seems silly not to wait and see
how things turn out, it might all be over in a few weeks, like Gen.
Fuller predicts.

On the same day she also wrote to Sydney,'(I may go to the Tyrol) as
I think to stay here would make too many difficulties for everybody.'
    The next day she wrote to Diana:

Your letter of the 30th just arrived.You can't think how thrilling
it is every time I hear the letterbox click, as I always expect every
letter to be the last that will get through … in case you didn't
hear the Führer's speech, this is what he said about England:
'Again and again I have offered England friendship and, when
necessary, the closest collaboration. But love cannot be offered
from one side only, it must find a return from the other'.

Hitler had in fact offered to defend Britain's Empire in return for
assisting Germany to gain Danzig and the Polish Corridor. Britain had reminded Hitler that they were bound by treaty to defend
Poland if she were attacked.
    By 29 August, the Wrede twins had gone home, leaving Unity
'alone with her wireless'[7]. Listening to the news became, for her, a
matter of life or death. While she continued to eat out, she sched-
uled her meals around news bulletins.
    On 1 September, the seven o'clock news announced the invasion
of Poland and the fact that Danzig had been incorporated into the
Reich. Even out shopping, Unity listened to the Führer's speech on
the car radio. It was hot and sunny in Munich so Unity sunbathed

on her balcony while the (nameless) *putzfrau* came to clean her apartment and the radio replayed Hitler's speech about Danzig.

Pryce-Jones assumed Unity lunched at the Osteria Bavaria through force of habit and because she was 'unable to tear loose from haunts of the past'. But he forgets that over the years she had made many friends there, not all political or Nazi, whose company she still enjoyed. In the afternoon, having changed into a bathing suit, she lay on her balcony in the hot sun and wrote replies to letters from Diana and Janos.

It was to be her last letter to him and referred in part to his astrological calculations. It read, 'My darling … I am horrified to hear that the critical day is the 7th because I can't bear it if the crisis drags on until then. Surely, we must know what England is going to do sooner than that.' Unity's impatience was understandable, as the accuracy of Janos' prediction of whether and when Britain would declare war on Germany had now literally become a matter of life or death.

In the evening Unity slowly dressed and walked to the Vierjahreszeiten cellar where she took supper, again amongst regular acquaintances. Meanwhile, the Wehrmacht continued to 'shoot back' while advancing into Poland. Back in her apartment, she listened to the English news.

★   ★   ★

The British ultimatum to Hitler, to withdraw the German Army from Poland, was not delivered until nine o'clock on the morning of Sunday 3 September; two hours later there had still been no reply. Thus, Britain finally declared war against Germany, three days after the start of the invasion, by which time Poland, as such, no longer existed and thus there was nothing left for the British to defend other than the basis of a 'just case for war'.

That same morning 'Unity received a message that there was a telegram for her at the British consulate'[8]. Having walked round to collect it, she found her parents' confirmation that Britain had declared war on Germany that morning. Immediately she went home and replied:

> Darling Muv and Farve, I came round to the Consulate to get your telegram and hear that war has been declared. So this is to say good-bye. The Consul will kindly take this to England and send it to you. I send my best love to you all and particularly to my Boud when you write. Perhaps when this war is over, everyone will be friends again, and there will be the friendship between Germany and England which we have so hoped for. I hope you will see the Führer often when it is over. With very best love and blessings, Bobo. Fondest love to Blor. And I do hope Tom will be all right.

Her next communication was with Rudi Simolin, who remembered:

> On Saturday, Erna and I came back from the Salzburg festival. The soldiers were already mobilised, and were mobilising further ... on the Sunday morning Bobo telephoned me, just at 11 o'clock, and said there would now be a war ... I asked her what she was going to do. I would be coming into Munich from Seeseiten on Monday morning. I urged her not to do anything until then and we would think what should be done for the best. There was no need to shoot herself at all, I told her, I beseeched her to wait until we could meet ... the war might be over soon...

> On Monday I got a letter from her enclosing her keys ... in it she had written that she had to kill herself and what I ought to do with her money and possessions. I went to the flat, and it had already been sealed. They had put a seal of paper over the keyhole. And then I went to Adolf Wagner in the Kaulbachstrasse, whose house I had visited with my cousin that time a few months before. I went to ask what had happened.

While it is difficult to tell exactly how the rest of Unity's story unfolded, Mary Lovell seemed to think, 'Her next act was to go to Gauleiter Wagner's office and ask if she was to be interned as an enemy alien. He assured her that she was not and even offered to obtain some petrol for her car.' But the strain of indecision was becoming obvious and 'he was sufficiently concerned to order that she should be discreetly followed'.

His suspicions were confirmed a little while later when she returned to Wagner's office in her car, handed him a 'large, heavy envelope' and left before he had a chance to speak with her. Lovell continued:

> In it he found a suicide note saying that she was unable to bear the thought of a war between England and her beloved Germany, a sealed letter for Hitler, and her two most precious belongings: the signed framed photograph of Hitler which she took with her even when she travelled back and forth to England, and her special Party badge.

Wagner sprang into action and immediately alerted the Sicherheitsdienst (SS intelligence service). Apparently, 'Everything was set in motion to prevent misfortune. But Unity had vanished.'

In subsequent conversations with Kathleen Atkins, Unity had no difficulty recounting the details of her 'attempted suicide', though she said she had found the whole idea of dying alone to be extremely sad, 'as if one were somehow ashamed of what one were doing'. And Unity was anything but ashamed or sad. Only the waiting and indecision had threatened her resolve. Now the time had come, she was so proud and so excited that there was no room for fear. All fear had been driven from her by 'the most powerful man in the world' and the memory of her numerous 'little deaths'.

She would like to have shot herself over lunch at the Osteria, but she could not be sure that someone would not stop her before she could 'complete the job'. She needed somewhere that she would be amongst people, but not people that would recognise her. Somewhere where she could be reassuringly anonymous. She had decided on the Englischer Garten, just inside the park, a few yards from the Königinstrasse, and close to the Haus der Kunst, an art gallery that had been built under Hitler's direction.

There, after a brisk walk from the gauleiter's office she sat down on a bench in the warm sunshine and took the small pistol from her coat pocket. Unity had previously told Gaby that she wished she had asked for 'something larger. Something in black.' The tiny, chrome-plated, pearl-handled gun looked more like an ineffectual toy than an instrument of death, and as she pressed the pistol to her temple she hoped it would prove capable of taking her on the next great adventure.

As she proudly lifted her head, she found herself looking straight into the pale blue eyes of a small blond-haired child, who, while walking in the park with his mother, had been fascinated by the woman in black, sitting on a bench. The boy was dressed all in white – his shirt and shorts, even his socks and sandals, were white, radiant in the bright summer sun. The power of the beauty and innocence in the child's gaze frightened Unity as she recognised the threat to her resolve. So she closed her eyes and everything went black. Then 'someone' pulled the trigger and everything went white.

8

THE NEXT GREAT ADVENTURE

1939–48

Those who restrain their desires do so
because theirs are weak enough to be restrained
William Blake

Unity was correct in questioning the suitability of the Walther 6.35, but for its ballistic rather than its aesthetic qualifications. To kill oneself with a .25 bullet from such a small pistol requires considerable care and attention, as such a tiny projectile is easily deflected by the bone of the skull, which is what appears to have happened in this case. The generally accepted, though rather suspicious, description of the bullet that had 'entered her right temple, ploughed its way through her brain and ended up near the back of her head'[1] was somewhat questionable; had it followed this trajectory, Unity would almost certainly have died. But Unity lived; suggesting that the injury may have been considerably less serious than claimed.

The responsibility for her lack of success may also not necessarily have been entirely hers, for there is evidence to suggest that a third party had been instructed to assist her and in so doing ironically contributed to the failure of the whole enterprise. Many years later, Michael Prodger of *The Sunday Times* described it rather elegantly as 'not quite suicide, but a wished for death by another's hand'. Unity would even write to Jessica, 'You know that I got shot in the head … that paralysed my right arm and right leg.' The latter part of the statement was somewhat exaggerated unless she enjoyed quite remarkable powers of recovery. The allegation that Unity had been shot by the Germans was awarded further credibility when 'Uncle Jack (the 4th Lord Redesdale) Mitford docked in New York on the Lancastria in February 1940 and told reporters that Unity's bullet wounds were not self-inflicted, and his niece's memory was a blank about the incident.'[2]

Innocent of her necromantic commitment, Gauleiter Wagner's fear of the consequences of having to admit to failing to adequately protect Unity, even from herself, appeared to be the most obvious reason for the delay in informing Hitler of the incident and it was not until later that evening that someone bucked up sufficient courage to inform the Führer. But far from being angry he displayed quite remarkable concern for her welfare, ordering immediate treatment by the best doctors at the Chirurgische Universitäts-Klinik. This was particularly puzzling as one would have thought that it might have been in everyone's interest, both mortal and transcendental, to hasten her end. Particularly if, as was also claimed, she was at this stage still in a coma. Gaby Bentinck was told by various members of the diplomatic community that Hitler was convinced by Goebbels of the propaganda value of his actions.

There were also conspiracy theorists who suggested Unity may have been 'assisted' in her suicide attempt by either an enemy within the top echelons of the Nazi Party who objected to her privileged position, or a British agent. Certainly, her refusal to leave Germany despite the outbreak of war was causing the British government increasing embarrassment and could have been an incentive for her elimination. Perhaps more likely was the involvement of Janos

Almasy who, having already been subject to her blackmail threats and unaware that Hitler had approved of his sexual adventures with Unity, still feared for his own safety as long as she remained alive. Meanwhile, Hitler put a stop to any media speculation by ordering a media blackout and giving the event the status of a state secret.

'The clinic on the Nussbaumstrasse was part of the university medical faculty, and its excellence justified its reputation … Dr Reiser had been little older than Unity when he had to look after her. He was lecturer in surgery in the university clinic, and private assistant to Professor Magnus.'[3]

Flowers were sent by Goebbels, Ribbentrop, several gauleiters and Hitler. Some say he only visited her once, others insisted he returned on several occasions. He was also said to have spoken with Professor Magnus concerning the prospects of recovery and the possibility of extracting the bullet, but the professor seemed to think that while there was a reasonable chance of recovery, operating might endanger Unity's life and could not be guaranteed to be successful.

According to Doctor Reiser:

> We had also warned Hitler that she was not speaking. He accepted that. He went in and stayed about a quarter of an hour, and when he came out he asked those of us waiting outside in attendance whatever had we meant by telling him that she wasn't speaking. She had found her tongue with him all right. Of course we asked what she had said, and he answered, 'She would like to go back to England'. And then Hitler said he would set things in motion so that somehow she would be able to travel home.

Even this evidence is somewhat suspicious as it was of course quite unthinkable that either the doctor or the professor would have asked the Führer what he and Unity had talked about. After the war, however, they would have been free to make whatever claims they chose, including whether they personally had abandoned the Hippocratic oath. Even if they *had* asked, he would certainly not have told them how distraught Unity was about her failure to achieve his wishes. Nor about his placating her by insisting how it had obviously not been meant to be, but that she must retain her faith and accept his conviction that in the fullness of time they would meet again 'on the other side'.

Later she was said to have told Sydney that Hitler offered her a choice: accept German nationality and stay in Munich, or return to England. She said she would like to go back to England for a few weeks, then return to Munich. An arrangement that he would have known would have been quite impossible. It was also claimed that Unity made another, even less effective, attempt to take her own life by swallowing her swastika brooch, which Gauleiter Wagner had returned to her amongst her personal effects.

Of course, at this point in time the Mitfords would still have had no real idea of what had happened, though they would obviously have been aware that all was not well. Nancy wrote to Deborah, 'Tell Muv I have written to the Duchess of Aosta and asked her to find out from the "wop" consul in Munich how and where Boud is.' But on 2 October, Janos' brother Teddy apparently sent a rather veiled telegram (presumably via the American Embassy) to the Redesdales to tell them that Unity had been ill but was now recovering. The same embassy supplied further news that, 'Unity was in a surgical hospital in Munich and making a good recovery from an attempted suicide.'

As always, rumours abounded concerning Unity and her fate. On 5 November 1939, Prince Nicholas Orloff, an English-speaking White Russian radio announcer who had fled Berlin, gave an interview to the *Sunday Dispatch* stringer in Belgrade, telling him that Unity had shot herself dead, which put a stop to all the secrecy if not the speculation.

Meanwhile, the clinic was informed by the Bavarian Ministry of the Interior that Unity was to be returned to England via Switzerland, from where she would be collected by English doctors. A special railway carriage was to be prepared, in which she would be accompanied by a Sister of Mercy and the young Doctor Reiser. With the health of the patient now dramatically improved and the Sister attending to Unity's nursing requirements, there was little chance of the Doctor being required, other than in an emergency, so their trip soon qualified as a welcome interlude. But he was also about to be presented with an entertaining travelling companion, as he later recalled:

> One day a Hungarian count rang up out of the blue and said that he knew the Redesdales very well and wanted to come too. He had spoken to the Innenministerium and had been given permission to travel with us. Professor Magnus had no objection, so the count came too, which was very nice for me.

'The Count' may of course have been offering his support in the hope that he could try once again to assist Unity in crossing over to the 'other side' on a more permanent level. But, fortunately for Unity, the opportunity never presented itself. In fact, Almasy ended up spending more time alone with the Doctor than he did with Unity:

> We had this large railway carriage to ourselves, with a bed in it specially arranged for transporting the wounded … The count and I went to the dining car on the train, for he liked his food. I had the money from the Ministry of the Interior to pay expenses for myself and the count at a hotel. We came to Berne. An ambulance was waiting. Unity was transferred into it and went on to the clinic of Professor Matti.

Janos then phoned Lord Redesdale and handed the phone to Unity who plaintively asked, 'When are you going to come and get me?' It was the first they knew of her arrival in Switzerland and while they frantically sprang into action Janos offered to stay and look after Unity while Lord Redesdale and the British Government organised the travel formalities. Doctor Reiser sadly returned to Munich.

Lord Redesdale was apparently deeply concerned that Unity would be arrested on arrival in England, so he 'went to see Oliver Stanley, the Secretary of State for War to explain that she was desperately ill and he would rather she stayed in Switzerland than suffer arrest'[4]. Fortunately, Stanley was a relative of the Mitfords and a close personal friend of Oswald Mosley. It was Gaby Bentinck's opinion, or those diplomatic chums of her husband, that it had been Stanley who was responsible for exaggerating Unity's injuries. Her staying in Switzerland would of course have saved everyone a great deal of expense and inconvenience. But David was soon reassured and supplied with all the necessary documentation to enable Sydney and Debo to set off for Berne by aeroplane on 27 December, and to return on New Year's Eve with Unity, safely unchallenged. The achievement of these arrangements in just three days would have been remarkable in peacetime, but with war having only recently been declared and hostilities commenced, it was miraculous; the plans had quite obviously been given top priority by the Foreign Office.

Unfortunately, they hadn't reckoned on the attention of a zealous MI5 operative in the form of Guy Liddell, who expressed his suspicions in his diary the day before Unity's arrival in Folkestone. 'We (MI5) had no evidence to support the press allegations that she was in a serious state of health and it might well be she was brought in on a stretcher in order to avoid publicity and unpleasantness to her family.' He became particularly aggrieved when the home secretary intervened, and his suspicions appeared confirmed when, on 8 January, he recorded, 'A report on Unity Mitford has now been received from the Security Control Officers [MI5 officers who interviewed new arrivals]. Apparently there was no signs of any bullet wound.'

Liddell was also to become involved in an investigation of the Right Club, which he believed to be operating a German spy ring. However, it was obviously considered a step too far and he was soon being accused of being a double agent. The resulting investigation came up with no incriminating evidence, other than by association, but effectively ended his career.

Meanwhile, British newspapers and newsreel companies had become obsessed by the Unity Mitford story, particularly when it was 'revealed' that Unity would be brought home in her own first-class carriage, with twenty pieces of luggage in a special guard's van, at a cost to her parents of £1,600. This was at a time when a three-bedroom house cost £300 and when £5 a week, or £260 a year, was considered a good wage.

In Folkestone, which was more awash with press and security than sailors, Unity was loaded into a private ambulance and headed off towards London with car loads of reporters in hot pursuit. Press sabotage soon caused the ambulance to break down (according to Sydney, 'There is no doubt in my mind that the Press and Cinema Company [Pathe News] arranged it') and the vehicle was forced to return to Folkestone. Here the family spent the night in a small hotel while continuing to be hounded by the journalists, who constantly raised their offers of payment for a story and clutched at the smallest crumbs of information. Predictably, it was a situation that infuriated Lord Redesdale, whose refusal to comment did not last very long.

'I am not ashamed of Unity,' he roared at the *Daily Mail*. 'I have been offered £5,000 for her story. I would not take £ 25,000.' In fact, Lady Redesdale had already sold the *Daily Express* an interview on their way back through Paris.

While Unity was being carried up the steps of the Folkestone Hotel, the press even managed to get a few words from Unity herself. 'Are you pleased to be home, Miss Mitford?' someone called. 'I'm very glad to be in England, even if I'm not on your side,' she replied.

Debo later claimed that Unity had lost two stone and was all eyes and matted hair, although there was no evidence of this from photographs of her. She claimed that every jolt was agony for her. Of this there was also no evidence. Furthermore, there was no sign of the bullet wound, which may have contributed to the fact that Unity was obviously considered in insufficient danger to be taken to a major London hospital. Instead, she was driven to the Radcliffe Infirmary in Oxford, the Mitfords' power base, 'to be attended by Professor (later Sir) Hugh Cairns, one of the foremost neuro-surgeons of his day', who gave a rather vague statement that made no mention of any 'lodged bullet'[5]. 'Her general health is good and the wound from which she suffered in Germany in September and for which she was skilfully treated in Germany, has healed in a normal and satisfactory manner. After consultation it has been decided that no operation is advisable or desirable.'

Further suspicions would be raised much later when it came to light that in police reports carried out on the instructions of the Home Office in 1941, the Chief Constable of Oxford Constabulary confirmed the fact that, 'Although stress had been made on the medical aspect of the case, no full medical report had even been obtained, and it was also clear that most of the information available had been obtained second and third hand and little of it had been confirmed.'

★   ★   ★

There was no explanation as to why Unity might have spent nearly four weeks at the infirmary if she was no longer ill. Presumably it was a secure environment in which she could wait for the fuss to die down.

On 5 February 1940 Unity was moved from the Radcliffe to Old Mill Cottage, owned by Sydney, situated on the outskirts of High Wycombe. For some months afterwards the cottage was given police protection. But neither the public nor the press were happy about her apparent immunity.

The *Daily Mail* listed Unity Mitford as one of the things that were most annoying about life in wartime Britain. The *Daily Mirror* stated, 'the Mitford girl who has openly been consorting with the King's enemies (surely a treasonable offence?) goes scot-free. Why? God and the House of Lords only know.'

For some reason, despite the fact that various newspapers and politicians wanted to know why Unity was never questioned by any of the security and/or intelligence agencies, the only person to make any official investigation were the local police who, in 1941, made discreet inquiries following suggestions from the Home Office. Yet Unity was never interviewed directly, unlike Lord Redesdale, Professor Cairns of the Radcliffe Infirmary in Oxford and a certain Mrs Phillimore of Old Farm, Swinbrook, whose only qualification appeared to be that, according to the local police, she was 'a person of high social standing and worthy of confidence'.

Despite the fact that MI5 had reason to believe that Unity was soon touring round the country picking up RAF pilots and 'interrogating' them, the police insisted this was untrue. When, in October 1941, MI5 confirmed that Unity was indeed having an affair with a test pilot called John Andrews, they relocated the man from Brize Norton to Scotland and no further mention was made of the issue. Herbert Morrison, the Home Secretary, still refused to imprison Unity. This may have had something to do with the fact that his prime minister was Unity's cousin, Winston Churchill. This partisan behaviour was not particularly unusual. After the war, Winston also assisted Coco Chanel, a fully fledged Nazi agent, code-named 'Westminster', in avoiding retribution; largely as a result of his and his friend the Duke of Westminster's friendship and relationship with Coco.

While this type of situation may have had much to do with the high esteem awarded the privileged classes at the time, it may also have been because, with a few obvious exceptions, 'Military Intelligence' was still a misnomer.

In November 1940, Brian Howard, like many highly intelligent homosexuals of the day, was given a job at the Ministry of Home Security, otherwise known as MI5. When he spoke to his superior officer about a specific member of the establishment who, according to Brian, still had dangerous fascist sympathies, the officer reacted by saying, 'Don't be ridiculous, he went to Eton with me!' Such a reaction being the norm rather than the exception.

Lady Redesdale, meanwhile, remained totally convinced by the value of fascism and made no attempt to disguise her continued sympathy for Hitler, convinced that he was 'doing more for the German people than the democratic system (was) doing for England'. She also insisted on telling anyone who cared to listen, 'we shall lose the war'. But she was not alone in her opinions or her insistence on her freedom to voice them. Virtually all the leading English aristocratic fascists remained at large, presumably to avoid government embarrassment.

Forty years later, Jonathan Guinness made a particularly interesting observation concerning Unity's freedoms in his book *The House of Mitford*:

> There were protests about Unity's treatment in *The Times* and in both Houses of Parliament ... the fact was that Unity had enraged too many people. It must be remembered in particular that the Jewish community, whom she had publicly insulted, and with whose deadly enemies she was identified, were disproportionately represented in the cinema and press.

It sounded uncomfortably similar to the type of statement made by the Nazis in justification of their anti-Semitic policies, particularly when voiced by the ex-chairman of the ultra right-wing Monday Club's Immigration and Repatriation Policy Committee. Jessica Mitford described her nephew Jonathan as 'a dangerous neo-Nazi'.

Most of the British elite were said to have eventually recognised the malevolence of the Nazis, and rallied to mutate into patriotic supporters of Churchill's government and its uncompromising anti-German position; but this they did only once it became obvious that Germany was going to lose the war and that Hitler had taken against the German aristocracy (as the German aristocracy took against him).

What was left of the French aristocracy supported the fascist Vichy government while the leader of the monarchist movement, Charles Maurras, described the German invasion and suppression of the French Republic as a 'divine surprise'.

*   *   *

Contrary to Sydney's refusal to abandon her commitment to fascism and her sympathy for the Nazis, Lord Redesdale displayed unusual expediency by voicing his rapidly revised political views in the *Daily Mirror*; views that as a peer of the realm he felt it his duty to adjust, as soon as war was declared. 'By 17 March 1940, Nancy could write to Mrs Ham: "He is more violent now against Germany than anybody I know, and against any form of peace until they are well beaten."'[6] Apparently the Hun was 'filthy' again.

The Redesdales had planned to take Unity to Inch Kenneth, their island on the east coast of Scotland, but as a result of national security concerns only Lord Redesdale was given permission to go. He blamed Sydney for this, believing that had she spent less time airing her pro-Nazi views and more time currying sympathy for Unity's brain damage, there would have been no such problem. But Lady Redesdale, like Diana, was uncompromising.

It seems likely that despite the right friends and relatives in high places, it was Lord Redesdale's recanting that saved Unity, and the Mosleys' refusal to do so that guaranteed the continuation of their incarceration.

Eventually, in the spring of 1940, the tensions between the Redesdales became insurmountable and David decided to go to the island without Sydney, 'taking the under-parlour maid, Margaret Wright, as his housekeeper'[7]. She was also a trained nurse who looked after David, first at Inch Kenneth and later at Redesdale Cottage, until his death in 1958. But the Mitford girls, strong in their conviction that Margaret was committing the cardinal sin of treating them as her equals, refused to accept her.

Following the Redesdales separation, 'Sydney decided to return to Swinbrook, reasoning that everyone in the area had known Unity from childhood so she was unlikely to be attacked or harmed'[8]. The locals, she felt, also 'knew their place' and as a result were far less likely to reveal unwanted information to the press, while they would continue to treat Lady Redesdale with respect and deference, regardless of her political views. Having sold all their property in the village, Sydney decided to 'rent the old "fishing cottage" next door to the Swan Inn, for the summer and took on a Mrs Timms [the landlord's wife], as a "daily"'. Initially, Nanny Blor helped with the nursing, but when Unity's health began to improve Blor returned home to her family.

Unity now became increasingly aware of the atrocities that were taking place in Germany, yet displayed no signs of repentance, while family and friends came to believe that her atheism was being replaced by her apparently new obsession with religion. What they failed to realise was that Unity had never been an atheist; she just believed in another deity and her apparently new 'obsessional fixation on religion' was nothing more than a manifestation of her determination to continue her worship of Adolf Hitler at every opportunity in every house of god, regardless of its denomination. This was certainly the opinion of Kathleen Atkins while James Lees-Milne described her life as a 'gradually dissolving fantasy existence'.

If the priests and vicars had known to whom she was praying, they would doubtless have been considerably less welcoming. But perhaps they did know, for presumably as a result of the exorcism of necromantic influence by ecclesiastical pressure, with the assistance of Blake and Milton, the priests eventually managed to replace Hitler with 'their' God, or at least thought they had, after Unity was finally confirmed by the Bishop of Dorchester, who may or may not have noticed that she still possessed somewhat of a fixation concerning death.

With Mosley and Diana incarcerated as Nazi sympathisers under the Emergency Powers Act in 1940, there was a public outcry when, following pressure on Churchill by Tom Mitford, Mosley was moved from Brixton to join Diana in Holloway a year later. It was hardly surprising that many, including Diana, must have remained somewhat mystified as to why Unity was allowed to enjoy her freedom. Her other sisters realised that in order to assure Unity's continued avoidance of Diana's fate, they would be well advised to encourage the belief that, having turned the gun on her own head, poor sick Unity, destroyed by the bullet, had already paid the ultimate price for the error of her ways.

As Unity's health improved even further she became increasingly mobile, but while her family admitted to her being capable of taking the bus into Oxford, they were less prepared to mention the fact that she also drove a car by herself and paid visits to friends and family, as well as lovers.

It was also less well known that Unity spent some time staying at 'The Garage', the Mitfords' London house in Rutland Gate, Knightsbridge. This gave Nancy, who was living near the Regent's Park Canal and working in Heywood Hill's bookshop in Curzon Street, greater opportunity to fit Unity into her social life:

> Harvey Nichols was within walking distance, we'd lunch there and were always looking through the *Matrimonial Times* for a husband for her. We'd shriek with laughter about it … She'd ring up or pop into the shop two or three times a week at that stage, she'd be sent to spend the afternoon in the Curzon cinema … They kept her very short of money.

What they didn't shriek with laughter about was the fact that from October 1940 the main house in Knightsbridge was sequestered for homeless people, in particular the victims of German bombing raids on London. Ironically, they were mainly Jewish. This apparently upset Unity 'no end'; Nancy claiming, 'She says if she had all the money in the world, she would not ever live in the house after the Jews have had it.' Unity appears to have been persuaded by her father to be somewhat less forthright about such things.

There can of course be no doubt that Unity suffered some physical and mental incapacitation, but this seemed to have been less severe than the authorities and the public were led to believe.

It's also quite possible that it was at least partially the result of mental rather than physical trauma. Perhaps her greatest mental anguish came in fact from the sudden termination of everything that her exotic mental and physical life in Germany had comprised.

So successful was the family's determination to convince everyone that Unity was suffering from considerably more brain damage than was actually the case, that from time to time she even began to doubt her own sanity. 'Am I mad?' she once asked Nancy, who replied, 'Of course you are, darling Stonyheart, but then you always were.'

*   *   *

The Mosleys were released from detention in November 1943, and on 29 July 1944 Unity was finally granted permission to visit Inch Kenneth. Until the end of her life, she would spend her summers there.

Being almost treeless, the island possesses a wild beauty that, particularly in the winter, could generously be said to be an acquired taste. Sydney loved Inch Kenneth and visited it as often as she could. But Unity hated it. She missed the social interaction, cinemas and churches of Oxford and London, let alone all that she had left behind in Germany and Austria. Unsurprisingly, Unity failed to appreciate the seemingly constant Inch Kenneth wind and rain, prevalent even in the summer, and the company of midges and goats, which made her extremely grumpy and a trial to be with. Even getting to the island was a major challenge.

The overnight train to Oban was pleasant enough, but the crossing to Mull on the Lochinvar steamer was often 'lumpy' and uncomfortable. Then there was the 15-mile-long narrow, winding road to the coastal hamlet of Gribun, followed by the further, often extremely challenging mile of sea to be crossed in *The Puffin*, their motor launch, piloted by her ladyship's boatman, before finally arriving at the island.

The quite remarkably unattractive, white, four-storey, bow-fronted Inch Kenneth house is more reminiscent of the English Home Counties than the wild, western coast of the Scottish Highlands. And while Lady Redesdale was said to have liked to rear sheep, cattle, goats and hens between tending the garden and making her own bread, butter and cheese, life was not perhaps as primitive as one might believe; this despite the lack of telephone, mains electricity or anything other than the most basic plumbing. A resident husband and wife looked after the house and helped tend the animals, while Sydney also brought her own cook from High Wycombe and laundry was sent down to Harrods in Knightsbridge by rail, to be returned with the type of provisions not readily available in the Western Isles.

In the spring of 1944, 'Sydney, Unity and Debo, leaving behind her two small children, went up to stay with David on the island. It was not a happy visit.' David was now virtually dependent on Margaret Wright, his 'strong-minded' nurse and companion. The 'politically based antagonisms between the Redesdales'[9] erupted constantly and it was to be the last time they would be together at Inch Kenneth, David preferring to spend his time with Margaret at Redesdale Cottage in Northumberland, where his mother Clementine had spent her last years.

*　　*　　*

In 1945 a war ended in which some 60 million people had died, though there was still no record of the main perpetrator having personally taken any lives, apart from his own. For Unity, Diana, Sydney and Tom it was the end of a dream. For the latter it was also the end of his life. For having been 'unwilling' to take part in the invasion of Germany he was posted to Burma where he was shot by a sniper. But while the family all suffered from tremendous grief at his passing, it did little to unite them.

Tom was also deeply mourned by lovers of both sexes. '"Beloved, handsome Tom", Lees-Milne wrote when he heard, "who should have been married with hosts of beautiful children; Tom, caviar to the general ... but to me the most loyal and affectionate of friends. It is hell".' The core of his grief lay in the fact that Tom had been his first love at Eton. "'On Sunday eves before Chapel at five, when the toll of the bell betokened that all boys must be in their pews", Lees-Milne recorded in his diary, "he and I would, standing on the last landing of the entrance steps, out of sight of the masters in the ante-chapel and all the boys inside, passionately embrace, lips to lips, body pressed to body, each feeling the opposite fibre of the other ... when Tom left Eton it was all over. He never again had any truck with me and turned exclusively to women".' Or that was what Lees-Milne chose to believe.

While the family seemed quite prepared to celebrate Tom's bisexuality, the closest any of them could get to admitting that Pam was a lesbian was Jessica's description of her as a 'you-know-what-bian'.

After divorcing Derek Jackson, Pamela Mitford had finally admitted to her sexual preference for women and spent the following forty-three years living with Giuditta Tomassi, an Italian horsewoman. For some inexplicable reason the Mitfords obviously found the whole thing too embarrassing for words.

The year 1945 also saw Nancy publish *The Pursuit of Love*, featuring the Mitfords, minus the politics, as the Radlett children. The book was a tribute to her lover, Lieutenant Colonel Gaston Palewski, the Free French major of Polish Jewish descent, who had so transformed her life.

In her letters to Decca, Nancy had 'casually mentioned the book' that she would describe as her autobiography.

To her friend Evelyn Waugh, Nancy explained that although people might think she had copied from his recently published success, Brideshead Revisited, in that she was relating the narrative in the first person, her book was 'about my family, a very different cup of tea, not grand and far madder. Did I begin writing it before Brideshead or after – I can't remember'.

According to Charlotte Mosley, it was also 'her first truly accomplished novel. It was an instant success, selling in huge numbers, and almost for the first time the name "Mitford" appeared in the press unattached to scandal.'

By 1945 Debo somewhat indirectly inherited the role and title of Duchess of Devonshire after her husband Lord Andrew Cavendish's older brother was killed and he became the Duke of Devonshire; an identical situation to that which had served to raise David Freeman-Mitford to the peerage.

But the most traumatic event as far as Unity was concerned was the death of Adolf Hitler by his own hand while she remained mortal, which underlined the fact that she had failed in her responsibilities as his Valkyrie. No amount of praying to her Christian god could overcome her profound sense of failure, futility and anger. Sydney bore the brunt of her angst, for no better reason than she spent most time with her. Particularly when they were staying on Inch Kenneth.

On 4 October 1945, Deborah wrote to Diana:

Darling Honks. I have been here for a week with Elizabeth and Anne [Cavendish] and at first Muv was really quite cheerful and so was Bobo, but after a day or two when they got used to us being here Birdie became furious with everyone and everything and Muv became silenter and silenter and she seems so sad and everything seems so pointless for her ... I think Muv would be more or less alright looking after Bobo if only Bobo wasn't so beastly to her, she never leaves her alone for a minute and as you know, is exactly like a child in that she has to be entertained the whole time and poor Muv can never sit down to read or enjoy herself for a moment. I do think we all ought to try and help her make some arrangement about Bobo which would leave Muv free, even for a few weeks or months, as I really do think the strain on her is too much, she looks so thin and tired and utterly miserable.

By 1948 Unity appeared to be in full grasp of her faculties while her physical health was considerably improved. So much so that according to Mrs MacGillivray, 'Unity and her mother were out in the boat a lot, the two of them, Unity rowing.' The wind, tide and soft but tedious summer rain cannot have made pulling a heavy boat across the choppy, dark loch waters an entirely clement experience, but presumably Sydney felt obliged to accompany her short-tempered daughter.

It must have been a considerable relief when she was considered fit enough to stay with friends while Sydney visited America. On her return, Sydney moved back once again to Inch Kenneth with the ever more trying Unity. The relationship between mother and daughter was becoming increasingly complex and strained. For while refusing to hand over the responsibility of looking after Unity to either Diana or Pam, Sydney professed to being increasingly concerned that Unity would outlive her and doubted that her sisters would be prepared to take on the amount of personal care involved. However, this was somewhat contradictory to Unity's hopes and intentions, manifest in her increasing habit of conducting her own funeral services in the island's old ruined chapel.

*　　*　　*

In mid-May 1948, three weeks after she arrived back on the island from southern England with her mother, Unity developed a feverish chill and was put to bed. There was no telephone on the island, only a very crude signalling system. 'At Gribun the postmaster would hang a large black disc on Sydney's garage door [where the postmaster kept an old Morris Minor] to signal that mail or parcels were awaiting collection, and Sydney scanned for signals every day with her binoculars.' It was a remarkably dangerous means of communication, particularly if Unity, or anyone else on the island for that matter, should have an accident or suffer from some debilitating illness. 'There was a similar device on the island to summon help in an emergency, but although the doctor was called, high winds and a rough sea prevented him from reaching Inch Kenneth for several days and during this time Unity's condition worsened.'[10]

Unity apparently complained of severe headaches and attacks of vomiting. Then, one morning, she suddenly looked up and announced loudly to God or her Führer, 'I am coming.' Sydney later said that her heart sank at this; though considering the way in which she had been treated by Unity, it might not have been any great surprise if she, albeit guiltily, enjoyed a degree of relief. There was also another threat to Unity's survival. When the doctor arrived on the island, he treated Unity with sulphathiazole, a drug that was used for the treatment of gonorrhoea, which, without displaying any symptoms, can lead to the development of meningitis. However, due to her belief in Christian Science, Sydney did not agree with conventional medicine and had already proved more than capable of throwing prescribed drugs out of the window when no one was looking. This could have been a contributing factor to Unity's temperature remaining 'obstinately high', and by the third day the doctor noticing that the scar on Unity's right temple was 'bulging and tender'.[11]

Suspecting a cranial abscess, the doctor called in a consultant; he diagnosed meningitis and Unity was transferred from the island to the mainland, an extremely unpleasant start to what must have been a nightmare journey:

> They arrived at the West Highland Cottage Hospital in Oban at midnight on the evening of 27 May and Unity was treated with penicillin. Arrangements were made to move her to the neurosurgery unit at Killearn Hospital on the following morning, but before she could be loaded into the ambulance she had an epileptic fit. She remained unconscious until she died at 10 o'clock that night. It was concluded that she had died of pneumococcal meningitis, caused by an infection in the site of the old head wound.[12]

An autopsy was suggested but deemed unnecessary by Professor Cairns who had remained Unity's consultant since her return from Germany; he was the only one who had ever taken any X-rays.

Sydney, with a considerable amount of help from her retinue of staff, had been responsible for Unity's well-being for nearly eight years and her death so soon after Tom's was a cruel blow. But it could also have been seen as a blessing. Unfortunately, the guilt that Sydney experienced for having wished Unity dead would haunt her, literally, for the rest of her life.

The MacGillivrays, who looked after the house and grounds, noticed:

> Photos and albums of Unity's were lying in the drawing room and Lady Redesdale would think we'd known Unity before and would tell stories of her in the past. Afterwards she used to think Unity was around the house. Lady Resdesdale wouldn't come with us to Iona on one occasion, because she was sure Unity was outside the house, waiting for her.

But while the MacGillivrays were left with their memories of reality, 'Brand Mitford' proceeded to set the record straight. As Mary Lovell says, '"Her only consolation", Sydney wrote to a friend, "was something Unity had said to her while she was ill: "No one ever had such a happy young life as I did up to the war".'

David travelled up to Oban from Northumberland, before he and Sydney accompanied the coffin on the long journey south, by train, to Swinbrook. Unity was buried on 1 June 1948, close to the church, to the accompaniment of her chosen hymns. Most of the family attended, including the Mosleys, which did little to please many local village people, while on her tombstone Sydney had ordered the epitaph, 'Say not the struggle naught availeth.' The title of a poem by Arthur Hugh Clough, it doubtless reflected the feelings of the exhausted Sydney rather than the dreams of Unity, for whom Richard Wagner's words 'Imagination creates reality' may have better suited.

EPILOGUE

I had always been somewhat baffled by the public appeal of the Mitfords but I now realise that it was not so much *who* they were as *what* they represented and *when* that gave them their allure. Despite the unmistakable signs that the sun was setting on both the British Empire and the future of the privileged classes, for many English the teens, twenties and thirties of the twentieth century were a golden period in our history and the Mitford girls symbolised all that was Great about Britain's young, glamorous aristocracy.

They were also a wonderful source of aspiration for the burgeoning middle class; particularly the newly urbanised women who dreamt of marrying into the peerage and learned the language of 'U' and 'Non-U' by heart while planning their ascent of England's mysterious social pinnacles. Only one of the Mitford girls actually married a peer of the realm and the aforementioned linguistic barometer was, as you now know, coined not by Nancy Mitford, as is so often claimed, but by Alan S.C. Ross, a professor of linguistics at Birmingham University. It could of course have been their well-mannered duplicity and abject snobbery that aspirants found so appealing and delightfully typical of the Mitford ilk.

As wealth became increasingly important in defining one's social position, the fascination with the Mitfords took on a greater degree of camp nostalgia. But with signs of a re-emergence of the social significance of aristocratic status, particularly in Austria and Germany, the original motivation for the appreciation of the Mitfords appears to be making a comeback.

Having immersed myself in their undoubtedly fascinating world for some time, I now also understand why so many people, regardless of their motivation, retain their affection for the Mitford girls by insisting on viewing them in the same spirit as Nancy; rather superficially, with a good deal of humour and a fair degree of imagination.

In-depth research makes it considerably more difficult to appreciate the Mitfords, as it becomes increasingly evident that they were, in fact, right-wing fascists and malicious bullies, vehemently committed to Nazi principles.

After the war, they remained largely unrepentant and their papering over the cracks in their fascist past with dismissive abandon can almost be considered predictable. What is less so, and of far greater concern, is the fact that so many journalists and authors appear to have been so easily persuaded to *aid and abet* the Mitfords' efforts in refusing to accept any responsibility or guilt in supporting and encouraging a regime that was responsible for so much death, destruction and suffering.

Unfortunately, I have also become convinced that given the right political, social and financial conditions and a suitably persuasive leader, the racial and military savagery that took place during the Mitford years could quite easily be repeated. In Germany or Britain. Though I still believe there to be considerably less risk of a totalitarian regime being accepted by the English.

We still have a rather contradictory relationship with the Germans, whom we pretend to dislike while secretly respecting and even admiring them. This was never more evident than in 1947 when the British public displayed remarkably little concern for the fact that the heir to the throne saw fit to marry the product of German aristocracy, thinly disguised as a Greek naval officer.

Many Germans, on the other hand, still display remarkably little regret for the actions of their forebears but a grudging appreciation for all things English. However, for some inexplicable reason they appear quite determined to deny the very existence of Unity Mitford, let alone her relationship with Adolf Hitler.

From the evidence and opinion supplied to me over the years, particularly by Baroness Gaby Bentinck, Marie-France Reilly, Milly Howard-Brown and my mother, Kathleen Atkins, I firmly believe that Unity was a highly intelligent woman who, like Hitler, lived in a world of advanced fantasy, and that it was the culmination of the fusion of their fantasies that transcended and appeared to defy social logic. And of the latter, I wonder how many people appreciate the fact that Hitler probably never actually killed anyone, despite being responsible for the deaths of millions. It was his genius in the art of persuasion that was so dangerous and that also, I believe, led to Unity's attempted suicide.

Whether the blame is laid at the Führer's feet or at the Germans' does not alter the fact that, apart from Jessica, the Mitfords were so committed to Nazi ideology and determined to accept Hitler as a man of limitless charm that it would not be difficult to believe that their real ambition, or certainly Lady Redesdale's and probably Diana's, had in fact been the marriage of Unity to their beloved Führer. At the height of British appeasement in 1938, the intensity of interaction between the Mitfords and Hitler was certainly a persuasive indication of the parents' marital ambitions, if not the Führer and his Valkyrie.

When both this formalised union and Unity's suicide failed to materialise and she was forced to return to England, it was her family's privileged social position that saved her from the ignominy of even the mildest interrogation, let alone the type of incarceration to which Diana and Oswald Mosley were subjected; though even in their case, the relationship between Winston Churchill and the Mitfords would eventually result in their dispensation, if not their recantation.

But notwithstanding my tarnishing of their reputation, the global fascination for the Mitford girls will doubtless 'kick-on' and they will continue to delight.

BIBLIOGRAPHY

de Courcy, Anne, *Diana Mosley*, Chatto and Windus, 2003. Written with the consent of Diana who insisted it be published after her death. The book shows a marked degree of understanding towards Diana's intransigence concerning her fascist beliefs.

Channon, Chips, *Chips*, Phoenix, 1967.

Devonshire Deborah, *Wait For Me! Memoirs of the Youngest Mitford Sister*, John Murray, 2010. Contains remarkably little concerning fascism or her sisters' relationship with Adolf Hitler. It is edited by Charlotte Mosley.

Fest, Joachim C., *Hitler*, Vintage, 1974.

Guinness, Jonathan (with Catherine Guinness), *The House of Mitford*, Phoenix, 2004. First published in 1984, it strongly argues the Mosley case. According to Mary Lovell, when Jonathan became chairman of the ultra-conservative Monday Club (1970–72), Decca branded him forever as a dangerous neo-Nazi.

Jennings, Charles, *Them and Us*, The History Press, 2007.

Lovell, Mary S., *The Mitford Girls*, Abacus, 2001. Lovell displays a considerable degree of sympathy for the Mitfords' fascist cause.

Mitford, Jessica, *Hons and Rebels*, Phoenix, 2003 (first published 1960). Mildly critical of her family's political sympathies, it was still authorised by all the surviving members of the family. Thus it contains few surprises and many omissions.

Mosley, Charlotte (ed.), *The Mitfords, Letters Between Six Sisters*, Fourth Estate, 2007. Unsurprising gaps in the letters, particularly those from Unity during her period in Germany.

Murphy, Sophie, *The Mitford Family Album*, Sidgwick and Jackson, 1985 (out of print). Murphy is the younger daughter of Deborah Mitford and the 11th Duke of Devonshire. She not only mentions Unity's interest in SS officers but also names Eric Widemann, a 'part-time' SS officer, as Unity's steady boyfriend for several years. She also mentions one of Hitler's adjutants, Stadelmann, as another of her lovers.

Petropoulos, Jonathan, *Royals and the Reich*, OUP, 2006.

Pryce-Jones, David, *Unity Mitford – A Quest*, Weidenfeld, 1976 (new edition 1995). The only other biography of Unity. Apparently due to his family connections with the Mitfords, Pryce-Jones compromised himself by admitting to having failed to include certain details that he believed, with admirable consideration capable of 'causing distress or embarrassment'. The surviving Mitfords were still upset by the book, which is now out of print.

Pugh, Martin, *Hurrah for the Blackshirts*, Pimlico, 2005.

Theweleit, Klaus, *Male Fantasies*, Polity Press, 1977.

SOURCES

Sources include my mother, who gained intimate knowledge of the Mitfords' 'goings-on' while her father was practising as a doctor in Burford; my friend Baroness Gaby Bentinck whose German industrialist family, the Thyssens, owned Rechnitz Castle, next door to Almasy Castle where Unity spent a great deal of time with her aristocratic Austrian Nazi lover. Gaby also married a Dutch diplomat called Baron Adolphe Bentinck, whose ambassadorial friends passed on yet more details to both her and her companion, Marie-France Railey. My grandmother, Milly Howard-Brown (first married to Frederick Litchfield, and remarried a Jewish Hungarian playboy who also went under the name Count von Schossberger), was also witness to Unity's extraordinary behaviour by her involvement with the Almasy crowd in pre-war Vienna, Munich and Venice. She spent the war years in South Africa, returning to spend the rest of her life in Nice, on the Cote d'Azure; every August being spent in England.

NOTES

1 Dawn of the Daughters of Albion 1264–1906

1 Guinness, Jonathan, *The House of Mitford*, Phoenix, 1984.
2 Ibid.
3 Ibid.
4 Ibid.
5 Ibid.
6 Ibid.
7 Ibid.
8 Jennings, Charles, *Them and Us*, The History Press, 2007.
9 Ibid.
10 Ibid.
11 Guinness, *The House of Mitford*.
12 Ibid.
13 Ibid.
14 Ibid.
15 Pugh, Martin, *Hurrah for the Blackshirts*, Pimlico, 2005.
16 *Metapedia*, 2012: www.metapedia.org.

17 Guinness, *The House of Mitford*.

18 Ibid.

19 Ibid.

20 Ibid.

21 Ibid.

22 Ibid.

23 Ibid.

24 Ibid.

25 Ibid.

2 The 'Golden' Years 1904–18

1 Lovell, Mary S., *The Mitford Girls*, Abacus, 2001.

2 Guinness, Jonathan, *The House of Mitford*, Phoenix, 1984.

3 Ibid.

4 Ibid.

5 Ibid.

6 Petropoulos, Jonathan, *Royals and the Reich*, OUP, 2006.

7 Guinness, *The House of Mitford*.

8 Ibid.

9 Ibid.

10 Ibid.

11 Ibid.

3 Fascism and Fantasy 1918–30

1 Guinness, Jonathan, *The House of Mitford*, Phoenix, 1984.

2 Ibid.

3 Ibid.

4 Ibid.

5 Ibid.

6 Jennings, Charles, *Them and Us*, The History Press, 2007.

7 Devonshire, Deborah, *Wait for Me!* John Murray, 2010.

8 Petropoulos, Jonathan, *Royals and the Reich*, OUP, 2006.

9 Finestone, Jeffrey, *The Last Courts of Europe*, J.M. Dent & Sons Ltd, 1981.

10 Petropoulos, *Royals and the Reich*.

11 Pugh, Martin, *Hurrah for the Blackshirts*, Pimlico, 2005.

12 Petropoulos, *Royals and the Reich*.

13 Laqueur, Walter, *Weimar*, G.P. Putnam's Sons, 1976.

14 Lovell, Mary S., *The Mitford Girls*, Abacus, 2001.

15 Ibid.

16 Petropoulos, *Royals and the Reich*, 2006.

17 Theweleit, Klaus, *Male Fantasies*, Polity Press, 1977.

18 Lovell, *The Mitford Girls*.

19 Ibid.

20 Ibid.

21 Ibid.

22 Guinness, *The House of Mitford*.

23 Ibid.

24 Petropoulos, *Royals and the Reich*.

25 Jennings, *Them and Us*.

26 Ibid.

27 de Courcy, Anne, *Diana Mosley*, Chatto and Windus, 2003.

28 Pugh, *Hurrah for the Blackshirts*.

29 Ibid.

30 Guinness, *The House of Mitford*.

31 Ibid.

32 Ibid.

33 Ibid.

34 Lovell, *The Mitford Girls*.

35 Guinness, *The House of Mitford*.

36 Ibid.

37 Jennings, *Them and Us*.

38 Ibid.

39 Manning, Frederic, *The Middle Parts of Fortune*, Leonaur Ltd, 2007.

40 Lovell, *The Mitford Girls*.

41 Pryce-Jones, David, *Unity Mitford*, Weidenfeld, 1976.

42 Ibid.

43 Ibid.

44 Lovell, *The Mitford Girls*.

45 Ibid.

46 Ibid.

47 Ibid.

48 Ibid.

49 Ibid.

50 Pryce-Jones, *Unity Mitford*.

51 de Courcy, *Diana Mosley*.

52 Ibid.

4 Dancing on the Edge 1930–34

1 Jennings, Charles, *Them and Us*, 2007.

2 Ibid.

3 Ibid.

4 de Courcy, Anne, *Diana Mosley*, Chatto and Windus, 2003.

5 Craig, Gordon A., *Germany 1866–1945*, Oxford Paperbacks, 1978.

6 Mitford, Jessica, *Hons and Rebels*, Phoenix, 2003.

7 Guinness, Jonathan, *The House of Mitford*, Phoenix, 1984.

8 de Courcy, *Diana Mosley*.

9 Ibid.

10 Petropoulos, Jonathan, *Royals and the Reich*, OUP, 2006.

11 Guinness, *The House of Mitford*.

12 *Action*, 1931.

13 Pugh, Martin, *Hurrah for the Blackshirts*, Pimlico, 2005.

14 Laqueur, Walter, *Weimar*, G.P. Putnam's Sons, 1974.

15 Pugh, *Hurrah for the Blackshirts*.

16 Fest, Joachim C., *Hitler*, Vintage, 1974.

17 Koshar, Rudy, *German Travel Culture*, Berg Publishers, 2000.

18 Guinness, *The House of Mitford*.

19 Ibid.

20 Mosley, Oswald, *The Greater Britain*, Black House Publishing Ltd (2012 edn), 1932.

21 Mitford, *Hons and Rebels*.

22 Lovell, Mary S., *The Mitford Girls*, Abacus, 2001.

23 *The Daily Express*, 1932.

24 Lovell, *The Mitford Girls*.

25 Ibid.

26 Pryce-Jones, David, *Unity Mitford*, Weidenfeld, 1976.

27 de Courcy, *Diana Mosley*.

28 Pryce-Jones, *Unity Mitford*.

29 Ibid.

30 Ibid.

31 Jennings, *Them and Us*.

32 Pryce-Jones, *Unity Mitford*.

33 Lovell, *The Mitford Girls*.

34 de Courcy, *Diana Mosley*.

35 Pryce-Jones, *Unity Mitford*.

36 Ibid.

37 Ibid.

38 Ibid.

39 Ibid.

40 Ibid.

41 Ibid.

42 Guinness, *The House of Mitford*.

43 Ibid.

44 Ibid.

45 de Courcy, *Diana Mosley*.

46 Pryce-Jones, *Unity Mitford*.

5 Bavarian Rhapsody 1934–36

1 Guinness, Jonathan, *The House of Mitford*, Phoenix, 1984.
2 Pryce-Jones, David, *Unity Mitford*, Weidenfeld, 1976.
3 de Courcy, Anne, *Diana Mosley*, Chatto and Windus, 2003.
4 Guinness, *The House of Mitford*.
5 Ibid.
6 Ibid.
7 Mosley, Charlotte (ed.), *The Mitfords: Letters Between Six Sisters*, Fourth Estate, 2007.
8 Mitford, Jessica, *Hons and Rebels*, Phoenix, 2003.
9 Ibid.
10 Lovell, Mary S., *The Mitford Girls*, Abacus, 2001.
11 Pryce-Jones, *Unity Mitford*.
12 Guinness, *The House of Mitford*.
13 Theweleit, Klaus, *Male Fantasies*, Polity Press, 1987.
14 Guinness, *The House of Mitford*.
15 de Courcy, *Diana Mitford*.
16 Pryce-Jones, *Unity Mitford*.
17 Guinness, *The House of Mitford*.
18 de Courcy, *Diana Mosley*.
19 Ibid.
20 Williamson, Henny, *The Phoenix Generation*, Faber and Faber, 2011.
21 de Courcy, *Diana Mosley*.
22 Lovell, *The Mitford Girls*.
23 Guinness, *The House of Mitford*.
24 Pryce-Jones, *Unity Mitford*.
25 Ibid.
26 Ibid.
27 Lovell, *The Mitford Girls*.
28 Pryce-Jones, *Unity Mitford*.
29 Ibid.
30 Ibid.

31 Lovell, *The Mitford Girls*.

32 Ibid.

33 de Courcy, *Diana Mosley*.

34 Pryce-Jones, *Unity Mitford*.

35 Ibid.

36 de Courcy, *Diana Mosley*.

37 Lovell, *The Mitford Girls*.

38 Petropoulos, Jonathan, *Royals and the Reich*, OUP, 2006.

39 Pugh, Martin, *Hurrah for the Blackshirts*, Pimlico, 2005.

40 Channon, Chips, *Chips*, Phoenix, 1967.

41 Petropoulos, *Royals and the Reich*.

6 The Great Affair 1936–38

1 Mitford, Jessica, *Hons and Rebels*, Phoenix, 2003.

2 Guinness, Jonathan, *The House of Mitford*, Phoenix, 1984.

3 Pryce-Jones, David, *Unity Mitford*, Weidenfeld, 1976.

4 Lovell, Mary S., *The Mitford Girls*, Abacus, 2001.

5 Ibid.

6 Guinness, *The House of Mitford*.

7 David Pryce-Jones. *Unity Mitford*. 1976.

7 Ride of the Valkyrie 1938–39

1 Pryce-Jones, David, *Unity Mitford*, Weidenfeld, 1976.

2 Ibid.

3 Ibid.

4 Guinness, Jonathan, *The House of Mitford*, Phoenix, 1984.

5 Lovell, Mary S., *The Mitford Girls*, Abacus, 2001.

6 Guinness, *The House of Mitford*.

7 Pryce-Jones, *Unity Mitford*.

8 Guinness, *The House of Mitford*.

8 The Next Great Adventure 1939–48

1 Guinness, Jonathan, *The House of Mitford*, Phoenix, 1984.

2 Pryce-Jones, David, *Unity Mitford*, Weidenfeld, 1976.

3 Ibid.

4 de Courcy, Anne, *Diana Mosley*, Chatto and Windus, 2003.

5 Pryce-Jones, *Unity Mitford*.

6 Hastings, Selina, *Nancy Mitford*, Hamish Hamilton Ltd, 1985.

7 Lovell, Mary S., *The Mitford Girls*, Abacus, 2001.

8 Ibid.

9 Mosley, Charlotte (ed.), *The Mitfords: Letters Between Six Sisters*, Fourth Estate, 2007.

10 Lovell, *The Mitford Girls*.

11 Ibid.

12 Ibid.

INDEX

INDEX

INDEX

INDEX

INDEX

INDEX

Gibson Bowles) 12, 49, 71, 96,
98, 101, 102, 126, 152, 153, 154,
159, 160, 163, 168, 181, 214–5,
216, 233, 242, 245, 251, 257,
258, 288, 292, 295, 305, 306,
308, 310–11, 312, 313, 316, 321,
325
Redesdale, Northumberland 13
Redesdale Cottage 48, 312, 316
Redwitz, Baroness 175, 276
Reinhardt, Oskar 235
Reiser, Dr Helmut 304, 306
Ribbentrop, Anneliese von 234
Ribbentrop, Joachim von 217, 233,
234, 257, 272, 304
Richardson, Mary 148
Riddell, Lord 260
Riefenstahl, Leni 173, 227
Right Club 103, 280, 307
Rodd, Peter 160, 161, 225
Rodzianko, Joan (née Farrer) ('Rudbin',
'Robin') 99, 100, 139, 142
Röhm, Ernst 131, 172, 184, 211,
254, 267, 274
Romilly, Esmond 173, 240, 257, 258
Romilly, Nellie (née Hozier) 101,
173, 259
Rosenberg, Alfred 148
Ross, Professor Alan S.C. 62, 323
Rothermere, Lord 80, 133, 154, 155,
183, 199, 237, 281

Rousseau, Douanier 51, 84
Royal Air Force 261, 310
Royal Yacht Squadron 28
Rubinstein, Arthur 133
Rumbold, Sir Anthony 154
Russell, Lady Patricia 284
Rutland Gate 93, 94, 289, 293, 314
SA (Sturmabteilung, Storm Division)

64, 129, 131, 157, 172, 181, 223,
263, 273, 274
Saxe-Coburg-Gotha, Duke Carl
Eduard von (formerly Duke of
Albany) 63, 233, 237
Sadomasochism 145
Salomon, Ernst von 118
Sandhurst Royal Military Academy
25, 34
Sandys, Duncan 232
Sauerbruch, Professor Ernst
Ferdinand 175
Schaub, Julius 271, 272
Schirach, Baldur von 254
Schleicher, General Kurt von 146
Schloss Buch, Bavaria 296
Schloss Fantaisie, Bavaria 277
Schmeling, Max 230
Schönerer, Georg Ritter von 22
Schopenhauer, Artur 97
Schwarz, Franz Xaver 129
Secret Intelligence Service (SIS,
MI6) 128
Sefton, 2nd Earl of 16
Shaw, George Bernhard 44, 125
Shelley, Percy 85
Simolin, Rudolfine (later von St
Paul) ('Rudi') 294, 299
Simon, Sir John 215
Simpson, Henry 113
Sinclair, Sir Archibald 237
Sitwell, Edith 110, 111
Sitwell, Georgia 110, 111, 138
Sitwell, Osbert 110, 111
Sitwell, Sacheverell 110, 111
Social Darwinism 21, 40
Speer, Albert 272
Spencer, Stanley 140
Spiegel, Baron 268
SS (Schutzstaffel, Protection or Shield

347

INDEX

If you enjoyed this book, you may also be interested in ...

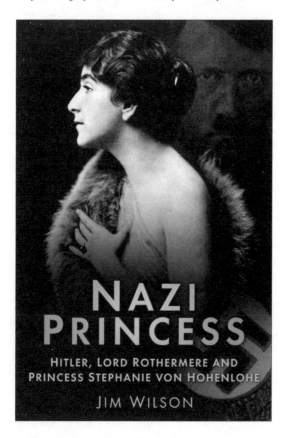

Nazi Princess

Jim Wilson

Stephanie von Hohenlohe lived a controversial life. Born to a middle-class Viennese family and of partly Jewish descent, after marriage to (and divorce from) a prince of the Austro-Hungarian Empire, she became a close confidante of Hitler, Goering, Himmler (who declared her an 'honorary Aryan') and von Ribbentrop. Author Jim Wilson uses recently declassified MI5 files and FBI memos to examine what motivated both Stephanie and Rothermere, shedding light on the murky goings-on behind the scenes in Britain, Germany and the USA before and during the Second World War.

978 0 7524 6114 4

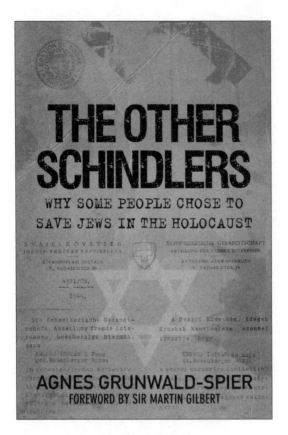

The Other Schindlers

Agnes Grunwald-Spier

In the midst of the extermination of the Jews in the Second World War, courage and humanity overcame evil. While 6 million Jews were murdered by the Nazi regime, some were saved through the actions of non-Jews. As a baby, Grunwald-Spier was saved from the horrors of Auschwitz by an unknown official, and has collected the stories of thirty individuals who rescued Jews, providing a new insight into why they were prepared to risk so much for their fellow men and women. This is an ultimately uplifting account of how some good deeds really do shine in a weary world.

978 0 7524 5967 7